The Smart Shopper's Cookbook

The Smart Shopper's Cookbook

by Loyta Wooding

NASH PUBLISHING, Los Angeles

OTHER BOOKS BY LOYTA WOODING

The Cooking Collectarium
Meals on Wheels

Illustrations by Ann Bruce Chamberlain

Copyright © 1972 Loyta Wooding

All rights reserved. No part of this book
may be reproduced in any form or by any means
without permission in writing from the publisher.

Library of Congress Catalog Card Number: 71-186892
Standard Book Number: 8402-1248-8

Published simultaneously in the United States and
Canada by Nash Publishing Corporation,
9255 Sunset Boulevard, Los Angeles, California 90069.

Printed in the United States of America.

First Printing.

For Evelyn and Elmer John

Contents

The
Smart Shopper's
Cookbook

Foreword

Today's homemaker is faced with the constant challenge of keeping the wolf away from her door. To be sure, this wolf is well fed by our contemporary standards, but the struggle to balance the food budget is never-ending and would strain the imagination of even a marketing expert.

With the cost of living continuing its upward climb like a well-inflated balloon, and no relief is in sight, the average homemaker could burn out a computer (if she could afford to buy one, that is) just trying to find out how to keep her expenditures down. What makes her job doubly difficult is the fact that her family has developed champagne tastes over the past fat years, but Dad's paycheck and those stock dividends are now on a beer level.

Economizing does not mean gnawing on a chop bone and sopping up your gravy; nor do we wish to turn you into a top sergeant in the army of food stretchers, doling out rations of bread and water. Besides, you've got to keep up appearances, no matter what, and never let the Joneses know that you're stretching your food dollars. No, that will never do! Never should there be even a soupçon of a hint that the Beef Wellington you served so proudly the other night, was the Chuck Roast Special; that the three-day-old leftover cake found its way into the elegant Tipsy Trifle, or that you're buttering up the boss with garlic margarine.

Impossible to accomplish? No, not at all! If you are really determined to cut your food costs, and who isn't, you must change your way of kitchenery—

that is, planning meals, shopping for food, and cooking the food, are all a matter of patience, organization, and advance planning. And this is something that you have to do all by yourself so that your family and friends will retain the illusion that you are a smart housewife, superlative cook, and a magician!

To begin with, you accept the fact that you can't change prices themselves, that even if the majority of the homemakers got together and boycotted the markets, they still would not succeed, but you can make every dollar you pay out do more for you. For it's what you pick, how you shop, and how you prepare what you have bought that counts toward making you a Cordon Bleu genius with Yankee thrift ingredients.

The Smart Shopper's Cookbook is not going to teach you how to cook. We assume that you know how. What we will teach you is how to budget your resources and take advantage of your grocer's specials, for successful cookery begins in the market. Furthermore, your time is important, and we have taken this into consideration, too. Whether you are a full-time homemaker with community work commitments, or a career woman helping to alleviate the burden of rising costs, we're not going to push you back into the kitchen to slave over the stove for endless hours, as many frugal-fare cookbooks imply you have to do, and for which, we are sure, you have neither the time nor the inclination.

We are aware, of course, that economical cuts of meats do need extra cooking time, but if preparation of the meals is planned in advance, this presents no problem. Today's homemaker is a talented wizard in her kitchen and we are here providing her with helpful guidelines for selecting and preparing meals which are appetizing and nutritious as well as economical.

You will note that we have included more beef recipes than any other variety of meat. We would like to assure you that we did this simply because the thriftier cuts of beef are more economical—and who can beat hamburger for universal popularity? It can be prepared in so many ingenious ways that it can make any low-cost dish high fashion and high adventure.

In the flavor department, we offer tomatoes in many forms along with occasional dashes of wine. These two ingredients, blended with other seasonings, can transform any ordinary dish into a culinary triumph, and we don't think any kitchen should be without them.

So here's the secret of how to eat high while spending low. Start planning tomorrow's meal from among the 450 recipes and 125 menus that follow. All recipes have been tested by the author and are for four servings, unless otherwise specified, so that you may halve or double them with equal ease.

We offer suggestions for breakfasts and lunches which are based on an all-around good nutritional pattern. Use these only as guidelines in serving them according to your family's needs and preferences.

What concerns us most is the main dish because this is the most important item in meal planning. It is the hub around which the rest of the meals are built, and it often carries a large proportion of the cost of the meal. Usually, the main dish is the main source of protein as well.

In some homes, noon is the time for the big meal of the day; in others, it is only at night that the family can gather around the dinner table; in still others, where everyone is physically active, a big meal may be needed both noon and night. But whenever the meal may be eaten, the dishes described here will help you to use a variety of economical foods to supply the protein and other nutritional foods your family needs at the lowest possible cost.

Play it smart: make a game of getting the most out of your food dollar. Pretty soon you'll come up with extra dollars you can spend on luxuries you thought you could not afford.

Loyta Wooding

Introduction

HOW TO MAP OUT A MEAL

The foods which each person requires are called nutrients. Each day your meals should supply you with:

        . . . Proteins for growth

        . . . Minerals and vitamins to keep the body functioning properly

        . . . Carbohydrates and fats for energy

The Basic Four Chart developed by the Department of Agriculture can serve as a guideline to well-balanced daily meals. Plan to include at least minimum servings from each category.

DAILY FOOD GUIDE

Milk Group

Children, 3 to 4 cups
Teen-agers, 4 or more cups
Adults, 2 or more cups

Vegetable-Fruit Group

4 or more servings:
Include a citrus fruit or other fruit or vegetable important for vitamin C.

**Vegetable-Fruit Group
(continued)**

A dark green or deep yellow vegetable for vitamin A—at least every other day.
Other vegetables and fruits, including potatoes.

Meat Group

2 or more servings:
Beef, veal, lamb, pork, poultry, fish, eggs.
As alternatives—dry beans, dry peas, nuts.

Bread-Cereal Group

4 or more servings:
Whole grain, enriched or restored.

What we eat makes a big difference in how we feel and act. The amount of food is not the only important aspect of what we eat. It is also essential to have the right foods so that there is a proper balance of all the different food elements the body needs to carry on its daily functions.

Food has three big jobs:

1.   It provides energy and heat so that we can breathe, walk, work, and play.

2.   It builds, maintains, and repairs our muscles, bones, skin, and internal organs, repairs the wear and tear on the bodies of adults, and helps children to grow big and strong.

3.   It keeps our bodies regulated and running smoothly—helping our food to digest properly, making sure we get the most good from the air we breathe, the proper body regulation from the hormones and internal secretions we produce, and that our hearts pump the blood to every section of our bodies—thus helping our tissues and organs to function properly.

Here are some pointers on how to use the daily food guide:

1.   Choose at least the minimum number of servings from each of the four food groups.

2.   Select additional foods to round out your meals from foods listed in the four groups and from others. These additional foods should add enough calories to complete your food-energy needs for the day.

3.   Try to have some meat, poultry, fish, eggs, and milk at each meal.

Naturally, there are reasons for including foods from each group every day.

The milk group is our best source of calcium and also provides high-quality protein. Use milk in food and to drink: whole milk, skim milk, buttermilk, evaporated milk, dried milk, or cheese.

Vegetables and fruits furnish vitamins and minerals for growth and to keep the body functioning properly. They provide the two vitamins that are more likely to be in short supply if you do not make an effort to obtain them each day—vitamin A and vitamin C. Vitamin A is needed for growth, normal vision, and healthy condition of skin and other body surfaces. Vitamin C is needed for healthy gums and body tissues.

The following foods are good sources of these vitamins:

Vitamin A

Dark green and deep yellow vegetables and a few fruits:

Vegetables	*Fruits*
Broccoli	Apricots
Carrots	Cantaloupe
Chard	Mango
Collards	Persimmon
Cress	Pumpkin
Kale	
Spinach	
Sweet potatoes	
Turnip greens and other dark green leaves	
Winter squash	

Vitamin C

Vegetables	*Fruits*
Asparagus	Cantaloupe and Melon
Broccoli	Grapefruit
Brussels sprouts	Guava
Cabbage, raw	Mango
Collards	Orange
Mustard greens	Papaya
Peppers, green and sweet red	Strawberries, fresh
Potatoes	Tangerine
Sweet potatoes, cooked in their jackets	Watermelon
Spinach	
Tomatoes	
Tomato Juice	

The meat group really offers an opportunity for variety. In addition to all types and cuts of meat, poultry, fish, and shellfish, this group includes eggs, dry beans, dry peas, lentils, nuts, peanuts, and peanut butter. These foods are important because of their protein content. As a bonus, they are also good sources of iron and all of the B complex vitamins.

Breads and cereals should be whole grain, enriched or restored. The only way to know is to read the labels on these products.

This group includes rolled oats, rice, noodles, macaroni and spaghetti, cornmeal, grits, crackers, flour and all baked goods if made with enriched flour or whole-grain flour. These foods are valued for protein, iron, B complex vitamins, and calories which they contribute to the daily diet.

You'll have no need for expensive food supplements in the form of pills or tonics if you are eating properly and you have no vitamin deficiency due to a bodily malfunction—an adequate diet will provide all the nutrients you will need during the day.

If cutting down calories enters the picture here, it is best to reduce the caloric intake by serving the dieter smaller portions, rather than attempt to eliminate some foods and substitute others. To plan thrifty wholesome meals, a homemaker has to learn to use all foods properly and, therefore, also, that the best way to reduce is to serve everything, cut down to half the average serving.

A calorie is a unit of measurement. It is not a unit of weight, like an ounce, nor is it one of size, like an inch; it is a unit of energy value. The amount of energy, and hence of calories, that an adult requires varies according to the amount he expends. An inactive person may utilize less than 1800 calories a day, whereas one engaged in manual labor may need as many as 4500. If fewer calories are taken in than required, the normal adult draws upon his reserves of fat and, then, when the fat is used up, of protein. If too many calories are taken in, he stores them in the form of fat.

Children require a sufficient number of calories, not only to provide for the overabundant amount of energy they expend, but also to build their growing muscles, bones, and organs. A child, when he reaches the stage when he is allowed to eat solid foods, has the same basic minimum nutritional needs as his parents except that he requires additional protein, some of which can be supplied by his daily intake of milk.

TO MARKET... TO MARKET...

No general would dream of going into battle unprepared, and neither should the homemaker who is embarking on a food-shopping expedition. She'll be defeated before she even starts if she sails into a supermarket unprepared and makes up her mind, then and there, about what she'll have for dinner. Her budget is in trouble before she has even started wheeling her cart down the aisles through the land of never-ending temptations.

A smart shopper, on the other hand, arrives on the scene with full ammunition—and we mean her shopping list.

Food costs are more flexible than any other household expenses. You can tighten the reins on your food bill when you need to, and let them out again when the difficult period is past. The trick is to know how to do this.

First, you must learn how to budget, and the only way to do it is to find out how much you're spending. You can do this in one of two ways. When you make up your shopping list, write down the prices of the items you plan to purchase by consulting the newspaper food ads; or, save the tapes the cashier at the checkout counter puts in the grocery bag. When you have accumulated enough for a month, add them up. And don't cheat! We mean, don't forget to include the extras like the special ice cream you pick up at your favorite ice-cream parlor because Nettie's makes the best pistachio ice cream in town, or the cheese you pick up at the Italian grocer's every other week. They're foods and they should be included in your budget list. And don't be too concerned about accounting to the last penny. Just get a rough estimate to use as a guideline.

Once-a-week marketing saves time, energy, and money if you have room to store the food. Buying perishables, such as dairy foods and vegetables, should be the only marketing chore done more often. The important thing is to create a marketing plan to fit your situation.

Now you're ready to make up the shopping list. It will be helpful if you keep a memo pad or slate on your kitchen wall. Use it for remember-to-buy items.

Study the newspaper food ads to see what foods are plentiful and specially priced. But no market-hopping, please! You'll waste more time, effort, and energy racing around to pick up special bargains than is worth the pennies you think you'll be saving. Most supermarkets feature specials every week, and they rotate them, which means that eventually you will get the bargain which is featured elsewhere—so find your favorite market and stick to it.

You are now ready for the second step: to plan your menus for a week, if that's possible, or at least for a few days in advance. Do include the weekend, when more meals will be prepared than at any other time. Even if you're a fair-to-middlin' planner, try to work two days in advance. Make a list of what you'll need to prepare these menus, and remember that the nice thing about the list is that it will not be too definite. It shouldn't pin you down to eat parsnips, for example, if they're one vegetable you can't abide but because it's a Special you feel compelled to buy it. Allow yourself plenty of flexibility because meals are a lot more fun if they include the foods everyone likes.

Now you should compare the cost. The only way to make a true comparison of the cost of two foods is to compare the cost per serving. Prices by weight may be misleading. For instance, a package of frozen lima beans weighs 12 ounces but contains 4 servings, while 1 pound (16 ounces) of fresh limas will only give you 2 servings.

Meat, poultry, and fish are the most expensive foods in your budget, accounting for 25 percent of your expenditures , and these should be checked carefully. Meats with much bone may have a lower price in the market per pound, but actually cost more than meat with less bone at a higher price.

So, finally, you make it to the market! The best time to do this is when the children are at school and your husband is at his office. Well, if the children are too young for school, by all means, take them along. They will intimidate you into purchasing a box of cereal which features a special toy advertised on the inescapable TV, and this won't be such a catastrophe, but a husband will absolutely ruin you. He'll pick up the can of Italian truffles he always wanted to try, or talk you into having turtle soup at a dollar a can just because his boss's wife served it at dinner the other night, and with a glazed eye, as unerring as a laser beam, he'll pass over the neatly stacked displays of Specials and head straight for the porterhouse and beef tenderloin section.

He may not know that a chicken has only two legs and this may be the reason he'll pick up the enticing package of six chicken legs (and nothing else) at one and a half times the price of a whole chicken. And just watch him at the produce section making a beeline for the hothouse strawberries, exotic papayas, and the out-of-season avocados.

So guard your shopping expedition's plans as secretly as General Eisenhower did the invasion of North Africa. If your husband is at home, lull him with a cold beer and a baseball game on TV, and just leave him behind; otherwise be prepared for the inevitable.

The most fatal mistake you can make (next to taking your husband, that is) is to go along with a neighbor to save the gas. You may save one-sixteenth of a gallon, but you'll end up buying something extra just to impress her with the fact that you're not budgeting, and there go your best-laid plans of rice and hen. So beware, and be prepared, like your seven-year-old Brownie, for as sure as rain and taxes, you'll be exposed to temptation.

If your neighbor squeals in ecstasy over the imported Baba au Rhum and takes a half dozen cans off the shelf, and then sweetly urges you to do the same, well, be the grande dame, by all means, but just take one can. After all, you may really want to try these Babas, and that one face-saving gesture is worth two Coffee Cake Specials any day. However, if you or your family don't like rum, for heaven's sakes, say so! Then, oh, very casually, reach for the imported Yorkshire Pudding package. You don't have to tell your neighbor that you can make some dandy popovers with it, in case you don't care for Yorkshire Pudding.

By the time the next shopping expedition comes around, you'll find it not only easier to plot and plan, but as exhilarating an experience as Perry Mason has when he cracks a hard case. You'll plan your strategy and execution to perfection each succeeding time, and this will mean extra quarters in the piggy bank you're hiding away in the back of the seldom-used coffee percolator your aunt sent you a few Christmases ago. That, further, you're plotting to purchase a snazzy little French blouse you've had your eye on for some time now at the Mademoiselle Boutique is really another story, and we have neither the time nor the inclination to delve into it just now. So let's get on with the food budget.

A FEW WORDS TO THE WISE

We call this part of the book the section of Twenty Commandments because there are many Thou shalts and Thou shalt nots to consider if you expect to emerge the victor in the Battle of the Budget.

Quantities to buy play an important role. How much you should buy depends upon three things: how many meals you eat at home, how much of each food group you require, and how much each member of your family is accustomed to eating. Then, to estimate the quantity you should buy, you'll need to know how many servings there are to the pound or package. The following list will give you this information on some of the most used foods:

Foods   Servings

Dairy Foods

Foods	Servings
Butter: 1 pound	2 cups, 32 tablespoons, or 48 medium pats
Cheese: 1 pound	12 to 16 slices or cubes, or 4 cups grated
Cream, light: ½ pint	1 cup, 16 tablespoons, or 4 average servings (over cereal, fruit, puddings, etc.)
Cream, heavy: ½ pint	1 cup, 16 tablespoons, or 2 cups whipped
Cottage Cheese: 1 pound	4 (½ cup) servings
Ice Cream: 1 pint	3 to 4 servings, depending on individual preference
Milk	4 cups in 1 quart

Meat, Poultry, Fish

Foods	Servings
Without bone - 1 pound	4 servings, when prepared separately or 5 servings made with other ingredients (stews, meat loaves, etc.)
With medium amount of bone - 1 pound	2 to 3 servings
With much bone and gristle (such as spareribs, short ribs, etc.) - 1 pound	1 serving

Vegetables

Fresh - 1 pound:	In ½ cup portions, serves:
Asparagus	4
Beans, lima	2
Beans, green	6
Broccoli	3 - 4
Brussels sprouts	4 - 5
Cabbage (raw, grated)	6
Cabbage (cooked)	4 - 5
Carrots (cooked)	5
Cauliflower	3
Onions (cooked)	4
Peas (in pod)	2
Potatoes	4 - 5
Rhubarb	4
Spinach	3 - 4
Squash	2 - 3
Sweet potatoes	3 - 4

Canned:

8 ounces	2
No. 303 can (1 pound)	4
No. 2 can	5
No. 2 can, vacuum	4
No. 2½ can	7

(Also, read labels.)

Frozen:

10- to 12-ounce packages	4

Other Packaged Foods

Cake mixes, pudding and gelatin desserts —	Watch for information on package
Juices, concentrated, 6 fluid ounces	6 servings

Also look for additional information under each category. However, don't overlook purchasing Specials in quantity whenever you can because you will obtain considerable savings for your future food bills. Sometimes a Special is offered by the manufacturer only once or twice a year, as an extra promotion, and you should be ready to take advantage of this windfall if you can store it safely even though you do not plan to use it for a while. This is where a freezer comes in handy: it keeps your assets in reserve, and eventually pays for itself.

Specials are offered quite frequently in convenience-packaged foods. Use these ready-to-makes, but use them wisely. Don't let them tempt you too far away from the good old cookbook beginning-from-scratch recipe. In prepared mixes, you buy time and service, as well as food, so some of them are likely to cost more than when they are prepared at home.

Here are your twenty specific guidelines to help you shop wisely:

1. Take advantage of seasonal foods. Spring lamb, fall and summer pork products, fruits and vegetables, are offered at special prices when the supply is plentiful. Be ready to plan meals using these foods, which means having true and tried recipes which will not fail.

2. Buy only what you need among vegetables and fruits unless you plan to cook them and freeze them. Nothing is more expensive than throwing away unused food.

3. Plan your menus to include the Specials of meat, fish, and poultry each week and you'll make significant savings.

4. Are your pet economies extravagant or real? Do you buy a large quantity of one food and then serve it so often that your family demands more expensive foods by way of reaction, or they don't eat it all? If you prepare double or more the quantity you'll need, be sure you freeze the unused portions and serve them a week or more later.

5. If you have a ventilated, dry-storage space, buy on-sale staples and canned food by the case, but only those items that you use regularly.

6. Save a few pennies in buying chicken by buying whole broiler-fryers and cutting them in pieces or quarters before freezing them. All you need is a sharp knife and a small cleaver.

7. Buy a large amount of ground beef when it's on sale. Then, before wrapping and freezing it, divide the meat into patties for hamburgers, and recipe-size portions for main dishes.

8. When planning to serve pot roast, compare the prices of chuck steak, bottom round, and rolled rump, and choose the cheapest, because all three cuts make excellent pot roast.

9. Pork shoulder steaks are similar to pork chops in appearance and flavor, but are often one-third less expensive.

10. Don't ignore the day-old-baked-goods counter. Cake, doughnuts, Danish pastries, and breads are usually sold at half the original prices and are just as good as the first day. Usually, heating in the oven for a few minutes (sprinkle a few drops of water on rolls) will restore their freshness, and you can always use cakes in trifles and puddings, doughnuts toasted and spread with peanut butter or jam, and breads for stuffing.

11. Use Grade B eggs for cooking sauces, puddings, custards, omelets, scrambled eggs, in any recipe where perfect appearance doesn't count. They have the same nutritive value as the Grade A. The same is true of brown eggs.

12. Many canned and condensed foods are often cheaper than those made from scratch without even taking into consideration the time it takes to prepare them. Take advantage of the excellent salad dressings, tomato and

other sauces, seasonings, dessert mixes, and refrigerated biscuits. Condensed soups make excellent sauces and are also ideal food extenders and binders.

13.   Try tasty cottage cheese and chives as a change from sour cream as a topping for baked potatoes. It's not only less expensive but has fewer calories, in case you're watching the scale.

14.   When turkeys are on sale, instead of a small turkey get a large one; it is usually priced at least 10 cents a pound less. Ask the butcher to halve or quarter it. Freeze part of it, raw or cooked, for use at a later time.

15.   Buy nuts in quantity when the price is low and freeze them for later use. Use them in puddings, cakes, pancakes, in vegetables, and as toppings for ice cream.

16.   Clip and save coupons from magazines, newspapers, and special offers dropped in your mail box, but use only those that fit your family needs. This holds true even if the package is offered free. If your family does not like it, you'll be wasting the eggs, milk, butter or margarine, going into it.

17.   Watch for penny sales and special two-fors. Buying three of a kind and getting the fourth one for a penny, or buying two items at a reduced price is a great saving.

18.   If you use a large quantity of fresh milk, buy the half-gallon containers for extra savings. Use powdered and evaporated milk for cooking and baking, concentrated milk instead of cream.

19.   Buy butter or margarine by the pound, not the quarter-pound. They are less expensive than the divided sticks.

20.   Check the price per unit weight of the giant economy-sized packages to be sure they are really a good buy. Sometimes a smaller size is cheaper. But don't pass up a larger, more economical can of a vegetable or fruit because your recipe calls for a smaller size. Use the leftover vegetable for another meal or tossed with another vegetable, to extend it, and the fruit might reappear as a molded salad or dessert.

THE HIDDEN PERSUADERS

There's more to economizing than budgeting your shopping list. What happens in your own kitchen will actually tell the story in the end, because food preparation is as important as purchasing the food itself, and giving your family the kind of meals they enjoy and the food they should have for their physical needs is a greater challenge than shopping for it.

Besides using only recipes that you know have been carefully tested and perfected, and following directions absolutely to the letter, there are other economies to be considered. Some are well-known and commonplace, and have been practiced all along, while others may be a complete surprise. You don't have to adhere to a strict schedule about using them, but it's good to know about some of them. The first kitchen rule is to make the most of your leftovers. They are the start of many a good meal and a challenge to your imagination. Try several ways to trick your family into thinking that you're serving them new dishes. Always store leftovers in tightly closed containers in the refrigerator, or in the freezer if you don't plan to use them in a few days. Here are several suggestions to persuade you to use every bit of leftover food:

• Transform yesterday's roast into a tempting scalloped dish for dinner. Just a few bits left? Don't throw them away! Combine them with cheese or vegetables for hearty sandwich fillings.

• Leftover vegetables get a ready welcome served in soups, casseroles, and as a garnish; try adding them to meat loaves. Grand in salads, too, either added to fresh vegetables, for a contrast, or molded in gelatin.

• Toast leftover sandwiches to give them new life. Simply slide them under the broiler for a few minutes on each side and serve them hot.

• If you have bits of fruits left over, combine several kinds in an upside-down cake, or serve as a sauce with pudding, or use in a gelatin mold.

• A bit of dried-out cake or a few dried cookies are wonderful when added to puddings; or, roll ice-cream balls in the crumbs and freeze.

• Add leftover cooked rice to griddle cakes, muffins, soups, stuffings for meat and poultry, and in making croquettes.

• Put those last few spoonfuls of mustard left in a jar to good use— mix 1½ tablespoons with ¼ cup of margarine. It's especially good on sandwiches.

• Use the liquid from canned vegetables, or the cooking liquid from fresh ones, to flavor soups and gravies and to moisten a meat loaf or a casserole dish.

• Leftover cooked carrots are great mashed and mixed with mashed white or sweet potatoes. They're high in nutritional value, too.

• If you have two or three leftover vegetables, but not enough of any one to serve them separately, combine them in a medium white sauce with bits of meat or fish and serve on toast for a really special lunch.

• Canned fruit juices lead a charmed life. After draining the fruit, the juices may be used combined with water or ginger ale as ice cubes for fruit punch, carbonated drinks, and iced tea; thickened with cornstarch, they are ideal sauces over toasted pound cake or puddings; mixed with salad dressing or French dressing to serve over fruit salad; and as part of the liquid in making gelatins.

• Stale bread, dried out in a slow oven until hard and crisp and then rolled, makes wonderful crumbs for casserole toppings, stuffings for meat, poultry, or fish, and for breaded chops.

• To freshen French or Italian bread, sprinkle the crust with a few drops of ice water, place in a paper bag in a preheated 350° F. oven for 10 minutes.

• Make Cornish pies using leftover meats and vegetables. Serve with heated canned tomato sauce or condensed mushroom or celery soup.

• Don't discard leftover mashed potatoes. Use as a frosting for cup-cakes by beating in confectioners' sugar and vanilla extract until well blended and of spreading consistency. Or line a casserole bottom with mashed potatoes and fill it with your favorite stew. Or use as a stew topping, sprinkled with grated Cheddar cheese and a tablespoon of chopped almonds. You can also mix in with pancakes, or add vegetables and form into patties, then fry in margarine until heated through.

• Leftover egg yolks or egg whites have many uses — egg yolks poached, then riced, make an attractive garnish; or mixed with pickle, relish, pimiento, and mayonnaise they make a delicious sandwich filling. Egg whites, beaten with sugar until stiff, make welcome garnishes for puddings, and glaze for bread or rolls.

• Save the rinds of oranges, lemons, limes, and grapefruits. Grate them and place in tightly covered jars. Store in refrigerator. Use as flavor-ings in frostings, sauces, puddings, and cakes.

• Ground leftover bologna, salami or sausage, added to ground beef will give an unusual flavor to hamburgers and meat loaf.

• Stir a little leftover oatmeal into a stew for added flavor and thicken-ing; or mix with pancakes. Or, shape into balls and fry in margarine, and sprinkle with cinnamon sugar.

• Trim fat from meat which needs to be browned, and use it instead of shortening to brown the meat.

• Combine leftover preserves or jellies with brown sugar and fruit juice and use as a glaze for ham.

• Use leftover sweet-pickle juice instead of vinegar when making the dressing for coleslaw.

• Save celery leaves, tender carrot tops, and green onion tops for use in stews, salads, and meat pies.

• Make toast cups from thinly sliced stale bread. Cut crusts, brush generously with melted margarine; press into large muffin cups. Toast in 350° F. oven for 10 to 15 minutes. Fill with creamed vegetable or meat mixture.

• Make easy canapés with leftover tuna fish. Moisten with mayon-naise, add a few drops of lemon juice and some minced parsley; serve on toast rounds or crackers.

• Chop leftover raisins, dates, or dried fruit, and add to bread puddings, or mix with apples when baking an apple pie.

Avant-Garde: The Menus

There's more to a meal than merely cooking it. The best-prepared dish will go unhonored if it is accompanied by unlikely companions.

The right kind of meal attracts the eye first, so good colors in foods should go together. Stay away from such combinations as creamed fish with mashed potatoes and corn. It all looks too bland. Instead, contrast the fish with color: serve it on golden triangles of toast and point up the creamy ivory color of the sauce with the bright green of peas and the orange of carrots. If you insist on mashed potatoes, then sprinkle them generously with paprika.

A good combination of textures is essential, too. Some foods should be crisp, some soft. The blandness of a cream-sauced dish should be accompanied by the tartness of a zesty salad to excite the palate.

If the meal is piping hot, the dessert should be cold—an ice cream, sherbet, or pudding. When you use a light entrée which is not very filling, make up for it by serving a luscious, rich dessert.

While repetition may have its virtues in some things, it adds nothing to meal planning. If you serve a fruit salad for dinner, don't serve fruit for dessert. Stewed tomatoes as a vegetable rule out a tomato salad.

Study your menu after you have planned it. Does it look good? Is there enough color? Is there something hot, something cold, something crisp, and something sweet? If there is, it all adds up to a perfect meal and it's bound to win you compliments.

Note: The asterisk in the menus that follow means that the recipe is given in this book. Look it up in the index.

Breakfast

Pineapple Juice
Waffles with Apple-Maple Syrup

Crisp Bacon

Lunch

Herb Omelet
Panned Potatoes

Tomatoes Vinaigrette
Cherry Pie

Dinner

Chicken Orientale*
Lettuce and Tomato Salad

Creamy French Dressing
Butterscotch Apple Dumplings*

Tips: Mix 1 cup canned applesauce, ½ cup water, ¼ cup brown sugar, and add a piece of cinnamon stick; bring to boil. Cook 3 to 5 minutes, stirring, until blended and heated. Stir in ½ teaspoon maple flavoring. Serve hot or cold.

Boil, drain and peel small new potatoes. Dip in thin cream and roll in seasoned fine bread crumbs. Place in baking pan and pour ¼ cup melted margarine on top. Bake 15 minutes in 400° F. oven, basting frequently.

Breakfast

Canned Apricots
Shirred Eggs

Danish Pastries

Lunch

Fish Fillet Parisienne
French Fried Potatoes

Tomato and Onion Salad
Sundae Treats

Dinner

Iloilo Chicken*
Whipped Potatoes
Tossed Green Salad

Blue Cheese Garlic Bread*
Hi-Hat Fudge Pudding*

Tips: Dip fish fillet in milk, then brush lightly on both sides with mayonnaise. Sprinkle with salt, pepper, and a dash of seasoned crumbs; broil quickly. Do not turn.

Prepare Sundae Treats ahead of time and keep plenty on hand. Line paper cups with thin strips of pound cake. Add 2 teaspoonfuls of a favorite jam, a generous ball of ice cream, another spoonful of jam; sprinkle with chopped peanuts. Freeze.

Breakfast

Cantaloupe
Cooked Whole Wheat Cereal

Raisin Toast with Honey

Lunch

Stuffed Green Peppers
Tossed Green Salad

Ice-Cream Cup Cake

Dinner

Veal au Vin*
Mashed Potatoes
Buttered Summer Squash

Shredded Lettuce with
  Thousand Island Dressing
Plum Betty*

Tips: Packaged seasoned stuffing and croutons make excellent bases for the stuffed peppers. Combine with cheese, leftover meats, and vegetables. Pour undiluted tomato soup over peppers; heat and serve.

Split cup cakes, top with slices of ice cream and chopped peanuts. Replace tops and freeze until ready to serve.

Breakfast

Fruit Cup
Western Omelet

Whole Wheat Muffins
Marmalade

Lunch

Open Grilled Sandwiches
Lettuce Wedges with Tabasco Dressing

Vienna Coffee Delight
Vanilla Cookies

Dinner

Bay Clam Chowder*
Salad Suprême*

Cloverleaf Rolls
Angel Ice-Cream Pie*

Tips: For the Open Grilled Sandwiches, toast one side of bread; on untoasted side place 1 slice of process American cheese, 1 slice of tomato, and 1 slice of crisp bacon. Broil until cheese is melted.

To bottled French dressing, add few drops of Tabasco sauce, lemon juice, and grated lemon rind.

Make extra-strong coffee, and chill. To serve, stir in partially whipped cream, top with stiffly whipped cream and a sprinkle of cinnamon and nutmeg. If, desired, sweeten coffee to taste.

Breakfast

Fresh Fruit Cup
Ready-to-Eat Cereal

Toasted English Muffins
Marmalade

Lunch

Tomato Pancakes
Romaine Salad

Herbed Cottage Cheese
Green Grapes with Caramel Sauce

Dinner

Swiss Steak Rhon*
Baked Turnip Puff*
Buttered Peas

Carrot Slaw
Easy Pumpkin Pie*

Tips: Prepare 1½ cups of a pancake mix with 1½ cups of milk according to package directions. Pour batter by spoonfuls onto hot greased griddle. Top each with a slice of tomato; season with salt and pepper. Pour another spoonful of pancake batter over tomato. Cook and brown on both sides.

Mix ½ cup brown sugar and 1 cup sour cream; spoon over grapes.

Breakfast

Baked Apple   Toast
Eggs Baked in Butter

Lunch

Date-Nut Cheese Sandwiches   Pineapple Hats
Buttermilk Shakes

Dinner

Tuna and Cheese Trianon*   Tossed Vegetable Salad
Buttered Asparagus   Peanut-y Bars*
Whipped Turnips

Tips: To make Buttermilk Shakes, combine ¾ cup orange juice, ⅛ teaspoon grated orange rind, 2 tablespoons sugar, and 1¾ cups chilled buttermilk; shake vigorously and serve.

Place a pineapple slice on individual plate for each serving. Top with vari-flavored sherbet; sprinkle with grated coconut.

Breakfast

Melon Slice   Sausage Patties
Tiny Jelly Rolls

Lunch

Lamb Chops   Ice Cream with Melba Sauce
Green Bean Succotash

Dinner

Tijuana Hamburg Pie*   Wilted Lettuce Salad*
Mashed Potatoes   Viennese Chocolate Cake*
Buttered Peas

Tips: For the Tiny Jelly Rolls, trim crusts off bread; spread bread slice thinly on one side with butter. Spread buttered bread with jelly and roll up securing roll with a wooden pick. Place on cookie sheet; brown under broiler, turning once.

Cook 1 package quick-frozen French-cut green beans and 1 package whole-kernel corn; drain. Add ¼ cup butter, 2 tablespoons sugar, ½ teaspoon salt and dash of pepper. Stir until well mixed.

Make Melba Sauce the easy way: combine 2 teaspoons cornstarch, ⅔ cup sugar, 1¼ cups crushed red raspberries, and ⅛ cup currants; cook, stirring constantly, over moderate heat until thickened and clear. Cool and serve.

Breakfast

Orange Juice   Broiled Sausages
Hot Farina   Blueberry Muffins

Lunch

Grilled Tuna and Cheese on   Health Salad
    Frankfurter Rolls   Snow White Cake

Dinner

Turkey Soup Parmentière*   Sliced Tomatoes
Country Omelet*   Oatmeal Rhubarb Crumble*
French Bread Chunks

Tips: Break or cut up lettuce and other greens. Toss with grated carrot, sliced radishes, chopped cucumber, and leftover vegetables. Serve with tangy Gorgonzola dressing.

Bake favorite flavor cake mix in a ring mold. Frost with sweetened and stiffly beaten whipped cream, garnish with cherries and nuts.

Breakfast

Cranberry Juice
Nut Buttermilk Pancakes

Bacon Curls
Syrup

Lunch

Cream of Pea Soup
Sardine Sandwiches

Crisp Greens Salad
Peach Pie

Dinner

Glazed Stuffed Ham Rolls*
Curried Carrots
Corn Muffins

Cabbage and Apple Salad*
Pink Cloud Pie*

Tips: Sprinkle 1 tablespoon of chopped nuts over each waffle before baking.
Drain sardines; mash. Add 3 ounces of packaged cream cheese, ¼ teaspoon salt, 1 teaspoon lemon juice, and ½ teaspoon Worcestershire sauce; mix well. Spread on bread.

Breakfast

Orange and Grapefruit Slices
Fried Rolled Oats

Bacon Strips
Coffee Cake

Lunch

French Beef Liver
Mashed Potatoes

Fruit Salad

Dinner

Moussaka*	Spinach and Celery Salad
French Fried Potatoes	Hot Milk Cake*

Tips: Place leftover cooked rolled oats in a greased mold. When cold, slice ½ inch thick. Dredge in flour and dip in beaten egg which has been thinned with 1 tablespoon water. Fry bacon until crisp; remove from fat and drain. Fry oatmeal slices in bacon fat, until brown on both sides.

Dip liver slices in French dressing; dust lightly with flour and fry.

Breakfast

Orange Juice	Bran Muffins
Scrambled Eggs Parmesan	

Lunch

Curried Chicken Salad	Cinnamon Rolls
Orange and Grapefruit Sections	Ice Cream

Dinner

Polenta Monte Bello*	Crusty Rolls
Deluxe Coleslaw*	Spice Cake

Tips: Scramble eggs and, just before setting, add 1 tablespoon grated Parmesan cheese for each serving.

Combine leftover chicken with celery, chutney, and curried mayonnaise.

Breakfast

Prune Juice	Corned Beef Hash Cups with
Toast	Baked Eggs

Lunch

Frankfurters
Creamy Corn

Green Salad
Ice Cream

Dinner

Oceania Fish Bake*
Buttered Broccoli
Tomato Cottage Cheese Salad*

Hi-Hat Fudge Pudding*
Cookies

Tips: Press slice of canned corned beef hash into a greased large muffin cup; drop in a raw egg. Bake in 350° F. oven until egg is set. Serve hot.

To a can (1 pound) of cream-style corn, stir in 2 beaten eggs, and ¼ cup evaporated milk; season to taste. Turn into greased baking dish and top with 3 tablespoons buttered crumbs. Bake until top is firm to touch.

Breakfast

Broiled Grapefruit
Swedish French Toast

Sausage Patties
Honey

Lunch

Waffled Peanut Butter Sandwiches
Cottage Cheese with Chives

Celery Sticks
Fruit Cup

Dinner

Meat Loaf Jardiniere*
Home-Fried Potatoes

Garden Fresh Salad*
Cracker Torte*

Tips: Add nutmeg and light cream in place of milk to French toast and brown in butter.

Make peanut-butter sandwiches, lightly butter outside slices and heat in waffle iron.

Breakfast

Baked Apple   Whole Wheat Toast
Cheese Omelet   Jelly

Lunch

Antipasto Platter   Chocolate Crunch Sundae
Tossed Green Salad

Dinner

Pork Cathay*   Lemon Cream Tarts*
Sliced Oranges and Bananas Salad   Fortune Cookies

Tips: Buy and bake a frozen pizza; cut into fourths. Arrange on luncheon plates with rolled slices of salami, cheese wedges, green pepper strips, sardines, and olives.

Combine ¾ cup chocolate sauce with ¼ cup coarsely ground peanut butter; thin to desired consistency with corn syrup or honey. Pour over ice cream.

Breakfast

Sliced Peaches   Toast with Grape Jelly
Rice Pudding

Lunch

Meat Loaf Sandwich   Fresh Fruit Platter
Minted Peas   Cheese Wedges

Dinner

Ring-A-Tuna*   Hot Rolls
Tomato and Cucumber Salad   Floating Island

Tips: Add a few pieces of plain mint candy to frozen peas; cook according to package directions.

Combine 2 tablespoons undiluted frozen limeade concentrate with 2 tablespoons honey, 2 tablespoons vegetable oil, and ½ teaspoon poppy seeds; sprinkle over fresh fruit.

Breakfast

Fresh Fruit	Toast
Eggs Any Style	Jelly

Lunch

Leftover Meat Loaf	Carrot and Celery Sticks
Harvard Spinach	Elegant Chocolate Pudding

Dinner

Veal Riblets Audubon*	Green Goddess Salad
Baked Potatoes	Apple Crisp*

Tips: Heat canned or leftover cooked spinach; drain. Stir in 1 tablespoon melted butter, 1 teaspoon minced onion, 1 teaspoon lemon juice; season to taste.

Make chocolate pudding (not instant) according to package directions; cool to room temperature. Fold in ½ cup cubed sponge cake and ¼ cup cut-up maraschino cherries. Chill, and serve with whipped topping.

Breakfast

Tomato Juice with Lemon	Sausage Patties
French Toast with Powdered Sugar	

Lunch

Chiliburgers	Confetti Cottage Cheese Salad
French Fried Potatoes	Pineapple Delight

Dinner

Ham Bake Amsterdam*   Aspic Avocado*
Carrot and Celery Sticks   Orange Sherbet

Tips: Sprinkle colored sugar lightly over cottage cheese to give it a festive touch.

Mix orange juice with marshmallow whip to desired consistency and serve over pineapple.

Breakfast

Grapefruit   Bacon Strips
Cornmeal Mush

Lunch

Beans and Franks   Carrot and Celery Sticks
Buttered Hard Roll   Sliced Peaches

Dinner

Beef Cardinale*   Cucumbers in Sour Cream
Gnocchi*   Fresh Pineapple Wedges

Tips: Bring 3 cups water to brisk boil, add 1 teaspoon salt, and slowly add 1 cup corn meal. Cook about 10 minutes. Reduce to simmer; cook until thick, stirring often. Serve hot with sugar and margarine.

Top hot beans and frankfurters with 1 tablespoon mixed ketchup and pickle relish.

Breakfast

Orange-Grapefruit Juice   Hot Ready-to-Eat Cereal with
Almond Coffee Cake   Warm Milk and Maple Sugar

Lunch

Fish Sticks in Toasted Frankfurter
Buns with Ketchup and Tartar Sauce

Marinated Mixed Vegetables
Pound Cake

Dinner

Bouillabaisse Americana*
Toasted French Bread

Tossed Green Salad
Skillet Fruit Cake*

Tips: For something unusual, place individual portions of your favorite ready-to-eat cereal on a square of foil and fold into a sealed packet. Heat in 375° F. oven for 10 minutes. Pour into heated bowl and serve with warm milk and maple sugar.

Cook a package of frozen mixed vegetables until just tender. Drain; add Italian dressing to cover. Marinate several hours in refrigerator. Partially drain; toss with lettuce.

Breakfast

Pineapple Juice
Creamed Toast with Poached Eggs

Marmalade

Lunch

Fish and Chips
Tossed Green Salad

Chocolate Trifle

Dinner

Mennonite Medley*
Spinach Toss

Toasted French Bread
Lemon Pie

Tips: Toast bread. Make 1 cup medium white sauce. Poach eggs; place on toast and pour sauce over all. Sprinkle with chopped parsley.

Prepare chocolate pudding according to package directions; cool slightly. In shallow dish, layer broken vanilla wafers, sliced bananas and chocolate pudding. Chill several hours; top with whipped topping.

Breakfast

Cranberry Sauce   Honey
French Toast

Lunch

Fruit and Cottage Cheese Salad   Deviled Eggs
Honey French Dressing   Cookies

Dinner

Pork Chops Valencia*   Crisp Greens with
Spinach with Sieved Egg   Avocado Dressing*
Baked Potato Boats   Ice Cream

Tips: A handy way to make many slices of French toast is to place dipped slices on greased baking sheet and bake in 500° F. oven for ten minutes or until browned.

Mash egg yolks with dry mustard and vinegar for an extra tangy flavor.

Breakfast

Apple Juice   Peaches
Ready-to-Eat Cereal   Toast and Jelly

Lunch

Herb Omelet   Merry Berry
Tangy Asparagus

Dinner

Smoked Pork Collins*   Fruit Salad with Sesame Dressing
Whipped Potatoes   Butterscotch Bread Pudding*

Tips: Heat canned asparagus in own liquid; drain. Add 2 tablespoons butter, melted, with 1 tablespoon lemon juice, and 1 teaspoon grated lemon rind. Season to taste.

For the Merry Berry Dessert make raspberry gelatin dessert as directed on package. Pour half of prepared mixture into a bowl and chill for future serving. Chill remainder until syrupy; add 1 package partially thawed frozen raspberries. Spoon mixture into seeded cantaloupe halves and chill until set.

Breakfast

Lemon Wedges with Lime
Australian Fried Eggs

Danish Pastries

Lunch

Soup
Ham Salad Sandwiches
Carrot and Celery Sticks

Potato Chips
Strawberry Gelatin

Dinner

Mock Chicken Legs Mamee*
Buttered Spaghettini
Fresh Asparagus

Lettuce and Cucumber Salad
Tropical Pie*

Tips: Serve fried eggs on heated leftover slices of beef or on fried bologna. Leftover ground ham, mixed with chopped pickle, celery, prepared mustard, and mayonnaise, makes ideal filling for sandwiches.

Breakfast

Orange Juice
French Toast

Honey

Lunch

Vegetable Soup with
    Frankfurter Chunks

Pink Lady Pears
Cookies

Dinner

Texan Breast of Lamb*
Buttered Lima Beans
Cheese-Stuffed Celery

Cucumber Sticks
Fruit Gelatin

Tips: Sauté frankfurter chunks in margarine and ¼ teaspoon dry mustard, then add to hot soup.

Heat canned pear halves in own juice with ¼ teaspoon cloves, 3 tablespoons brown sugar, and ⅛ teaspoon cinnamon. Chill. Serve pear halves topped with spoonfuls of partially thawed frozen raspberries.

Breakfast

Fruit Cup	Maple Sugar
Ready-to-Eat Cereal	Cinnamon Toast

Lunch

Hamburgers	Sliced Tomatoes and Cucumbers
Confetti Rice Bake	Raisin Pie Romanoff*

Dinner

Cheese Soufflé*	French Dressing
Tomato Vegetable Sauce*	Hot Rolls with Butter
Hearts of Lettuce	Honey Pecan Pie*

Tips: For Confetti Rice Bake, cook rice according to package directions and turn into baking dish. Stir in chopped green pepper, pimiento, and grated carrots. Add butter, and season to taste; top with grated cheese. Bake to heat through.

Make raisin pie; serve warm with a spoonful of sour cream and a sprinkle of brown sugar.

Breakfast

Sliced Bananas	Bacon Slices
Pancakes with Syrup	

Lunch

Sunny Sandwiches	Golden Eggnog
Potato Chips	Cookies

Dinner

Pennsylvania Dutch Supper*
Lettuce Wedges with
  Lemon Dressing

Hot Buttered Rye Bread
Fresh Fruit Platter

Tips: To make sandwich filling, use ½ cup each seedless raisins, shredded carrots, and cottage cheese, with ⅛ teaspoon salt and 1 tablespoon mayonnaise; mix well.

For each serving of eggnog, use 1 well-beaten egg, 2 teaspoons sugar, pinch of salt, 1 cup cold milk and dash of nutmeg; beat and serve.

Breakfast

Pineapple-Grapefruit Juice
Scrambled Eggs and Sausages

Toast

Lunch

Open Grilled Cheese Sandwiches
Jellied Cranberry Salad

Apple Pie

Dinner

Spiced Tomato Juice
Meat Loaf Chatelaine*
Buttered Broccoli

Tossed Green Salad
Scotch Shortbread*

Tips: Toast bread slices on one side. Cover lightly buttered untoasted side with Cheddar cheese. Place under broiler until cheese melts. Sprinkle with paprika, garnish with parsley and pickles. Serve at once.

Use canned whole cranberry sauce and chopped celery mixed with cubes of lime-flavored gelatin.

Breakfast

Grapefruit Juice
Hot Farina

Broiled Sausages
Toast

Lunch

Soup
O Sole Mio's

Tossed Green Salad
Kurt's Cookie Sandwiches

Dinner

Osso Buco*
Risotto Parmesan

Spinach and Tomato Salad
Cantaloupe with Ice Cream

Tips: For the O Sole Mio's, top slices of bread with slices of cheese; sprinkle with a little minced parsley. Add dash of oregano; spread with spoonful of cooked onion rings; top with thin slice of tomato and spoonful of chili sauce. Broil 3 minutes.

Put spoonful of marshmallow whip on top of big cookie; cover with another cookie.

Breakfast

Orange Juice
Toasted Waffles

Hot Applesauce

Lunch

Soup
Denver Sandwich

Cole Slaw
Prune Whip

Dinner

Stuffed Pork New Orleans*
Creamed Carrots

Caesar's Salad*
White Cake

Tips: Heat canned applesauce in saucepan, sprinkle with a little nutmeg and sugar, then spoon over toasted leftover or frozen waffles.

Whips are so easy to make—when puréed baby fruits are on sale buy several jars! Add a fluffy topping or a vanilla sauce.

Breakfast

Tomato Juice
Hot Cereal

Brown Betty Applesauce

Lunch

Bologna Slices Broiled
Southern Yams

Sliced Tomatoes
Ice Cream

Dinner

Onion Pie Hongrois*
Chef's Salad

Assorted Relishes
Strawberry Chiffon Cake

Tips: Spread canned applesauce in shallow baking dish; top with crumbled graham crackers, brown sugar, and dots of margarine. Broil until bubbly and browned.

Canned mashed yams are very inexpensive. Turn 1 can into a baking dish; stir in ⅛ cup chopped salted peanuts. Dot with margarine, sprinkle with brown sugar and bake 25 minutes.

Breakfast

Orange Juice
Pink Hot Cereal

Coffee Cake

Lunch

French Omelet
Buttered Peas

Laurel's Black-Bottom Pie

Dinner

Lamb Smetana*
Potatoes au Gratin
Glazed Carrots

Mixed Salad
Chocolate Brownies

Tips: Heat strawberry jam in top of double boiler. Spoon onto hot cereal in place of sugar. Top with thin pat of margarine and stir into hot cereal.

Prepare chocolate pudding according to package directions, adding rum flavoring; pour, cool, into baked and cooled pie shell. Repeat with vanilla pudding. Chill; top with whipped topping.

Breakfast

Fruit of the Season   Bacon Strips
New York Poached Eggs   Muffins

Lunch

Soup   Potato Chips
Chicken Salad Sandwiches   Jelly Roll Surprise

Dinner

Flank Steak Fiorio*   Romaine Salad
Buttered Thin Noodles   Ice Cream
Broccoli

Tips: Sprinkle eggs with a little mixed grated cheese and parsley just before serving.

Cut jelly roll into thick slices and sprinkle each with a little fruit juice. Wrap each slice individually in square of foil; place on cookie sheet and bake at 400° F. 10 minutes. Open and serve from foil, topped with vanilla ice cream.

Breakfast

Grape Juice   Toasted Raisin Bread
Hot Wheat Cereal

Lunch

Sloppy Joes*   Chocolate Cake
Citrus Salad

Dinner

Hamburger Romanoff*   Tossed Greens Salad
Mashed Potatoes   Cherry Pie à la Mode
Buttered Green Beans

Tips: Toast raisin bread, butter, and sprinkle with cinnamon and dash of nutmeg.

Mix orange and grapefruit segments with lettuce greens. Add grated lemon rind for extra sharpness.

Breakfast

Broiled Grapefruit Maraschino
Scrambled Eggs

Toast with Bacon Butter

Lunch

Soup
Cheesy Muffins

Sausage Patties
Chilled Fruit Cup

Dinner

Roast Lamb Shoulder*
Mashed Potatoes
Herbed Carrots

Tossed Salad
Gingerbread Squares with
Vanilla Ice Cream

Tips: Prepare grapefruit as usual, then spoon a tablespoon of maraschino syrup from jar of cherries over each half; broil.

Crumble 2 strips crisp bacon to ½ stick margarine; spread on hot toast.

Split and butter English muffins; toast under broiler. Top each half with a thin slice of cheese. Return to broiler for 30 seconds; serve at once.

Cut pared carrots into chunks; cook until tender. Drain; mix with salt, pepper, and margarine to taste; toss with minced parsley and a little dried dill.

Breakfast

Pineapple Chunks
Poached Eggs on Toast

Jelly

Lunch

Grilled Cheese Sandwiches
Carrot Sticks
Pickles

Peppy Cole Slaw
Two-Flavor Cupcakes

Dinner

Pork Tenderloin Slices
Lettuce Wedges with
  Mustard Dressing

Tomato Pies Ana*
Dutch Apple Crunch Pie*

Tips: Add a small, finely chopped, hot cherry pepper to the dressing before tossing your favorite cole slaw.

Split two flavors of cupcakes, then put back together again so that you have a vanilla top on a chocolate bottom. Spread with a spoonful of marshmallow whip to hold together.

Breakfast

Orange Juice
Scrambled Eggs California

Sweet Rolls

Lunch

Open-Face Frank and Bean Broil
Fresh Relishes and Pickles

Applesauce and Cookies

Dinner

Chicken Grazzia*
Buttered Poppy-Seed Noodles*

Waldorf Salad
Coconut Cake

Tips: Cook eggs to a soft scramble, then fold in several spoonfuls of cottage cheese and dot with tart jelly—serve hot.

Dice 3 frankfurters and combine with a can (1 pound) of pork and beans with tomato sauce. Heap mixture on toasted soft buns and top with a slice of cheese on each. Broil until cheese melts and beans sizzle.

Breakfast

Orange Juice
Ready-to-Eat High
  Protein Cereal

Milk
Banana
Cinnamon Toast

Lunch

Soup   Thrifty Sundaes
Dagwood Sandwiches

Dinner

Short Ribs and Limas Devon*   Tossed Green Salad
Peas and Pearl Onions   Coffee Ice Cream

Tips: Fill sandwiches with thin slices of leftover meat, cheese, tomatoes, lettuce, etc., making them thick and hearty.

Bake tart shells. Cool and fill with ice cream; top with crushed fruit and sprinkle with chopped nuts.

Breakfast

Fruit of the Season   Jelly
Poached Eggs Benedict

Lunch

Hamburgers à l'Oignon   Old-Fashioned Sugar Cookies
Lettuce and Tomatoes

Dinner

Persian Lamb Curry*   Toasted French Bread
Tossed Vegetable-Tomato Salad   Lemon Sherbet

Tips: For each serving, quickly fry ½ thin slice boiled ham and place on piece of toast. Top with poached egg and spoonful of mayonnaise; sprinkle with lemon juice.

Broil hamburgers; keep warm. Drain all but 2 teaspoons fat from heated skillet. Add 1½ cups thinly sliced raw onions; sprinkle with 1½ teaspoons sugar. Stir and cook until onions begin to turn yellow. Add 2 tablespoons water; cover and cook 3 to 4 minutes. Season to taste and serve hot.

Breakfast

Orange Juice
Sweet Rolls

Hot Rolled Oats with
   Brown Sugar

Lunch

Neptune Sandwich
Coleslaw

Peaches Parisienne
Almond Cookies

Dinner

Hot Tomato Juice
Egg Croquettes Malfel*
Buttered Asparagus

Mixed Salad
Apple Pie

Tips: Bake individual brown-and-serve French loaves as directed. Cut off and keep top, and remove white bread, leaving a shell about 1½ inches thick all around. Spread insides with mayonnaise; sprinkle lightly with celery salt. Fill with drained sardines, sliced cheese, sliced tomato, and shredded lettuce. Replace top and wrap tightly. Heat in oven 3 minutes and serve.

Thoroughly chill canned sliced peaches, adding just a touch of sherry flavoring. Sprinkle with toasted coconut shreds just before serving.

Breakfast

Grapefruit
French Toast with Syrup

Bacon Strips

Lunch

Double Beef-Burgers
Lettuce and Sliced Tomatoes

Snowflake Pudding

Dinner

Broiled Pork Chops
Macaroni and Cheese Suprême*
Buttered Peas

Lettuce Wedges with
   French Dressing
Chocolate Brownies

Tips: Divide 1½ pounds lean ground beef into 12 portions and pat each into a thin round. Combine 1 tablespoon minced parsley, 1 tablespoon minced onion, and 1 tablespoon chopped process American cheese with salt and pepper; heap in center of half the meat rounds. Top with remaining rounds; press edges together to seal. Broil on both sides.

Make favorite flavor instant pudding; stir in tiny white marshmallows and serve.

Breakfast

Sliced Oranges   Fried Bologna
Waffles with Buttered Syrup

Lunch

Welsh Rarebit on Toast   Mock Fruit Shortcake
Tomato and Cucumber on Lettuce

Dinner

Sorrento Meat Loaf*   Crisp Greens Salad
Whipped Potatoes   Pound Cake
Glazed Carrots

Tips: Coarsely chop tomatoes and cucumbers and toss with blue cheese dressing.

Bake refrigerated biscuits according to directions. Split biscuits; butter and lightly toast under broiler. Place two halves in each serving dish. Heap with diced bananas and chopped maraschino cherries; top with whipped topping.

Breakfast

Pineapple Juice   Toasted English Muffins
Ready-to-Eat Cereal   Jelly

Lunch

Meat-Loaf Sandwiches
Golden Coleslaw*

Judy's Pudding Cake

Dinner

Roast Chicken
Buttered Squash
Peas and Celery

Louisiana Tomato Aspic*
Butterscotch Brownies

Tips: Shred equal parts of carrots and cabbage. Add crushed pineapple to dressing and toss lightly.

Simmer canned peach slices with ¼ teaspoon mace, ⅛ teaspoon nutmeg and 1 teaspoon lemon rind with peach syrup. Spoon hot over toasted left-over pound cake slices.

Meat:
The Hub of Each Meal

When planning meals for your family, you should keep two things in mind. Give them the kind of meals they like, and give them the kind of nourishment they need.

It is easy to plan well-balanced meals around meat because meat goes such a long way toward meeting the body's nutritional needs. Every grade and cut of meat can be made tender and palatable by following certain guidelines that are the basic principles of meat cookery: the control of temperature in cooking, and the specific methods for cooking a particular meat and cut.

If you don't have a meat thermometer, it will be worth your while to invest in one. Inserted into the thickest portion of the cut, the thermometer is scaled to indicate various degrees of doneness for all types of meat—which would help you to cook it to perfection.

Knowing your way around the meat counter is a big help in solving your meal planning problems. Besides getting acquainted with your butcher, familiarize yourself with the various cuts. Roasts, chops, and steaks are wonderful because they're so easy to prepare, but we're going to slight them in this book because we believe it makes a lot more sense to spread your meat money over as many of the week's meals as possible, rather than on a few splurges.

Although you're usually able to find any meat you have in mind, when you shop it's well to remember that, like vegetables and fruits, there are seasonal patterns in marketing that make some meats better buys than others at certain times of the year. So watch your Specials!

The federal government offers two services to help you in meat buying: One is government inspection of all meat shipped interstate to make sure that it is wholesome; the other is meat grading. There are seven official U. S. government grades of meat, but only four are normally found in retail markets:

U. S. Prime — Refers to the highest grade, usually of beef, and is normally in very small supply. This term should not be used erroneously to describe a cut, as, for example, "prime" ribs.

U. S. Choice — Beef, veal, lamb, and mutton. Well marbled with fat and has a moderately thick fat covering.

U. S. Good — Has a fat covering somewhat thinner than U. S. Choice.

U. S. Commercial and Utility — Lower grades with thin fat covering, used for braising or cooking in liquid.

Pork is usually not graded at all.

Look for the U.S.D.A. inspection and grade marks used by the U. S. Department of Agriculture as buying guides.

A WORD ABOUT STEWS

Stews are natural-born meat-stretchers, and you can count on them to make the most of a bargain. Any low-cost cut of meat will make a fine stew. Remember, too, it's good managing to make enough to freeze for other meals. The following are good flavor combinations:

Beef Stew

Choose cuts from neck, brisket, flank, shank, chuck or heel of round.

For vegetables—choose from onions, carrots, turnips, celery, potatoes, green beans, cabbage. Use tomatoes as part of liquid.

For seasonings—choose from pepper, green pepper, minced celery tops, carrot tops or parsley, garlic, paprika, chili powder, Worcestershire sauce, ketchup, vinegar, clove, basil.

Veal Stew

Use cuts from neck, shoulder, shank, breast, flank.

For vegetables—choose from onions, green beans, parsnips, cauliflower, carrots, potatoes, celery, tomatoes, celery root.

For seasonings—choose from green pepper, bay leaf, celery tops, paprika, nutmeg, marjoram, savory.

Lamb Stew

Use cuts from neck, shank, breast or shoulder.

For vegetables—choose from onions, carrots, peas, potatoes or rice, celery, Lima beans, tomatoes, cauliflower, parsnips, leeks.

For seasonings—choose from pepper, dried mint, curry powder, thyme, savory, ketchup, minced carrot tops.

Pork Stew

Use cuts from shoulder or neck, or any lean pork.

For vegetables—choose from green beans, onions, potatoes, sweet potatoes, turnips, cabbage, Lima beans, celery.

For seasonings—choose from pepper, paprika, chili powder, sage, parsley, bay leaf, clove.

Ways To Serve Stews:

With Vegetables—Stews may be cooked without vegetables, then served with carrots, turnips, or potatoes.

With Potatoes—If potatoes are not cooked in stew, serve mashed, boiled, or baked potatoes to accompany stew, or serve sweet potatoes with pork or lamb stew.

With Noodles, Macaroni—Serve stew with well-seasoned noodles or macaroni instead of potatoes.

In Meat Pies—Turn a stew into a flavorful meat pie by topping it with a pastry crust.

In Shepherd's Pies—Turn stew into an elegant dish. Pile fluffy mashed potatoes over top, or pipe around edge.

As Stew With Dumplings—Plain or potato dumplings may be dropped by tablespoons on top of stew.

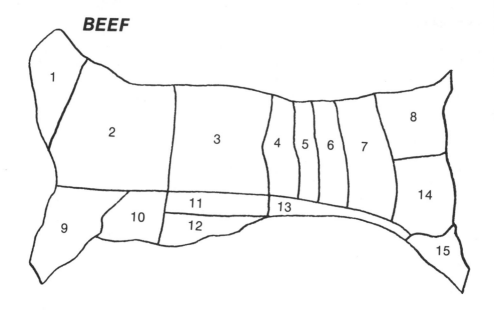

BEEF

1. *Neck:* soups, stews
2. *Chuck:* pot roasts, braised steaks, ground meat, stews
3. *Ribs:* roasts (standing or rolled)
4. *Club Steaks*
5. *T-Bone Steaks*
6. *Porterhouse Steaks*
7. *Loin End:* sirloin steaks or roasts
8. *Rump:* pot roasts
9. *Fore Shank:* soups
10. *Brisket:* fresh or corned beef
11. *Short Ribs:* for braising
12. *Plate:* soups and stews
13. *Flank:* flank steak
14. *Round:* pot roasts, braised steaks
15. *Hind Shank:* soups

Budgetwise, 60 to 65 percent of beef cuts are thrifty, and learning to use the less expensive cuts means cutting down on costs without cutting down on nutrition.

Learn to identify the expensive cuts:

Short Loin
. . . club steaks
. . . porterhouse steaks
. . . T-bone steaks

Loin End
. . . sirloin steaks
. . . roasts

Round
. . . braised steaks
. . . roasts

The inexpensive cuts are:

Neck
. . . for soups and stews

Chuck
. . . ground meat
. . . pot roasts
. . . steaks
. . . stews

Fore Shank
. . . soups

Brisket
. . . fresh or corned beef

Ribs
. . . roasts (standing or rolled)

Short Ribs
. . . for braising

Plate
. . . for soups and stews

Flank
. . . steak

Rump
. . . pot roasts

Hind Shank
. . . soups

Tips: To save money on chuck, buy a large cut at a lower price per pound and divide it for cooking in three ways: the rounded, boneless end for stew; the center with round bone for pot roast; and the remaining piece, sliced lengthwise into two Swiss steaks.

To tenderize chuck, rump, flank, brisket, cook slowly by the moist-heat method—braising or stewing.

Shank and knuckle bones can be sawed through by your meat cutter, or your butcher, and used in soup or stock preparation to add richness and flavor.

Sauerbraten

Meat becomes flavorfully tender when simmered in a vinegary sauce.

3½ to 4 pounds pot roast of beef
2 cups vinegar
2 cups water
2 medium onions, sliced
10 whole cloves

4 bay leaves
6 whole peppercorns
2 tablespoons salt
2 tablespoons sugar
2 tablespoons vegetable oil

Place meat in deep bowl. Combine remaining ingredients, except oil, blend well. Pour mixture over meat. Cover; place in refrigerator for 2 days; turn meat several times during this time. Remove meat; dry with absorbent paper. Heat oil in heavy saucepan; add meat and brown slowly all over, turning frequently to brown evenly on all sides. Add 1 cup of vinegar mixture. Cover tightly; cook over very low heat, about 3 hours or until meat is fork tender, adding more vinegar mixture, if necessary. Makes 8 to 10 servings.

Boston Bay Pot Roast

4 pounds chuck roast
1 teaspoon salt
⅛ teaspoon pepper
3 tablespoons flour
½ cup water

5 medium potatoes, pared
5 medium carrots, scraped
5 medium onions, peeled
3 tablespoons shortening

Heat oven to 325° F. Dredge meat with mixture of salt, pepper and flour; brown in hot shortening on all sides. Place meat in baking pan; add water. Cover; bake 3 hours. During last 45 minutes add vegetables. Check for doneness and serve. Makes 4 servings with leftovers.

Swiss Pot Roast

A newcomer with gusto, this is a take-off on Swiss steak, which is an exciting change.

¼ cup flour
1 teaspoon salt
¼ teaspoon pepper
3½ to 4 pounds beef pot roast
3 tablespoons shortening
2 cloves garlic, finely minced

⅓ cup chopped green pepper
½ cup chopped onion
1 small can chopped mushrooms,
  with liquid
1 can (10½ ounces) tomato soup

Combine flour, salt, and pepper; coat both sides of roast. Brown in hot shortening in heavy kettle. Add remaining ingredients. Cover; simmer over low heat 2 hours or until tender. Makes 6 servings.

Hawaiian Pot Roast

3 to 4 pounds beef chuck roast
1 large onion, sliced
1 cup canned pineapple juice
3 tablespoons soy sauce
1½ teaspoons ground ginger
½ teaspoon salt
4 stalks celery, sliced
4 carrots, sliced

2 small sweet potatoes, pared
    and thinly sliced
½ pound fresh spinach, cleaned,
    with stems removed
6 fresh mushrooms, thinly sliced
1 tablespoon cornstarch
2 tablespoons cold water

Place meat in shallow pan; cover with onion slices. Pour mixture of pineapple juice, soy sauce, ginger, and salt over it. Let stand 2 hours, turning meat once. Place meat in heavy kettle; add onion-and-pineapple mixture. Simmer, covered, 2½ hour or until meat is tender when pierced with fork. Add celery, carrots, and sweet potatoes; simmer 10 minutes longer. Arrange spinach and mushrooms on top; cook 5 minutes so that spinach is just wilted. Remove meat and vegetables to heated serving platter; keep warm. Combine cornstarch and water; stir into kettle drippings. Cook, stirring constantly, until thickened. Makes 6 servings.

Barbecued Pot Roast

Savory and tangy, this will become everyone's favorite.

1½ pounds beef for pot roast
1½ tablespoons fat
1 teaspoon salt
¼ teaspoon pepper
¼ cup water
½ cup tomato sauce
2 medium onions, thinly sliced

1 clove garlic, minced
1 tablespoon brown sugar
¼ teaspoon dry mustard
¼ teaspoon Worcestershire sauce
2 tablespoons lemon juice
2 tablespoons vinegar
2 tablespoons ketchup

Brown meat in hot fat in deep skillet; season with salt and pepper. Add water, tomato sauce, onions and garlic. Cook, covered, over low heat 1½ hours. Combine remaining ingredients; pour over meat. Continue cooking, covered, 1 hour longer or until tender. Remove meat to heated serving platter. Skim off fat. Serve gravy with meat.

Budget Sukiyaki

Do all the slicing ahead of time, arrange ingredients on a tray, and cook quickly in chafing dish or hibachi.

¾ pound tender sirloin steak,
   cut into paper-thin strips
1 tablespoon vegetable oil
½ cup thinly sliced cabbage
1 cup thinly sliced celery
½ cup washed and drained spinach
   leaves, with stems removed

4 green onions, thinly sliced
¼ pound thinly sliced
   fresh mushrooms
2 tablespoons Worcestershire sauce
¼ cup soy sauce
1 tablespoon red wine
1½ teaspoons sugar

Sear meat in vegetable oil until brown on both sides. Add remaining ingredients. Cook at high heat 3 minutes, stirring constantly. Reduce heat to low; simmer 5 to 6 minutes longer, stirring occasionally. Vegetables should be crisp tender.

Flank Steak Jubilee

If you must serve steak for a company meal, plan a flank steak which has no waste in bones and fat.

½ cup vegetable oil
¼ cup vinegar
1 tablespoon capers
½ cup chopped onion
1 bay leaf
1 teaspoon salt
⅛ teaspoon pepper

1 flank steak, about 1¾ pounds
¼ cup coarsely shredded
   sharp Cheddar cheese
1 tablespoon finely chopped parsley
1 tablespoon finely chopped
   celery leaves

Combine oil, vinegar, capers, onion, bay leaf, salt, and pepper in saucepan; bring to boil, cook 5 minutes. Place steak in large shallow baking pan; pour hot oil mixture over meat. Cover; refrigerate overnight, turning meat occasionally. Remove meat from marinade; place on board. Sprinkle with cheese, parsley and celery. Starting with long side, carefully roll meat into a tight roll. Cut crosswise into slices 1½ inches thick. Insert a metal skewer into each meat slice to hold roll together. Broil 3 inches from source of heat about 10 minutes, turning once. Makes 6 servings.

Swiss Steak Savory

¼ cup flour
¼ teaspoon ginger
¼ teaspoon marjoram
⅛ teaspoon oregano
⅛ teaspoon thyme
½ teaspoon salt
1 pound round steak,
    cut in small pieces

1 small kidney,
    cut in small pieces
½ teaspoon prepared mustard
1½ teaspoons Worcestershire
    sauce
1 cup water
4 small onions

Combine flour, ginger, herbs, and salt. Roll meat in mixture. Turn in heavy skillet. Add mustard and Worcestershire sauce. Pour in 1 cup water. Cover; bring to boil. Reduce heat; simmer 2 hours or until meat is tender. Add onions; cook 35 minutes longer or until tender.

Chef's Swiss Steak

1 pound round steak,
    cut 1½ inches thick
1½ tablespoons flour
¾ teaspoon salt
⅛ teaspoon pepper
1½ tablespoons shortening
½ cup chopped onion

¼ cup chopped celery
¼ cup mushrooms, coarsely chopped
1 cup canned tomatoes
½ can (6 ounces) tomato paste
1½ teaspoons Worcestershire sauce
1 beef bouillon cube

Sprinkle meat with combined flour, salt, and pepper on both sides, and pound meat with rim of saucer. Cut into serving pieces. Heat shortening in large heavy skillet; brown onion lightly and push to one side. Brown meat well on both sides. Stir in remaining ingredients. Simmer, covered, 2 hours or until meat is fork tender. Skim off fat. Serve meat with sauce on heated serving platter.

Flank Steak À La Creole

This is a wonderful homey dish with traditional bread stuffing and a rich Creole Sauce.

¼ cup chopped onion
1 teaspoon bacon drippings
2 cups dry bread cubes
¼ teaspoon salt
¼ teaspoon poultry seasoning

Dash pepper
1 flank steak, about 1¾ pounds,
   scored
Creole Sauce (recipe below)

Sauté 2 tablespoons chopped onion in bacon drippings until golden. Add bread cubes, salt, poultry seasoning, and pepper. Spread stuffing over steak; roll like a jelly roll and fasten with wooden picks. Lace with string. Brown on all sides in skillet. Add Creole Sauce, and simmer, covered, 1¾ to 2 hours or until tender. Add mushrooms; cook 15 minutes longer.

Creole Sauce

1¼ cups canned tomatoes
½ cup water
2 tablespoons minced green onion

2 tablespoons ketchup
¼ cup chopped green pepper
½ cup sliced mushrooms

Combine all ingredients and add to meat in skillet.

Swiss Steak Rhon

1½ pounds round steak,
   1½ inches thick
1 teaspoon salt
¼ cup flour
½ teaspoon garlic salt
¼ teaspoon pepper

2 tablespoons shortening
2 large onions, sliced
1 cup sliced celery
2 cups canned tomatoes
1 tablespoon Worcestershire sauce

Trim excess fat from steak. Combine salt, flour, garlic salt, and pepper. Roll steak in flour mixture and pound with the edge of a heavy saucer. Melt shortening in heavy skillet. Brown meat on both sides. Add remaining ingredients. Cover; simmer 1½ to 2 hours or until meat is tender.

Roman Minute Steaks

Have your budget and eat it, too! Minute steaks with herbed tomato sauce and mozzarella cheese give a festive Italian accent.

4 minute steaks, ¼ pound each
1½ tablespoons vegetable oil
1 small clove garlic, minced
1½ cups tomato sauce
½ cup water
1 teaspoon oregano

½ teaspoon basil
¼ teaspoon thyme
Dash pepper
4 thin slices mozzarella cheese
2 tablespoons chopped parsley

Brown steaks quickly in hot oil. Add garlic, tomato sauce, water, and seasonings. Simmer, uncovered, turning steaks occasionally until sauce is thick, about 45 to 50 minutes. Top each steak with a cheese slice. Skim off excess fat. Transfer steaks to heated serving platter; pour sauce over and sprinkle with parsley.

Steak Mirada

Chuck steak is always a good buy—sprinkle it with instant unseasoned tenderizer and serve it with a richly seasoned sauce.

1 chuck steak, about 1½ pounds
   and 1½ inches thick
8 small stuffed green olives

2 tablespoons prepared mustard
2 tablespoons bottled steak sauce
Continental Sauce (recipe below)

Make cuts into steak all around edge with a sharp knife; push olives deep into cuts. Place steak on rack in broiler pan. Combine mustard and steak sauce; brush evenly over top of steak. Broil to desired doneness. Turn; broil a few minutes longer. Serve with sauce.

Continental Sauce

½ cup apple juice
1 tablespoon finely chopped onion
1 tablespoon cider vinegar
1 teaspoon tarragon

2 egg yolks
½ cup melted margarine
Dash cayenne
1 teaspoon chopped parsley

Combine apple juice, onion, vinegar, and tarragon in small saucepan. Heat to boil. Reduce heat; simmer, uncovered, 10 minutes or until mixture measures ⅛ cup. Strain. Beat egg yolks slightly in top of double boiler; stir in about ⅛ cup of melted margarine. Place over simmering water. Beat in strained liquid, alternately with remaining melted margarine until smooth and well blended. Stir in cayenne and parsley.

Beef Bourguignon

Scrumptious feasting—this Continental favorite is tender, mild-tasting beef in an extra-rich gravy.

2 pounds round steak,
   cut in 2-inch cubes
2 teaspoons salt
¼ teaspoon pepper
1½ tablespoons flour
12 small white onions
½ pound salt pork, cut in cubes

½ teaspoon marjoram
¼ teaspoon thyme
1 cup dry red wine
½ cup water
2 carrots, thickly sliced
8 small new potatoes, pared

Dust steak with mixture of salt, pepper, and flour. Sauté onions and salt pork in heavy kettle until pork is crisp. Remove onions and salt pork; set aside. Add meat to kettle drippings; brown slowly on all sides. Add bits of salt pork, herbs, wine, and water. Simmer, covered, until meat is tender, about 1 hour. Add onions, carrots, and potatoes; cook 30 minutes longer. Makes 6 servings.

Flank Steak Fiorio

1½ pounds flank steak
½ teaspoon salt
¼ teaspoon pepper
⅓ cup grated Parmesan cheese
1 tablespoon chopped parsley
1 tablespoon chopped celery
1½ tablespoons shortening

1 clove garlic, minced
1 cup tomato purée
½ cup tomato sauce
4 slices lemon
½ teaspoon basil
½ teaspoon marjoram

Score both sides of flank steak about ⅛ inch deep. Sprinkle with salt, pepper, cheese, parsley, and celery. Roll up as for jelly roll; tie with string. Heat shortening in deep heavy skillet and sauté garlic. Brown flank steak on all sides. Add tomato purée and tomato sauce, lemon, and herbs. Cover; simmer 1 hour or until fork tender. Turn flank steak onto serving platter; remove string. Remove lemon slices from sauce; pour over meat.

Beef Jardiniere

For a hearty and economical family meal, here's an easy oven way with steak and vegetables.

1 chuck beefsteak, about 3 pounds	¼ cup wine vinegar
3 tablespoons flour	2 tablespoons ketchup
3 tablespoons vegetable oil	1 teaspoon salt
12 small white onions	1 teaspoon marjoram
6 medium carrots, scraped	¼ teaspoon pepper
3 small white turnips,	1 bay leaf
pared and sliced thin	
1 can (10½ ounces) condensed onion soup	

Heat oven to 375° F. Rub steak well with flour. Brown in oil in large skillet; transfer to shallow baking dish. Sauté onions, carrots, and turnips in drippings; arrange around steak. Stir remaining ingredients into skillet; heat to boiling. Pour over steak and vegetables. Bake, covered, 1½ hours or until meat is tender. Remove bay leaf. Place steak on heated serving platter; surround with vegetables and pour gravy over all. Makes 6 servings.

Cathay Short Ribs

2 pounds short ribs of beef	1 medium green pepper,
2 tablespoons flour	cut in chunks
1 teaspoon salt	½ cup sugar
⅛ teaspoon pepper	¼ teaspoon cinnamon
1 cup water	¼ teaspoon allspice
8 small onions	¼ teaspoon ground cloves
1 cup dried prunes	3 tablespoons vinegar
1 cup dried apricots	

Trim off some of the fat from short ribs; fry fat in skillet, remove and discard. Coat meat in mixture of flour, salt, and pepper; brown on all sides in hot fat. Drain off drippings. Cover skillet; cook over low heat 45 minutes. Add onions, prunes, apricots, and green pepper. Season with sugar, spices, and vinegar. Cook, covered, 1 to 1¼ hours longer or until meat and vegetables are tender.

Polynesian Short Ribs

A South Seas specialty served in Tahiti and adapted here to an economical and streamlined version.

3 pounds short ribs of beef
¼ cup flour
2 tablespoons shortening
1 can (10½ ounces)
    condensed beef broth
1 cup dried apricots
½ cup raisins

2 tablespoons brown sugar
2 tablespoons vinegar
¼ teaspoon cinnamon
¼ teaspoon cloves
⅛ teaspoon allspice
⅛ teaspoon mace

Dust ribs with flour; brown in shortening in large heavy skillet. Pour off excess drippings. Combine remaining ingredients; pour over ribs. Cook over low heat, covered, 2½ hours or until tender, turning ribs often.

Potted Short Ribs

3½ pounds short ribs of beef
2½ teaspoons salt
¼ teaspoon pepper
Flour
3 tablespoons vegetable oil

2½ cups water
1 pound green beans
8 small white onions
¼ teaspoon crushed red pepper

Sprinkle short ribs with salt and pepper; coat lightly with flour. Heat oil in large skillet; brown meat on all sides. Add water; cover, and cook slowly 1½ hours or until beef is tender. Clean beans and cut in slivers. Add to beef with onions and sprinkle red pepper. Continue cooking over low heat, covered, 35 to 40 minutes longer.

Southern Short Ribs

These short ribs accumulate a delicious, slow-baked flavor as they cook.

1½ teaspoons salt
½ teaspoon pepper
3 to 4 pounds short ribs of beef
1 can (8 ounces) tomato sauce

2 tablespoons molasses
2 tablespoons cider vinegar
1 teaspoon Worcestershire sauce
1½ tablespoons minced onion

Sprinkle salt and pepper on all sides of short ribs and place in 3-quart baking dish. Heat oven to 275° F. In small pan combine tomato sauce with molasses, vinegar, Worcestershire sauce, and onion; bring to boil and simmer 5 minutes. Pour over short ribs; cover and bake 3 to 4 hours or until very tender. Spoon off excess fat before serving.

Short Ribs and Limas Devon

1½ pounds short ribs of beef,
   cut into serving pieces
1 teaspoon salt
¼ teaspoon pepper
¼ teaspoon paprika
1½ tablespoons shortening
1 small onion, thinly sliced
¼ cup brown sugar

½ teaspoon dry mustard
1½ teaspoons flour
1 tablespoon vinegar
1 tablespoon lemon juice
⅛ teaspoon grated lemon rind
⅛ teaspoon thyme
¾ cup water
2 cups drained, cooked, dried limas

Heat oven to 400° F. Sprinkle short ribs with combined salt, pepper, and paprika. Heat shortening in skillet; brown ribs well and remove to 1½-quart baking dish. Sauté onion slices in remaining shortening until golden. Add onions to meat; pour off drippings. In skillet add brown sugar, mustard, and flour; stir until blended. Add vinegar, lemon juice and rind, thyme, and water; stir. Bring to a boil and continue stirring; pour over short ribs. Bake, uncovered, 1 hour or until meat is almost tender. Stir in limas; bake, covered, 25 minutes longer.

Goulash with Paprika Dumplings

A Hungarian specialty adapted to American tastes.

1 pound lean beef,
   cut into 1-inch cubes
¼ cup flour
1 tablespoon salt
⅓ cup shortening
¾ cup chopped onion
¼ cup diced green pepper

2 cups cooked tomatoes
¼ teaspoon red pepper
1 teaspoon paprika
¼ cup diced celery
1 cup carrot strips
Paprika Dumplings (recipe below)

Dredge beef cubes in flour and salt; brown in shortening in deep, heavy skillet. Add onion and green pepper; brown lightly. Add tomatoes and seasonings; cover, cook over low heat 30 minutes or until meat is tender. Add celery and carrots; cook 15 minutes longer. Prepare Paprika Dumplings, drop from a teaspoon on hot goulash. Cover; steam about 15 minutes. Makes 4 servings.

Paprika Dumplings

1 cup flour
1½ teaspoons baking powder
½ teaspoon salt

2 tablespoons melted shortening
½ cup milk
1 tablespoon paprika

Combine flour, baking powder, and salt. Add shortening and milk; blend lightly. Drop by spoonfuls on simmering goulash. Sprinkle with paprika.

Danish Beef Goulash

1 pound beef round steak
  cut in ½-inch cubes
2 tablespoons vegetable oil
2 teaspoons salt
⅛ teaspoon pepper
1 medium onion, thinly sliced
2 bay leaves

1 tablespoon brown sugar
2 cups boiling water
2 tablespoons flour
1 tablespoon paprika
¼ cup cold water
1 tablespoon vinegar

Lightly brown meat in vegetable oil in heavy skillet. Add salt, pepper, onion, bay leaves, sugar, and 2 cups water. Cook over low heat, covered, 1½ hours. Remove bay leaves. Combine flour, paprika, ¼ cup water, and vinegar; blend well. Gradually add to meat. Cook 10 minutes longer, stirring constantly until sauce is thickened.

Viennese Goulash

Goulash is that wonderful European dish which has as many variations as countries.

2 pounds chuck beef,
  cut into 1½-inch cubes
2 tablespoons shortening
1 cup chopped onion
1 tablespoon flour
1 tablespoon paprika
1½ teaspoons salt
¾ teaspoon rosemary

½ teaspoon thyme
½ teaspoon sage
1 clove garlic, minced
1 can (1 pound) tomatoes
1 can (8 ounces) tomato sauce
2 slices crisp bacon, crumbled
Poppy-Seed Noodles (recipe below)

Brown meat in shortening; add onion and sauté until tender. Stir in flour, paprika, salt, herbs, garlic, tomatoes, and tomato sauce. Simmer, covered

1½ to 2 hours or until meat is tender. Serve with Poppy-Seed Noodles; sprinkle with bacon. Makes 6 servings.

Poppy-Seed Noodles

1 package (6 ounces) noodles   2 tablespoons margarine
2 tablespoons poppy seeds

Cook noodles according to package directions; drain. Add poppy seeds and margarine; mix well.

English Boiled Beef

6 to 7 pounds beef chuck roast   1 bay leaf
1 onion, halved   2 tablespoons salt
1 carrot, sliced   1 teaspoon peppercorns
1 stalk celery, sliced   Brown Horseradish Sauce
4 sprigs parsley   (recipe below)

Place meat in large kettle; add onion, carrot, celery, parsley, bay leaf, salt, and peppercorns. Add enough water to cover meat. Bring to boil; reduce heat. Simmer, covered 2½ to 3 hours, or until meat is fork tender. Remove meat to heated platter; keep warm. Strain broth; measure 2 cups and skim off fat. Prepare Brown Horseradish Sauce and serve with sliced meat. Makes 8 to 10 servings.

Brown Horseradish Sauce

3 tablespoons margarine   ½ teaspoon minced onion
⅓ cup flour   ½ cup prepared horseradish
2 cups skimmed broth   ½ teaspoon salt

Melt margarine in small saucepan; blend in flour. Heat slowly, stirring constantly, until flour is browned. Remove from heat; stir in 2 cups skimmed broth and onion. Cook, stirring constantly, until sauce thickens and boils 1 minute. Stir in prepared horseradish and season with salt; heat thoroughly. Makes 2 cups.

Maine Corned Beef Dinner

If your food budget's feeling a pinch and your family's appetites seem to get bigger, try appeasing them with robust, economical foods such as the all-in-one Maine Corned Beef Dinner.

1 3½ to 4 pound corned beef brisket	1 stalk celery, cut up
1 medium onion, sliced	1 carrot, sliced
3 whole cloves	2 parsley sprigs
2 whole peppercorns	8 new potatoes, pared
1 small bay leaf	8 carrots, scraped
½ teaspoon rosemary	1 small head cabbage, cut in wedges
1 clove garlic	1 can (16 ounces) whole beets

Place corned beef in large deep kettle; cover with cold water. Add onion, cloves, peppercorns, bay leaf, rosemary, garlic, celery, sliced carrot and parsley sprigs. Bring to boil, then simmer, covered, 3 to 3½ hours or until meat is fork tender. Remove to heated serving platter; keep warm. Strain liquid from kettle; return 3 cups liquid to kettle. Add potatoes, carrot, and cabbage, placing cabbage on top. Bring to boil. Reduce heat; simmer, covered, 30 minutes or until vegetables are just crisp tender. Heat beets in small saucepan. Slice meat; arrange drained vegetables around it. Makes 8 servings.

Greek Onion-Beef Stew

All the good flavors mingle in this invigorating and nourishing dish.

1 pound beef-stew meat,	1 bay leaf
cut in 1½-inch cubes	1½ teaspoons salt
1 tablespoon shortening	½ teaspoon sugar
2 cups boiling water	¼ teaspoon pepper
1½ teaspoons lemon juice	¼ teaspoon paprika
½ teaspoon Worcestershire sauce	Dash allspice
1 clove garlic	4 carrots, quartered
1 small onion, sliced	16 small white onions

Brown meat on all sides in hot shortening in skillet; add water, lemon juice, Worcestershire sauce, garlic, sliced onion, bay leaf, and seasonings. Cover; simmer 2 hours, stirring occasionally. Remove bay leaf and garlic. Add carrots and onions. Cover; continue cooking 30 minutes or until vegetables are tender.

Chinese Stew

1 pound beef chuck, cubed
¾ teaspoon salt
1 tablespoon flour
2 tablespoons vegetable oil
2 medium onions, thinly sliced

2 stalks celery, cut in fine strips
6 water chestnuts, thinly sliced
1 green pepper, sliced in strips
4 whole mushrooms, sliced

Dust meat cubes with mixture of salt and flour. Heat 1 tablespoon of oil in heavy saucepan. Add meat; brown slowly on all sides. Cook over low heat, covered, 1 hour or until meat is tender. In heavy skillet, heat remaining 1 tablespoon oil. Add vegetables; cover and cook slowly until just soft, about 10 minutes. Add vegetables to meat and serve.

Zesty Stew With Horseradish Dumplings

1½ pounds beef-stew meat,
   cut in 1½-inch cubes
⅓ cup flour
1 teaspoon salt
¼ teaspoon pepper
¼ cup shortening
½ cup chopped onions
1 bay leaf
3 cups hot water

1 teaspoon Worcestershire sauce
4 stalks celery, sliced
6 small onions
6 medium carrots, sliced
4 medium potatoes, pared,
   quartered
Horseradish Dumplings
   (recipe below)

Coat meat with flour combined with ½ teaspoon salt and ⅛ teaspoon pepper. Brown slowly in hot shortening. Add onions, bay leaf, hot water, and Worcestershire sauce. Cover; simmer 2 hours or until meat is very tender. Add celery, onions, carrots, potatoes, and remaining ½ teaspoon salt and ⅛ teaspoon pepper. Simmer, covered, 25 minutes or until vegetables are tender. Drop Horseradish Dumplings by teaspoons on top of boiling stew. Cover; cook over low heat 20 minutes. Makes 6 servings.

Horseradish Dumplings

1 cup prepared biscuit mix
2 tablespoons chopped parsley
Dash marjoram

Dash oregano
1 teaspoon prepared horseradish
6 tablespoons milk

Combine biscuit mix with parsley, marjoram, and oregano. Mix horseradish with milk; add to biscuit mix mixture; blend well.

Sunshine Beef Stew

The secret of this stew is orange juice—and an everyday meal becomes an occasion.

2 pounds beef-stew meat
¼ cup flour
2 teaspoons salt
3 tablespoons shortening
1 clove garlic, finely chopped
1½ cups orange juice

1 teaspoon Worcestershire sauce
6 carrots, cut in pieces
1 medium onion, chopped
1 cup sliced celery
1 package (12 ounces) frozen
    lima beans

Coat meat with combined flour and salt. Brown on all sides in hot shortening in heavy skillet. Add garlic, orange juice, and Worcestershire sauce. Cover; cook over low heat 2 hours or until tender. Add carrots, onion, celery, and lima beans. Cook, covered, 10 minutes longer or until vegetables are crisp tender, stirring occasionally. Makes 8 servings.

Mennonite Medley

The original recipe was over one hundred years old; our version has been adapted to suit present-day tastes.

1 small cabbage, about 1¼ pounds
2 tablespoons margarine
1 tablespoon brown sugar
1½ cups beef broth
2 cups water
½ teaspoon allspice

¾ teaspoon salt
1 can (12 ounces) corned beef
1 slice whole wheat bread
1 egg, slightly beaten
2 tablespoons shortening

Remove outer leaves and cut cabbage into quarters; cut out core and heavy veins and chop finely. Melt margarine in saucepan; add cabbage and sugar. Brown over low heat until golden, stirring occasionally, about 30 minutes. Add beef broth, water, allspice, and salt; cover and simmer 30 minutes. Flake corned beef with fork. Separate bread into soft crumbs. Combine meat, bread, and egg; mix well. Shape into small balls. Fry quickly in shortening; add to cabbage and simmer 6 minutes.

Hash-Stuffed Potatoes

A perfect luncheon dish served with vinaigrette tomatoes and a tossed green salad.

4 large baking potatoes	1 teaspoon Worcestershire sauce
2 teaspoons vegetable oil	Dash nutmeg
1 can (1 pound) corned beef hash	¾ teaspoon salt
½ cup milk	¼ teaspoon celery salt
2 tablespoons margarine	¼ teaspoon pepper
¼ cup minced onion	½ cup grated sharp Cheddar cheese

Heat oven to 450° F. Scrub potatoes; dry thoroughly and rub skins with vegetable oil. Bake 1 hour or until done. Cut each potato in half lengthwise; scoop out potato into bowl leaving skins intact. Mash potato well and stir in hash. Heat milk and margarine in saucepan; add to hash and potato mixture, with onion, Worcestershire sauce, nutmeg, salt, celery salt, and pepper, and blend well. Heap mixture into scooped-out potato shells; sprinkle with cheese. Arrange on cookie sheet; bake 20 minutes or until thoroughly heated. Makes 8 servings.

Louisville Hash

5 medium potatoes, coarsely chopped	1 cup leftover dark brown gravy
2 medium onions, coarsely chopped	2 cups leftover cooked meat, diced
½ cup diced tomatoes	1 teaspoon salt
3 tablespoons shortening	¼ teaspoon pepper

Sauté potatoes and onions with tomatoes in shortening in a large skillet. Add gravy; cover and cook over medium heat for 25 minutes, stirring occasionally. Add meat and seasonings. Heat through, stir, and serve.

Sirloin Roast Iowa

Here's a meal-in-one special to satisfy your hungry family's clamoring for a good hearty dish that's thrifty, too.

3 to 4 pounds sirloin-tip roast
Flour
1 teaspoon salt
¼ teaspoon pepper
1 medium onion, sliced
2 bay leaves

1 clove garlic, minced
½ cup hot water
8 small onions, peeled
8 medium carrots, scraped
8 small potatoes, pared

Sprinkle meat lightly with flour and rub in. Brown slowly on all sides in deep, heavy, baking dish. Add sliced onion, bay leaves, garlic, and water. Cover; cook over low heat 2 hours or until almost tender. Add vegetables. Continue cooking, covered, 1 hour longer or until meat and vegetables are tender. Remove to warm platter. Thicken liquid with flour, adding water, if necessary. Makes 8 servings.

Beef Di Napoli

4 pounds beef for pot roast
2 tablespoons vegetable oil
1 medium onion, chopped
1 clove garlic, minced
1 teaspoon mixed herb seasoning
1 teaspoon salt

¼ teaspoon pepper
2 cans (8 ounces each) tomato
   sauce
Water
1 package (1 pound) spaghetti
¼ cup grated Parmesan cheese

Brown meat all over in vegetable oil in a heavy kettle. Add onion, garlic, herbs, salt, and pepper. Mix tomato sauce with 1 cup water; pour over meat. Simmer, covered, 3½ hours or until meat is tender, adding more water when necessary. Prepare spaghetti according to package directions. Remove meat to heated serving platter; slice. Skim fat from sauce and top with some of the sauce from the kettle. Toss remaining sauce with spaghetti and sprinkle with cheese; serve with meat. Makes 6 to 8 servings.

Beef Vindaloo

An exotic Indian dish with a spectacular flavor of the traditional spices of the country.

1 tablespoon ground coriander seed	3 tablespoons minced onion
½ teaspoon ground cumin seed	2 tablespoons margarine
1 teaspoon turmeric	½ cup water
½ teaspoon dry mustard	2 pounds shoulder of beef,
½ teaspoon red pepper	cut into 2-inch cubes
1 teaspoon black pepper	2½ cups hot water
½ teaspoon ground ginger	1½ teaspoons salt
¼ teaspoon instant garlic	2 tablespoons lemon juice
2 tablespoons cider vinegar	

Combine spices with vinegar; mix to a paste. Sauté onion in margarine; add spice mixture and ½ cup water and cook 2 minutes. Add meat; stir and cook 10 minutes. Add hot water. Simmer 40 minutes or until meat is tender. Add salt and lemon juice; cook 5 minutes longer. Serve plain or with fluffy rice. Makes 6 servings.

Beef À L'Indienne

Just a hint of curry makes all the difference to stew meat.

¼ cup flour	½ cup water
1 teaspoon salt	½ cup onion, chopped
¼ teaspoon pepper	Curry Gravy (recipe below)
1½ pounds beef-stew meat	2 cups hot cooked rice
3 tablespoons shortening	

Combine flour, salt, and pepper; coat meat cubes. Brown meat in hot shortening in heavy skillet. Add water and onion. Simmer over low heat, covered, 2 hours or until tender. Remove meat; measure drippings in skillet, adding water, if necessary, to make ½ cup. Make Curry Gravy; add meat and heat thoroughly. Serve over hot rice.

Curry Gravy

2 cups milk
1 teaspoon curry powder
¼ cup flour

½ teaspoon salt
2 tablespoons lemon juice
½ cup skillet drippings

Combine all ingredients; blend well. Cook over low heat, stirring constantly, until heated.

Spaghetti and Beef Rolls Romeo

Company-style main dish. Chuck may be sliced at the market, or you can do it yourself from a thick blade cut of which the chuck is a part.

1 cup creamed cottage cheese
1 can (3 ounces) sliced
   mushrooms, drained
1½ pounds beef chuck,
   thinly sliced
¼ cup vegetable oil
1 clove garlic, chopped
½ cup chopped onions

1 can (1 pound) tomatoes
1 can (6 ounces) tomato paste
¼ teaspoon oregano
Dash sage
1½ tablespoons salt
1 cup cooked peas
3 quarts boiling water
1 package (8 ounces) spaghetti

Combine cheese and mushrooms. Spread on meat slices. Roll up each and tie with string. Heat oil in large skillet; add meat rolls and garlic and cook until lightly browned. Remove rolls; add onions and sauté until lightly browned. Add tomatoes, tomato paste, oregano, sage, and 1½ teaspoons of the salt; mix well. Add meat rolls. Simmer, covered, 1 hour or until meat is tender. Add peas and heat thoroughly. Add remaining 1 tablespoon salt to rapidly boiling water in large saucepan; gradually add spaghetti so that water continues to boil. Cook, uncovered, stirring occasionally, until tender. Drain. Put in serving dish; spoon meat rolls over spaghetti and remove string. Pour sauce over meat. Makes 6 servings.

Beef Cardinale

An elegant dish, adapted to low-cost cookery, which can be doubled to serve as a company dinner.

2 tablespoons margarine
2 tablespoons vegetable oil
¾ pound small white onions
2 pounds chuck beef, trimmed,
    cut into 2-inch cubes
2 tablespoons flour
½ teaspoon Worcestershire sauce
2 teaspoons tomato paste

1½ cups red wine
⅛ teaspoon pepper
1 bay leaf
¼ teaspoon thyme
¼ teaspoon marjoram
⅛ teaspoon rosemary
¾ cup mushrooms, sliced
2 tablespoons chopped parsley

Heat oven to 325° F. In 2-quart baking dish heat margarine and oil. Sauté onions 5 minutes in oil and margarine; remove. Add beef; brown on all sides and remove. Discard all but 2 teaspoons of fat. Stir in flour, Worcestershire sauce, and tomato paste; blend until smooth. Gradually add wine, stirring constantly. Add meat, pepper, herbs, mushrooms, and 1 tablespoon parsley; mix well. Cover; bake 50 minutes. Add onions; bake 1 hour longer or until meat is tender. Turn onto heated serving platter; sprinkle with remaining parsley.

Texas-Style Chili

A new recipe for dyed-in-the-wool chili lovers.

1½ pounds diced lean beef
2 tablespoons vegetable oil
2 cups water
3 tablespoons chili powder
1½ teaspoons salt
5 cloves garlic, finely chopped
½ teaspoon cumin
½ teaspoon oregano

½ teaspoon red pepper
1½ teaspoons sugar
1 tablespoon paprika
1½ tablespoons flour
3 tablespoons cornmeal
2 cups cooked, seasoned,
    pinto beans

Sauté meat in oil in large kettle just until it loses its red color. Add water, cover, and cook over low heat 1½ to 2 hours. Add chili powder, salt, garlic, cumin, oregano, red pepper, sugar, and paprika. Cook 30 minutes longer. Stir flour and cornmeal into 1 cup water; add to meat mixture. Cook, stirring constantly, 5 to 10 minutes until thoroughly heated. Serve with pinto beans on the side.

Sweet 'N' Sour Beef Lanai

A Hawaiian treat made with leftover beef cubes.

1 can (1 pound 4 ounces)
  pineapple chunks
¾ cup water
2 chicken bouillon cubes
⅓ cup brown sugar
3 tablespoons molasses

¼ cup cornstarch
¼ cup vinegar
2 cups cubed leftover cooked beef
1½ tablespoons soy sauce
2 cups hot fluffy rice

Combine pineapple with liquid, water, bouillon cubes, brown sugar, and molasses; heat 5 minutes. Blend cornstarch with vinegar to a smooth paste; stir into pineapple mixture. Cook 1 minute, stirring constantly, until sauce thickens and boils. Add meat and soy sauce; heat thoroughly but do not boil. Serve on hot rice.

South Seas Beef

It's chuck beef, simmered fork-tender in a soy-seasoned sauce for an exotic flavor.

3½ to 4 pounds beef chuck roast
1 large onion, sliced,
  separated into rings
1 cup canned pineapple juice
3 tablespoons soy sauce
1½ teaspoons ginger
½ teaspoon salt

4 stalks celery, sliced
4 large carrots, sliced lengthwise
½ pound spinach, cleaned
8 fresh mushrooms, thinly sliced
1 tablespoon cornstarch
2 tablespoons cold water

Place beef with onion rings in shallow pan. Combine pineapple juice, soy sauce, ginger, and salt; pour over meat. Let stand 1 hour, turning meat once. Remove beef and onions to heavy kettle; pour pineapple mixture over all. Simmer, covered, 1½ to 2 hours or until meat is tender when pierced with fork. Reduce heat; add celery and carrots. Simmer 10 minutes longer. Arrange spinach and mushrooms on top; simmer 5 minutes more or until spinach is wilted and vegetables are crisp tender. Remove meat and vegetables to heated serving platter; keep hot.

Combine cornstarch with cold water and make a smooth paste; stir into pan drippings. Cook, stirring constantly, until gravy thickens and boils, about 3 minutes. Makes 8 servings.

GROUND MEAT

Sloppy Joes

1½ pounds ground beef
1 medium onion, chopped
½ cup ketchup
1 tablespoon prepared mustard
1 can (10½ ounces)
   chicken gumbo soup

1 cup water
1 can (3 ounces) mushroom bits
   and pieces, drained
¾ teaspoon salt
⅛ teaspoon pepper
6 sandwich rolls, toasted

Cook beef and onion in skillet until lightly browned, breaking up meat with fork. Add remaining ingredients, except rolls. Cover; bring to boil. Reduce heat; simmer 30 minutes. Serve on toasted rolls. Makes 6 servings.

Laurel's Lasagne

1 cup sliced onions
¼ cup vegetable oil
1½ slices white bread
3 tablespoons water
¾ pound ground chuck beef
¼ pound ground lean pork
1 egg
2 tablespoons chopped parsley

¼ teaspoon pepper
1 teaspoon salt
1 cup grated Parmesan cheese
1 can (8 ounces) tomato sauce
4½ cups canned tomatoes
1 package (1 pound) lasagne
1¼ pounds ricotta cheese
½ pound mozzarella cheese

Sauté onions in oil in heavy skillet until lightly browned; remove. Soak bread in water; squeeze thoroughly to remove excess water. Combine meat, egg, parsley, pepper, salt, and ¼ cup Parmesan cheese; add bread and mix well. Gently shape into small balls. Sauté in oil left in skillet until brown all over; remove. Add tomato sauce and tomatoes to skillet; simmer, covered, 1½ hours. Add meat balls and onions; simmer, uncovered, 1 hour longer. Cook lasagne according to package directions; drain. Heat oven to 350° F. Into a 15 × 12 × 2-inch shallow baking pan, spoon enough sauce and meat balls to cover bottom. Top with crisscross layer of lasagne; then with half of ricotta. Top with ½ of mozzarella and ⅓ remaining Parmesan cheese. Repeat layers, ending with sauce. Top with remaining Parmesan. With sharp knife, make 6 to 8 deep gashes down through surface of lasagne. Bake 40 minutes or until bubbling.

Beef Monaco

1 pound ground lean beef	1½ cups tomato sauce
¼ teaspoon onion salt	¼ teaspoon oregano
¾ teaspoon salt	¼ teaspoon pepper
6 slices peeled eggplant	1½ cups grated process
Vegetable oil	American cheese
3 cups drained cooked lima beans	2 tablespoons chopped parsley

Blend beef with salt and onion salt; shape into 6 thin patties. Brown eggplant lightly in hot oil. Remove from pan. Brown beef patties. Heat oven to 350° F. Place limas in shallow baking dish. Blend tomato sauce with oregano and pepper; pour ½ cup over lima beans. Sprinkle with ½ the cheese. Top with eggplant, more sauce, and ¼ cup cheese. Place beef patties on top. Pour remaining sauce; sprinkle with remaining ½ cup cheese, and parsley. Bake 25 to 30 minutes until bubbly and hot. Makes 6 servings.

Cheapie Beef Ragout

Smart is the cook who has a thrifty mainstay meal for the days the budget just won't budge—and this dish is good even on payday.

1 pound ground beef	5 whole allspice
1 cup soft bread crumbs	1 bay leaf
1 egg	½ teaspoon sugar
¼ cup milk	⅛ teaspoon pepper
1 teaspoon salt	12 small carrots, scraped
1 tablespoon vegetable oil	1 package (7 ounces) frozen
1 can (12 ounces) mixed	French-style green beans
vegetable juice	

Mix meat, bread crumbs, egg, milk, and ½ teaspoon salt in medium bowl; form into 12 small balls. Brown in oil in large skillet; drain off excess fat. Reduce heat; stir in vegetable juice, remaining ½ teaspoon salt, allspice, bay leaf, sugar, and pepper. Push meat to one side of pan and arrange carrots in space. Simmer, covered, 30 minutes; add frozen green beans. Cook 15 minutes longer or until beans are just tender.

Beef À La Grecque

2 pounds ground beef
4 medium onions, chopped
2 cloves garlic, minced
1½ teaspoons salt
¼ teaspoon pepper
2 beef bouillon cubes

1½ cups hot water
1 can (6 ounces) tomato paste
½ cup dry red wine
1 can (1 pound) potatoes, diced
2 bay leaves
3-inch stick cinnamon

Heat oven to 350° F. Cook meat in large skillet, breaking it up with fork, with onion, garlic, salt, and pepper until beef loses red color. Add cubes to water and dissolve. Pour over meat in skillet. Add remaining ingredients; bring to boil. Turn into 1½-quart baking pan. Cover, bake 1¼ hours. Makes 6 servings. Remove bay leaves and cinnamon stick.

Beef Pielets Diablo

Seasoned ground beef baked inside a pastry jacket makes an unusual food—served plain or with hot tomato sauce.

1 pound ground beef
1 small onion, grated
1 egg
½ cup soft bread crumbs
1 tablespoon ketchup

½ teaspoon Worcestershire sauce
1 teaspoon salt
⅛ teaspoon pepper
1 package (6 ounces) piecrust mix

Combine beef and onion in bowl; shape into large patty and place in medium skillet. Brown 5 minutes on each side; break up into small chunks with fork. Beat egg slightly in bowl; stir in bread crumbs, ketchup, Worcestershire sauce, salt, and pepper. Drizzle over meat chunks. Cook, stirring constantly, 1 minute; cool.

Heat oven to 400° F. Prepare piecrust mix according to package directions. Roll out half to a 12-inch square on a lightly floured board; cut into four 6-inch squares. Spoon about ¼ cup meat mixture onto center of each; fold over to make a triangle. Press edges firmly with fork to seal. Repeat with remaining half of pastry and meat mixture to make 8 pielets. Place on cookie sheet. Bake 20 minutes or until pastry is golden. Remove to wire racks to cool 3 minutes. Serve hot, plain or with tomato sauce.

Cheese Hideaways

¾ pound ground beef
¼ pound lean ground pork
2 tablespoons light brown sugar
2 tablespoons marmalade
2 tablespoons finely chopped onion
2 tablespoons chopped parsley
1 teaspoon dry mustard
½ teaspoon savory

¾ teaspoon salt
¼ teaspoon pepper
1 cup cracker crumbs
2 eggs, slightly beaten
½ pound process cheese spread
2 tablespoons margarine
1 cup sour cream
¼ teaspoon tarragon

Combine beef, pork, 1 tablespoon sugar, marmalade, onion, parsley, mustard, savory, salt, pepper, cracker crumbs, and eggs; mix lightly until well blended. Cut half of cheese into 24 cubes. Insert a piece of cheese into the center of a tablespoonful of meat mixture. Form into a ball, enclosing cheese completely. Repeat until all ingredients are used. Heat margarine in large skillet; cook meatballs slowly until well browned. Melt remaining cheese in top of double boiler; gradually blend in sour cream and remaining 1 tablespoon brown sugar. Stir in tarragon. Pour over meatballs; cover and cook until heated through. Makes 8 servings.

Pepper-Ring Patties

This variation on an old theme proves to be a colorful and inviting manner of sprucing up ground beef.

1 pound ground beef
1 can (2 ounces) mushroom
    stems and pieces
Milk
¾ cup soft bread crumbs
2 tablespoons chopped onion
1 teaspoon Worcestershire sauce

1 teaspoon salt
⅛ teaspoon pepper
1 egg, beaten
2 large green peppers
2 tablespoons ketchup
2 tablespoons grated
    American cheese

Heat oven to 350° F. Drain mushrooms; reserve liquid. Add enough milk to make ½ cup. Combine meat, mushrooms, liquid, bread crumbs, onion, Worcestershire sauce, salt, pepper, and egg. Remove ends and seeds from green peppers. Cut each into 3 one-inch rings. Place green-pepper rings in shallow baking pan. Pack meat mixture into pepper rings. Bake 35 minutes. Combine ketchup with cheese; spoon over patties. Bake 10 minutes longer. Makes 6 servings.

Baked Eastern Kibbeh

½ cup cracked wheat
Water
1 pound ground beef
2 medium onions, finely chopped
1 teaspoon salt
⅛ teaspoon allspice

⅛ teaspoon cloves
⅛ teaspoon cinnamon
¼ cup pine nuts
½ pound ground lamb
¼ cup margarine

Wash cracked wheat in cold water; soak it 1 hour. Heat oven to 450° F. Grease a 12 × 8 × 1½-inch baking pan. Brown beef and 1 onion in skillet; add salt, spices, and pine nuts. Cook, stirring frequently, until pine nuts are golden brown. Mix ground lamb with remaining 1 onion; knead 2 minutes. Squeeze excess water from cracked wheat; add to lamb mixture. Divide into two equal parts. Spread one half of lamb mixture on baking pan. Spread, on top of this, beef mixture and cover with remaining lamb mixture; press gently and smooth to keep even. Cut kibbeh into squares in pan. Dot each square with margarine. Bake 35 to 40 minutes or until done. Let stand 5 minutes in pan before serving. Makes 6 servings.

Sauce-Crowned Meat Ring

Everyone will wonder what the secret ingredient is in this tasty and flavored ground-meat dish.

¼ cup coarse dry bread crumbs
1 bottle (7 ounces) lemon-lime
   carbonated beverage
2 pounds ground beef
2 eggs, slightly beaten
1 cup chopped onion

1 clove garlic, minced
2 teaspoons salt
1½ teaspoons dill weed
⅓ cup Worcestershire sauce
½ cup chili sauce
Dash Tabasco

Heat oven to 350° F. Soak bread crumbs in beverage. Add ground beef, eggs, onion, garlic, salt, and dill weed; mix lightly but thoroughly. Pack into deep 1½-quart ring mold. Turn out onto a shallow baking dish. Brush meat ring generously with all but 1 teaspoon of Worcestershire sauce. Bake 45 minutes, basting occasionally with pan drippings. Blend remaining 1 teaspoon Worcestershire sauce with chili sauce and Tabasco; spoon topping over meat; bake 15 minutes longer. Makes 6 servings.

Indian Samosas

2 cups flour
2 tablespoons margarine
1 teaspoon salt

5 tablespoons yoghurt
Samosa Filling (recipe below)
Vegetable oil

Combine flour, margarine, and salt; using two knives or pastry blender, cut into mixture until it resembles bread crumbs. Add yoghurt, a little at a time, kneading the flour into a stiff dough. Gather into a ball. Roll out into a thin round circle about ⅛ inch thick. Cut in half. Cut each half into two portions. Divide stuffing in equal parts; fold each half into a cone, pinching edges to seal and folding over the mouth of the cone. Fry in hot vegetable oil until crisp and medium brown. Makes 4 cones. Fill with Samosa Filling, below.

Samosa Filling

1 tablespoon butter
1 small onion, chopped
1 small tomato, chopped
½ pound ground beef

1 tablespoon mixed herbs
¼ teaspoon turmeric
1½ teaspoons lemon juice

Melt butter in skillet; sauté onion and tomato until soft. Add remaining ingredients; mix well. Cook 10 minutes.

Salisbury Steaks

1½ pounds ground beef
1 egg, beaten
⅔ cup evaporated milk
½ cup fine cracker crumbs
1½ teaspoons salt

¼ teaspoon pepper
1 teaspoon dry mustard
¼ cup finely chopped onion
½ cup finely chopped green pepper
Mushroom Sauce (recipe below)

Combine all ingredients, except mushroom sauce; mix well. Form into 8 equally long rolls. Broil, 3 inches from source of heat, 5 to 7 minutes on each side, turning to brown evenly. Add to Mushroom Sauce; heat 15 minutes.

Mushroom Sauce

¼ pound mushrooms
5 tablespoons margarine
3 tablespoons flour
1 cup milk
½ teaspoon salt

½ teaspoon paprika
1 small clove garlic, minced
1 beef bouillon cube
¼ cup hot water

Wash mushrooms and slice thin; set aside. To make a cream sauce, melt 3 tablespoons margarine in saucepan; blend in flour. Slowly add milk, stirring constantly, and cook until thickened. Season with salt, paprika, and garlic. Dissolve bouillon cube in hot water. Sauté mushrooms in remaining 2 tablespoons margarine until tender but not browned. Add cream sauce and bouillon mixture to mushrooms; mix well. Cook 5 minutes.

Applesauce Meat Ring O' Day

A juicy meat-loaf dinner with bright vegetables in mounds in the center.

2 pounds ground beef
¾ cup chopped onion
2 eggs, slightly beaten
1 cup fine dry bread crumbs
½ teaspoon oregano
½ teaspoon basil

1½ teaspoons salt
1 can (1 pound 1 ounce) applesauce
¼ cup sherry wine
Green Bean Succotash
  (recipe below)

Heat oven to 375° F. Combine all ingredients, except Green Bean Succotash; blend well. Turn into a 10-inch ring. Bake 1 hour. Remove from oven; let stand 5 minutes. Unmold on heated serving platter; fill center with Green Bean Succotash. Makes 8 servings.

Green Bean Succotash

½ cup water
1 teaspoon salt
1 package (10 ounces)
  frozen cut green beans

1 package (10 ounces)
  frozen whole kernel corn
1 tablespoon margarine

Bring water and salt to a boil; add beans and corn. Cover, cook according to package directions or until beans are just tender. Drain well. Toss lightly with margarine.

New York Casserole

1 large onion, chopped
1 clove garlic, minced
1 tablespoon margarine
1 pound lean ground beef
1 can (10½ ounces)
   condensed tomato soup

1 cup canned creamed corn
½ teaspoon salt
⅛ teaspoon pepper
1 package (8 ounces) noodles,
   cooked
½ cup grated Parmesan cheese

Heat oven to 350° F. Sauté onion and garlic in margarine in skillet until soft. Add beef; cook until redness disappears. Stir in tomato soup and corn; season with salt and pepper. Alternate meat mixture, noodles, and cheese in casserole, ending with cheese. Bake 20 minutes.

Mock-Steak Joubey

Food budget low? Try everyday ground meat in company dress.

2 pounds ground round beef
½ pound ground lean pork
1 package dry onion soup mix
2 tablespoons Worcestershire sauce

2 cups stuffing mix
1½ cups tomato juice
4 strips bacon
Hot Steak Sauce (recipe below)

Combine all ingredients except bacon and Hot Steak Sauce, and blend well. Shape meat into a steak shape about 1-inch thick. Use a strip of carrot to mark the bone in the steak. Wrap bacon around the outer edge of the steak where layer of fat would be located. Fasten bacon with wooden picks. Brush meat with Hot Steak Sauce. Broil about 10 minutes on each side. Use 2 pancake turners to turn meat carefully. Brush meat with sauce frequently. Serve hot with remaining sauce. Makes 8 servings.

Hot Steak Sauce

½ cup margarine
¼ cup minced onions
2 tablespoons Worcestershire sauce

3 tablespoons ketchup
¼ teaspoon dry mustard
½ teaspoon salt

Combine all ingredients. Heat to boil.

Stuffed Cabbage Rolls

8 large green cabbage leaves
Boiling, salted water
⅔ cup raw regular rice
2 tablespoons shortening
1 pound ground beef
⅔ cup finely chopped onions
2 teaspoons Worcestershire sauce

1 teaspoon salt
⅛ teaspoon pepper
⅛ teaspoon poultry seasoning
⅛ teaspoon oregano
1 can (10½ ounces)
   condensed tomato soup
1 soup can milk

Heat oven to 350° F. Drop cabbage leaves in boiling, salted water and cook until they are soft enough to roll. Drain; cool. Cook rice in boiling salted water 15 minutes. Drain. Melt shortening; lightly brown meat and onions. Add rice, Worcestershire sauce, salt, pepper, poultry seasoning, and oregano. Divide mixture among cabbage leaves. Roll up, making neat packets of each. Place in baking dish with seam side underneath. Pour combined tomato soup and milk over rolls. Cover; bake 1 hour.

Beef Leban

2 tablespoons margarine
2 tablespoons vegetable oil
2 small onions, minced
2 cloves garlic, minced
1 pound lean ground beef
2 beef bouillon cubes
½ cup hot water

½ teaspoon paprika
1 can (6 ounces) tomato paste
1 teaspoon allspice
1 teaspoon salt
¼ teaspoon pepper
3 tablespoons wine vinegar
Turmeric Rice (recipe below)

Melt margarine in skillet; add vegetable oil. Sauté onions and garlic until soft. Add meat; stir until well separated and lightly browned. Dissolve bouillon cubes in hot water; combine with paprika, tomato paste, allspice, salt, and pepper. Add to meat mixture; mix well, stirring constantly. Add vinegar. Cook over moderate heat until liquid is nearly gone. Turn onto heated serving platter; surround by rice.

Turmeric Rice

1 cup rice
¼ teaspoon salt
½ teaspoon vegetable oil

½ teaspoon turmeric
½ teaspoon butter

Prepare rice according to package directions adding remaining ingredients.

Beef Pinwheel

An old favorite transformed into a mouth-watering dish.

1 pound ground round beef	2 tablespoons ketchup
1½ teaspoons salt	⅓ cup dry bread crumbs
1 tablespoon Worcestershire sauce	3 cups chopped cooked cabbage
1 egg, well beaten	½ cup chopped sautéed onions

Heat oven to 350° F. Grease a shallow baking pan. Combine meat, salt, Worcestershire sauce, egg, ketchup, and bread crumbs; blend well. Roll out meat between 2 sheets of waxed paper into an oblong about ½ inch thick. Spread with cabbage mixture. Roll like a jelly roll. Place in baking pan. Bake 40 to 45 minutes. Serve plain or with canned cream of vegetable soup, heated to boiling, as a sauce.

Hobo's Banquet

When the money budgeted for food is about spent, try this good hearty meal—the vegetable dish requires only ½ pound of ground beef, and with a fruit slaw and a chocolate pudding, it will indeed be a banquet.

2½ cups sliced carrots	2½ cups cooked green beans
2½ cups diced potatoes	3 tablespoons margarine
½ cup chopped onions	3 tablespoons flour
1 teaspoon salt	Meat Puffins (recipe below)
2 cups boiling water	

Place carrots in small saucepan and potatoes and onions in medium saucepan; sprinkle ½ teaspoon salt in each and pour 1 cup boiling water in each pan. Cook, covered, 10 minutes or until just tender. Drain; reserve liquid. Heat oven to 425° F. Grease a 2-quart baking dish. Arrange carrots, potatoes, onions, and green beans in baking dish. Melt margarine in saucepan; blend in flour. Slowly stir in 2 cups vegetable liquid; cook until thick and clear and pour over vegetables. Bake 15 minutes. Serve with Meat Puffins. Makes 6 servings.

Meat Puffins

2 cups biscuit mix	⅓ cup chili sauce
½ cup milk	½ teaspoon prepared mustard
½ pound ground beef	½ teaspoon salt

Heat oven to 425° F. Grease muffin tins. Combine biscuit mix with milk; roll on floured board to ¼-inch thickness. Cut into 3-inch squares. Combine meat with remaining ingredients; stir until well blended. Place squares of biscuit dough in muffin tins so that corners stick up. Put a spoonful of meat mixture in center of each. Bake 15 minutes. Makes 9 squares.

Pastitsio

A Greek Islands specialty with a heavenly flavor. Served hot or cold, it's equally good.

1 package (1 pound) elbow macaroni
½ cup margarine
1 cup grated Parmesan cheese
¼ cup vegetable oil
¼ cup chopped onion
4 cloves garlic, mashed
1 pound ground chuck beef

1 teaspoon salt
1 teaspoon oregano
½ teaspoon basil
4 eggs
1 tablespoon flour
½ cup milk

Heat oven to 300° F. Cook macaroni according to package directions; drain well. Melt ¼ cup margarine in skillet; cook over moderate heat until it begins to brown. Add to macaroni with cheese; mix thoroughly and set aside. Melt remaining margarine in skillet adding oil and stirring well. Add onion and garlic; sauté until onion is lightly browned. Add meat. Cook and stir until meat is browned. Add salt, oregano, and basil. Combine meat mixture with macaroni. Pour into greased 3-quart baking dish. Beat eggs with flour and milk until well blended. Pour over macaroni mixture. Bake 30 minutes. Makes 6 to 8 servings.

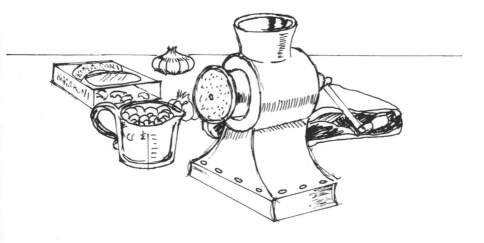

Onion Pie Hongrois

A favorite of many restaurants in Budapest, this dish is ideal for Sunday supper or dinner.

1 cup packaged biscuit mix	½ teaspoon celery salt
⅓ cup milk	¼ teaspoon pepper
1½ tablespoons margarine	1 tablespoon flour
½ cup thinly sliced onions	½ cup sour cream
½ pound ground chuck beef	1 egg, slightly beaten
½ teaspoon salt	1 teaspoon paprika

Heat oven to 375° F. Prepare biscuit mix according to package directions for biscuits; roll into 10-inch circle. Line a well-greased 8-inch pie plate just to edge of rim. Melt margarine in skillet; sauté onions until barely tender. Add beef; cook, stirring with fork to loosen meat, until it loses its color. Blend in salt, celery salt, pepper, and flour; cook, stirring, 3 minutes longer. Spread meat mixture evenly over biscuit dough in pie plate. Blend sour cream with egg; spoon evenly over meat; sprinkle with paprika. Bake 30 minutes or until knife inserted in center comes out clean.

Spaghetti Napolitano

A quick version of an all-time favorite made with beef and sausage.

½ pound ground beef	1 cup tomato sauce
½ pound bulk sausage, shaped into tiny balls	1 teaspoon salt
	Dash cayenne
1 cup thinly sliced onions	1 teaspoon Worcestershire sauce
¾ cup green pepper, cut in thin strips	¼ cup grated Cheddar cheese
	1½ teaspoons vinegar
1½ cups water	5 cups seasoned cooked spaghetti
2 bouillon cubes	

Separate meat into small pieces with fork in hot skillet and cook until red color disappears, tossing with fork. Remove meat; fry sausage balls until just browned and remove from skillet. Discard all but 1 tablespoon drippings. Add onions and green pepper; cover and cook over low heat 5 minutes. Add meat, water, bouillon cubes, tomato sauce, seasonings, cheese, and vinegar. Stir over low heat until bouillon cubes are dissolved; simmer 10 minutes longer. Add spaghetti and heat through. Makes 8 servings.

Polenta Monte Bello

Gay enough for a party, this dish does well for a hearty family meal, too.

¼ cup vegetable oil
½ cup finely chopped onion
1 small clove minced garlic
1 cup sliced mushrooms
1 pound ground beef
1 can (1 pound 12 ounces) tomatoes
1 cup finely chopped celery
2 sliced carrots
1 teaspoon salt

⅛ teaspoon pepper
⅛ teaspoon cloves
1 teaspoon oregano
½ teaspoon marjoram
Pinch cayenne pepper
1½ teaspoons lemon juice
1 beef bouillon cube
Polenta (recipe below)

Heat oil in large heavy skillet. Sauté onion, garlic, and mushrooms until light golden. Add meat; break up with fork and brown well. Add tomatoes, celery, carrots, seasonings, lemon juice, and bouillon cube. Mix well. Cover; simmer 1 hour, stirring occasionally.

Polenta

2 cups yellow cornmeal
3 cups cold water
3 cups boiling water

2 teaspoons salt
⅛ teaspoon pepper
1½ cups grated Parmesan cheese

Mix cornmeal and cold water in top of double boiler. Stir in boiling water, salt and pepper. Cook until smooth and thickened, stirring constantly. Add 1 cup cheese; mix well. Heat oven to 350° F. Spoon mixture into a buttered 2-quart baking dish. Sprinkle remaining cheese on top. Bake 20 to 25 minutes. Broil a few minutes until top is golden.

Frikadeller Pie

Bargain Day? Yes, when you take one pound of ground meat and stretch it into a very sturdy and delicious meal.

½ pound ground beef
½ pound ground lean pork
2 eggs
½ teaspoon salt
⅛ teaspoon pepper
1 tablespoon grated onion
½ cup tomato juice
1½ cups soft bread cubes

½ cup dry bread crumbs
1½ teaspoons chopped green onion
¼ cup milk
⅛ teaspoon marjoram
⅛ teaspoon thyme
½ cup chopped, pared apples
¼ cup seedless raisins

Heat oven to 350° F. Combine beef, pork, eggs, salt, pepper, grated onion, tomato juice, and dry bread crumbs; beat with fork until light. Combine bread cubes, green onion, milk, herbs, apples, and raisins. Spread half of meat mixture in bottom of 8-inch square pan. Spread fruit mixture over meat; cover with remaining meat mixture. Bake 1 hour. Cut into 4 large squares or eight small ones.

Oriental Beef Curry

Serve this exotic dish with pineapple chunks, salted peanuts, tomato slices, and fried onion rings.

1 pound ground chuck beef
1 tablespoon salt
¼ teaspoon pepper
2 tablespoons shortening
1 medium onion, chopped
1 teaspoon chili powder
1 tablespoon turmeric
1 tablespoon curry powder

½ teaspoon marjoram
½ teaspoon thyme
2 tablespoons flour
2 cups hot, cooked green beans,
    cup up
1¼ cups hot water
2 cups hot fluffy rice
1 tablespoon chopped parsley

Season meat with 1 teaspoon salt and pepper; form into 16 small balls. Heat shortening in skillet; brown meatballs on all sides. Remove to heated platter. In skillet sauté onion until tender. Combine spices with flour; add enough water to make smooth paste. Stir into onions; simmer 10 minutes, stirring constantly. Add beans and hot water; simmer, covered, 20 minutes. Add meatballs; simmer 10 minutes. Serve over rice; sprinkle with parsley.

Meatballs De Menthe

The heady flavor of fresh mint gives a piquant taste to these meatballs; if you don't have a mint bed already in your herb garden, run out to the nursery and buy a plant.

1 pound ground lean beef
½ pound ground lean lamb
1½ tablespoons finely
   chopped fresh mint
½ cup fresh bread crumbs
2 eggs
1 medium onion, finely chopped

1 teaspoon salt
⅛ teaspoon pepper
½ cup flour
6 tablespoons vegetable oil
1 can (1 pound) tomatoes
½ teaspoon basil

Combine beef and lamb. Add 1 tablespoon to meat mixture together with bread crumbs, eggs, onion, salt, and pepper. Blend and shape into balls 1½ inches in diameter; roll in flour. Heat oil in skillet; brown meatballs, turning them frequently. Pour off excess fat; add tomatoes, basil, and remaining ½ teaspoon mint. Cook, covered, 15 minutes or until done.

Gingersnap Meatballs

1 pound ground beef
1 egg
¾ cup soft bread crumbs
¼ cup water
¼ cup finely chopped onion
½ teaspoon salt
⅛ teaspoon pepper

1½ cups boiling water
2 beef bouillon cubes
⅓ cup brown sugar
¼ cup seedless raisins
2½ tablespoons lemon juice
½ cup coarse gingersnap crumbs

Combine meat, egg, bread crumbs, ¼ cup water, onion, salt, and pepper; shape into 1-inch balls. Combine boiling water with bouillon cubes, sugar, raisins, lemon juice, and gingersnap crumbs; stir until bouillon cubes are dissolved. Add meatballs; cook over low heat 10 minutes. Turn meatballs, spooning sauce over all; cook ten minutes longer, stirring occasionally. Makes 6 servings.

Sauerbraten Meatballs

Ground beef goes elegant with the snappy German sauce.

1 pound ground beef	½ cup water
½ cup finely chopped onion	1 bay leaf
1 egg, slightly beaten	8 cloves
1 teaspoon salt	6 peppercorns, crushed
⅛ teaspoon pepper	3 tablespoons brown sugar
1½ tablespoons margarine	8 gingersnaps, coarsely broken
½ cup wine vinegar	½ cup sour cream

Combine beef, onion, egg, salt, and pepper. Shape into 1½-inch balls. Melt margarine in skillet. Add meatballs; cook, turning, until evenly browned. Combine remaining ingredients, except sour cream; add to meatballs. Cook over very low heat, covered, about 30 minutes. Remove meatballs to heated serving platter. Strain liquid and return to skillet. Stir in sour cream; pour over meatballs.

Honan Beef Balls

1 egg	1 slice canned pineapple,
2 tablespoons flour	cut into 8 pieces
2 teaspoons salt	2 teaspoons cornstarch
½ teaspoon pepper	2 teaspoons soy sauce
1 pound ground lean beef	½ cup vinegar
¼ cup vegetable oil	½ cup sugar
1 cup chicken broth	2 cups hot cooked spinach,
	well drained

Combine egg, flour, ½ teaspoon salt, and pepper; beat with fork to form a batter. Shape meat into 1-inch balls; dip in batter. Heat vegetable oil in large skillet with remaining 1½ teaspoons salt; place balls in skillet and fry until browned. Remove and keep warm. Drain skillet, measure 1 tablespoon drippings and discard remaining oil. Add drippings, ½ cup chicken broth, and pineapple to skillet; heat 3 minutes. Blend cornstarch, soy sauce, vinegar, sugar, and remaining ½ cup chicken broth. Add to pineapple mixture; cook, stirring constantly, until thickened. Arrange spinach on heated serving platter; add meatballs on top. Pour sauce over all.

Danish Meatballs

Always a budget saver, ground beef is seasoned here with curry powder and cloves.

1 pound ground beef
1 small grated onion
¼ cup chopped parsley
1 egg
1 slice of bread, coarsely crumbled
½ teaspoon salt
¼ teaspoon marjoram
½ soup can water

1 can (10½ ounces)
  condensed tomato soup
1 tablespoon chopped green onion
⅛ teaspoon curry powder
Dash ground cloves
¼ teaspoon celery salt
2 cups hot buttered noodles

Combine ground beef, onion, parsley, egg, bread crumbs, salt and marjoram; mix well and set aside. Combine remaining ingredients, except noodles, in large heavy skillet. Heat to boiling, stirring frequently; turn off heat. Form seasoned beef into tiny bite-sized balls; drop them in sauce. Heat sauce to boiling. Cover skillet; simmer 5 minutes. Serve meatballs and sauce over buttered noodles.

Meat Loaf Jardiniere

1½ pounds ground beef
¼ cup milk
1½ cups soft bread crumbs
¼ cup chili sauce
3 tablespoons Worcestershire sauce
1 unbeaten egg
5 slices cooked crumbled bacon

3 tablespoons finely chopped onion
1 teaspoon salt
¼ teaspoon pepper
¼ teaspoon thyme
4 slices raw bacon
Mushroom Sauce (recipe below)

Heat oven to 350° F. Combine beef with remaining ingredients, except raw bacon and Mushroom Sauce; mix well. Pack into 9 × 5 × 3-inch loaf pan. Lay raw bacon slices on top. Bake 1 hour. Serve with Mushroom Sauce. Makes 8 servings.

Mushroom Sauce

1 cup thin cream sauce
½ teaspoon salt
½ teaspoon paprika
½ small clove garlic, minced

1 beef bouillon cube
2 tablespoons hot water
¼ pound chopped mushrooms
2 tablespoons margarine

Combine cream sauce with salt, paprika, and garlic. Dissolve bouillon cube in hot water; add to sauce. Sauté mushrooms in margarine; add to sauce. Simmer 5 minutes, stirring constantly. Makes 1½ cups.

English Meat Loaf

A meat loaf that's different! It's marked into servings before cooking.

3 cups cooked rice
2 pounds ground beef
½ cup diced green pepper
¼ cup chopped onion

1¼ cups canned tomatoes
1 tablespoon salt
¼ teaspoon pepper

Heat oven to 375° F. Mix together all ingredients; turn into an 11 × 7-inch baking dish. Score top of loaf with knife to mark off servings. Bake 1 to 1¼ hours, or until done. Makes 8 servings.

Sorrento Meat Loaf

Versatility plus! Why not prepare two meat loaves? Serve one plain, hot from the oven; heat some in foil for another meal and serve with Surprise Gravy; and keep any leftovers cold for luncheon sandwiches.

1 cup tomato juice
1 egg, slightly beaten
2 cups soft bread crumbs
¾ teaspoon salt
⅛ teaspoon pepper
1 teaspoon poultry seasoning

1 medium onion, minced
1 tablespoon parsley, minced
3 pounds ground beef
4 skinless frankfurters
Surprise Gravy (recipe below)

Combine first eight ingredients; mix well and let stand in refrigerator 20 minutes. Heat oven to 350° F. Add ground beef to refrigerated mixture; mix well. Pat half of mixture equally into two 8½ × 4½ × 2½-inch loaf pans. Place 2 frankfurters on top lengthwise in each pan; add remaining mixture on top. Bake 1 hour. Makes 12 to 14 servings.

Surprise Gravy

1 can (10½ ounces)
  condensed mushroom soup
¼ to ⅓ cup water

Dash nutmeg
2 to 4 tablespoons drippings

Pour off drippings from meat loaf; skim top and measure remaining 2 to 4 tablespoons. Pour soup into pan; stir in drippings and nutmeg along with enough water for desired thickness. Heat; stirring constantly. Makes 1½ cups.

Meat Loaf Chatelaine

2 pounds ground beef
½ cup fine dry bread crumbs
½ cup chopped onion
2 tablespoons chopped parsley
1 tablespoon chopped celery
1 can (10½ ounces)
  condensed chicken gumbo soup

1 tablespoon Worcestershire sauce
1 egg, slightly beaten
1 teaspoon salt
⅛ teaspoon pepper

Heat oven to 350° F. Combine all ingredients; mix thoroughly. Shape into a loaf. Place in shallow baking pan. Bake 1 to 1¼ hours. Makes 8 servings.

Lemon Barbecued Beef Loaves

A quickly prepared meal is a good trick for a cook to keep up her sleeve. This one combines ground beef with a tangy barbecued flavor.

1½ pounds ground beef
¼ cup lemon juice
½ cup milk
1 egg, slightly beaten
4 slices stale bread, finely diced
¼ cup chopped onion

2 teaspoons seasoned salt
½ cup ketchup
⅓ cup brown sugar
⅛ teaspoon allspice
4 lemon slices

Combine beef with lemon juice, milk, egg, bread, onion, and salt; mix well. Shape into 4 individual loaves. Heat oven to 350° F. Grease a shallow baking pan; place meat loaves in pan. Bake 15 minutes. Combine remaining ingredients, except lemon slices; heat 1 minute. Place a lemon slice on each loaf. Continue baking 30 minutes longer, basting frequently with sauce.

Meat Loaf Ricottaki

Who said there's nothing new under the sun? Here's a brand-new way to serve ground meat which will win a round of applause.

1 pound lean ground beef
1 cup soft bread crumbs
½ cup grated Romano cheese
3 eggs, beaten
1 cup chopped onion
1½ tablespoons parsley flakes
1 teaspoon crushed basil

1¼ teaspoons salt
¼ teaspoon pepper
2 tablespoons dry bread crumbs
½ pound ricotta cheese
¼ teaspoon marjoram
2 tablespoons vegetable oil

Heat oven to 350° F. Lightly grease a 9 × 5 × 3-inch loaf pan. Combine meat, soft bread crumbs, Romano cheese, 2 eggs, onion, parsley flakes, basil, 1 teaspoon salt, and pepper; mix well. Sprinkle loaf pan with dry breadcrumbs. Turn half the meat mixture into pan. Combine ricotta cheese with remaining egg, marjoram, and remaining ¼ teaspoon salt; mix well. Spread over meat layer. Top with remaining meat and spread to completely cover cheese layer. Generously brush top with oil. Bake 1 hour. Makes 6 servings.

Meat Loaf A Là Judy

Cottage cheese and oats make this an extra-special filling for meat loaf— for company dinners add your favorite mushroom sauce.

1 pound ground beef
1 cup large-curd
   cream-style cottage cheese
½ cup quick-cooking rolled oats
1 egg
¼ cup ketchup
2 teaspoons prepared mustard

2 tablespoons chopped onion
1 tablespoon chopped celery
1 tablespoon chopped parsley
1 teaspoon salt
⅛ teaspoon pepper
⅛ teaspoon thyme
⅓ cup grated Parmesan cheese

Heat oven to 350° F. Combine all ingredients, except Parmesan cheese; mix thoroughly. Lightly pack meat mixture into an 8-inch square pan. Bake 20 minutes. Sprinkle top with cheese; bake 10 minutes longer. Let stand 5 minutes; cut into squares. Makes 6 servings.

Family Meat Loaf

The tomato sauce makes a tasty gravy for this meat loaf.

1 pound ground beef
1 cup cracker crumbs
  (about 12 crackers)
½ cup chopped onion
2 tablespoons chopped
  green pepper

2 tablespoons chopped celery
1 egg, slighty beaten
1 teaspoon salt
⅛ teaspoon pepper
½ cup milk
1 can (8 ounces) tomato sauce

Heat oven to 350° F. Combine meat, cracker crumbs, onion, green pepper, celery, egg, seasonings, and milk. Mix well. Press mixture together until it forms a round shape. Place in 2-quart casserole; pour tomato sauce over top. Cover; bake 1 hour. Makes 6 to 8 servings.

Brazilian Meat Loaf

Coffee is used in Brazil in many ingenious ways and here's one of them.

1 egg, beaten
¾ cup strong, cold coffee
½ teaspoon oregano
½ teaspoon marjoram
1½ teaspoons salt

⅛ teaspoon pepper
2 cups soft bread crumbs
1 onion, minced
1 tablespoon chopped celery
2 pounds lean beef, ground

Heat oven to 350° F. Combine egg, coffee, oregano, marjoram, salt, pepper, and bread crumbs; let stand 10 minutes. Add onion and beef; mix well. Pack into greased 9 × 5 × 3-inch loaf pan. Bake 1½ hours. Makes 8 servings.

Meat Loaf Wellington

With meat loaf enjoying such popularity, here's a new interesting variation, capped with a savory liver paste, under pastry.

1 medium onion, minced	¼ teaspoon pepper
2 stalks diced celery	¼ pound liverwurst
2 tablespoons margarine	1 tablespoon ketchup
2 pounds ground lean beef	1 teaspoon prepared mustard
1½ teaspoons salt	1 (8 ounces) package pie crust mix

Heat oven to 400° F. Sauté onion and celery in margarine until soft. Add to beef with salt and pepper. Shape in a roll about 9 inches long. Mash liverwurst; blend in ketchup and mustard. Prepare pie crust mix according to package directions. Roll out a rectangle about 10 × 12 inches. Spread center of rectangle with liverwurst mixture. Place meat roll on liverwurst mixture; bring pastry up over meat; seal, leaving ends open. Place roll seam side down on baking sheet. Cut gashes on top to indicate slices. Bake 30 to 35 minutes or until pastry is lightly browned. Makes 8 servings.

Peachy Meat Loaves

Delicious and unusual, these individual meat loaves are festive and flavorful on a bed of rice.

4 canned cling peach halves	1½ teaspoons finely chopped onion
16 whole cloves	⅛ teaspoon dry mustard
1½ tablespoons brown sugar	⅛ teaspoon black pepper
1 egg	½ pound lean ground beef
5 tablespoons fine dry bread crumbs	½ cup ground cooked ham
5 tablespoons milk	2 cups hot cooked rice
1 tablespoon ketchup	

Heat oven to 350° F. Insert 4 cloves in each peach half. Divide sugar among 4 greased custard cups; place peaches, cup sides up, on sugar. Beat egg lightly; blend with crumbs, milk, ketchup, onion, and seasonings. Blend in beef and ham. Fill cups with meat mixture. Bake 45 minutes. Invert cups to remove loaves; serve, peach side up, on bed of rice.

Tropical Hamburger

1 cup shredded coconut
½ pound ground beef
¼ teaspoon nutmeg
1 teaspoon salt
1 cup pineapple juice

2 tablespoons lemon juice
½ cup water
2 tablespoons cornstarch
Fried noodles

Brown coconut in skillet until crisp. Stir in ground beef and cook until lightly browned. Add nutmeg and salt. Combine pineapple and lemon juice with water and cornstarch; blend well. Stir into meat mixture. Stir and heat 5 to 10 minutes. Serve on fried noodles.

Tijuana Hamburg Pie

¼ cup finely chopped onion
½ cup chopped green pepper
1 pound ground beef
¼ cup vegetable oil
1 can (8 ounces) tomato sauce
2 tablespoons ketchup

1 teaspoon chili powder
1 teaspoon salt
¼ teaspoon pepper
¼ teaspoon oregano
Flaky Biscuits (recipe below)

Heat oven to 400° F. Sauté onion, green pepper, and meat in vegetable oil in heat-and-serve 9-inch skillet, separating meat with fork into small pieces. Add tomato sauce, ketchup, chili powder, salt, pepper, and oregano. Roll biscuit dough to fit skillet. Place over top of meat mixture. Bake 25 minutes or until biscuit top is lightly browned. Turn out onto heated serving plate, crust side down.

Flaky Biscuits

2 cups flour
3 teaspoons baking powder
1 teaspoon salt

⅓ cup vegetable oil
⅔ cup milk

Combine flour, baking powder, and salt; mix well. Combine vegetable oil and milk; pour all at once over entire surface of flour mixture. Mix with fork to make a soft dough. Shape lightly with hands to make a round ball. Knead lightly 10 times or until smooth. Pat out to ½-inch thickness.

Hamburger Romanoff

½ cup minced onion
¼ cup margarine
1 pound ground chuck
1 clove minced garlic
2 tablespoons flour
1 teaspoon salt
¼ teaspoon pepper

¼ teaspoon paprika
1 pound sliced mushrooms
1 can condensed cream
  of chicken soup
1 cup sour cream
2 tablespoons chopped parsley

Sauté onion in margarine until golden. Stir in meat, garlic, flour, salt, pepper, paprika, and mushrooms; sauté 5 to 6 minutes. Stir in soup; simmer, uncovered, 10 minutes. Stir in sour cream. If desired, serve over hot mashed potatoes; sprinkle with parsley.

Whipped Hamburgers

1½ pounds ground beef
2 tablespoons flour
1½ teaspoons garlic salt
½ teaspoon garlic salt
¼ teaspoon pepper

¼ teaspoon marjoram
⅛ teaspoon thyme
Dash Tabasco
1 can (8 ounces) tomato sauce
2 cups hot mashed potatoes

Heat oven to 425° F. Grease a baking sheet. Combine beef, flour, salt, garlic salt, pepper, herbs, and Tabasco. Beat mixture vigorously 5 minutes. Slowly add tomato sauce, beating constantly. Drop by tablespoonfuls onto baking sheet. Bake 20 minutes. Make a nest of ½ cup mashed potatoes on individual plate; place a hamburger in each center and serve.

Arizona Hamburgers

1 pound lean ground beef
½ cup red wine
1 tablespoon capers, drained
¾ teaspoon salt
⅛ teaspoon pepper
1 small onion, minced
1 teaspoon sage

½ teaspoon marjoram
½ teaspoon oregano
½ teaspoon chili powder
1 egg
Vegetable oil
2 cups hot buttered green noodles

Combine meat with wine, capers, salt, pepper, onion, herbs, and chili powder; mix well. Let stand at room temperature 1 hour. Add egg; mix well. Shape into 8 small patties. Fry in deep oil 2 or 3 minutes each side. Turn onto absorbent paper. Serve over hot buttered green noodles.

Southern Blueburgers

1 clove minced garlic
3 tablespoons vegetable oil
3 tablespoons soy sauce
3 tablespoons ketchup
1 tablespoon vinegar
1 tablespoon brown sugar

1 pound ground beef
¼ cup crumbled American
  blue cheese
4 slices pineapple
8 squares hot corn bread
  made from mix

Combine garlic, oil, soy sauce, ketchup, vinegar, and brown sugar in saucepan; heat to boil. Remove from heat; let stand to cool. Shape ground beef into 8 thin square patties. Marinate beef patties in spicy mixture for 2 hours. Spoon 1 tablespoon cheese on each of four patties; top with remaining patties and seal edges well. Broil to desired doneness, turning once. Broil pineapple 2 minutes or until just tinged with brown. Place pineapple and blueburgers between squares of hot corn bread. Spoon 1 teaspoon spicy mixture on each square.

Hamburgers Mexicaine

1 large ripe avocado,
  peeled and pitted
1 large tomato, peeled
2 small canned green
  chillies, seeds removed
1 tablespoon vegetable oil
1 teaspoon vinegar

¾ teaspoon salt
½ cup minced onion
2 pounds ground lean beef
¾ teaspoon chili powder
1 cup hot cooked rice
1 cup hot canned kidney beans

Combine avocado, tomato, chillies, oil, vinegar, and ¼ teaspoon salt; mash together thoroughly until smooth. Add onion; blend well. Shape meat into 6 round patties. Season with remaining salt and chili powder. Broil to desired doneness. Serve topped with avocado mixture with rice combined with kidney beans. Makes 6 servings.

Hamburger Benedict

1½ pounds ground lean beef
1 teaspoon salt
¼ teaspoon pepper

12 hot cooked asparagus spears
Hollandaise Sauce (recipe below)
4 cooked shrimp

Shape meat into 4 round patties. Sprinkle both sides with salt and pepper. Broil to desired doneness. Arrange asparagus on top of each hamburger. Top with Hollandaise Sauce. Garnish with shrimp.

Hollandaise Sauce

4 egg yolks
3 tablespoons hot water
½ cup soft margarine

½ teaspoon salt
Dash pepper
2 tablespoons lemon juice

In top of double boiler beat egg yolks and hot water until slightly thickened. Add margarine, stirring constantly, until smooth and thickened. Add salt, pepper, and lemon juice. Stir and serve at once.

Hamburger Pizza

1½ pounds ground lean beef
¾ teaspoon salt
⅛ teaspoon pepper
1 can (8 ounces) tomato sauce
1 teaspoon oregano
6 flat anchovy fillets, chopped
1 package (8 ounces)
   mozzarella cheese

3 hot Italian sausages,
   sliced, sauteed
3 tablespoons grated
   Parmesan cheese
6 sliced stuffed olives
2 tablespoons chopped parsley
2 cups hot cooked spaghetti

Pat meat out into a circle about ¾ inch thick on a baking sheet lined with aluminum foil. Sprinkle with salt and pepper. Broil almost to desired doneness. Remove from broiler; spread with tomato sauce. Sprinkle with oregano and anchovy. Top with slices of mozzarella cheese and sausage. Sprinkle with Parmesan cheese. Broil until cheese melts and browns. Garnish with olives and parsley. Cut into wedges and serve with spaghetti. Makes 6 servings.

New England Hamburgers

1 onion, thinly sliced
¼ cup celery tops, sliced
1 tablespoon margarine
Dash Tabasco
¼ teaspoon dried thyme
¼ teaspoon salt
⅛ teaspoon pepper

1 can (1 pound) Boston-style
  baked beans
½ pound ground chuck beef
1 tablespoon soy sauce
1 tablespoon honey
¼ teaspoon celery salt
1 tablespoon butter

Heat oven to 350° F. Sauté onion and celery in margarine in skillet 5 minutes; add Tabasco, thyme, salt, and pepper. Heat beans; stir in onion mixture. Combine meat, soy sauce, honey, and celery salt; shape into 1-inch balls. Sauté balls in butter until browned. Arrange ⅓ beans in 1½-quart casserole; top with ⅓ meat balls; repeat layers until all ingredients are used. Bake, covered, 20 minutes.

Tennessee Hamburger Stew

A savory blend of meat and vegetables gives this dish a distinctive flavor.

1 pound ground beef
1 tablespoon margarine
1 onion, sliced
1½ teaspoons salt
¼ teaspoon pepper
1 tablespoon steak sauce
1 can (1 pound 3 ounces) tomatoes

3 medium potatoes,
  pared and sliced
3 medium carrots,
  scraped and thickly sliced
2 stalks celery, diced
4 split hot biscuits

Brown beef lightly in margarine, stirring with fork to break up meat. Add onion; cook 5 minutes longer. Add remaining ingredients, except hot biscuits; bring to boil. Reduce heat; simmer, covered, 30 minutes or until vegetables are tender. Serve on biscuits.

VEAL

Veal is a very young beef. Its meat is delicious and may be prepared in many ways. The European meat is more delicate than our American variety mainly because fodder is expensive in Europe. This means that the calves are killed as soon as they are weaned and, being milk-fed, their flesh is extremely white and firm in texture as compared to the American meat where the calves are put out to pasture to graze and are killed when they are older.

Veal is the main meat of Italy, Switzerland, and Germany. It is not used as widely in America because it is only available seasonally. Veal welcomes savory sauces because it is bland and has very little fat.

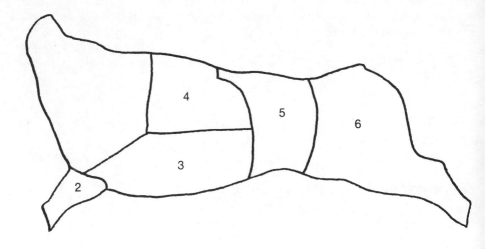

Learn which are the economical cuts of veal and use the meat whenever it is available.

Inexpensive cuts

1. *Shoulder:*   rolled shoulder, roast, blade steak, arm steak, and arm roast.
2. *Shank:*   stew meat, ground meat (excellent for meat loaves and patties).
3. *Breast:*   stew meat, boneless roasts, ground meat.

Expensive cuts

4. *Rib:*   crown roast, rib chop, rib roast.
5. *Loin:*   sirloin steak, loin chop, kidney chop.
6. *Leg:*   rump roasts, cutlets, center-cut roasts, heel-of-round pot roasts.

Tip: Arm roast has excellent meat and is economical.

Stretch veal breast by making a pocket and stuffing it, before roasting or braising.

Sweet and Sour Veal Vlodich

Savory meat, ready to fall apart at the touch of a fork in a smooth sweet-and-sour sauce.

1 veal knuckle, cracked	1 tablespoon flour
1 pound boneless stewing veal	1½ tablespoons vinegar
1 quart water	½ teaspoon sugar
2 small sliced onions	Dash nutmeg
½ cup chopped celery leaves	1 egg, well beaten
1½ teaspoons salt	2 tablespoons chopped parsley
⅛ teaspoon pepper	

Place veal knuckle, meat, water, onions, celery leaves, salt, and pepper in large deep kettle. Bring to boil; reduce heat, cover, and simmer 1½ hours. Strain stock. Remove meat; discard bones and vegetables. Return strained stock to saucepan; boil until reduced to 2 cups. Make a smooth paste of flour and vinegar and add to stock. Cook until thickened, stirring constantly. Add meat, sugar, and nutmeg. Heat thoroughly. Stir in egg; cook 2 minutes. Turn onto serving platter; garnish with chopped parsley.

Peruvian Veal

3 pounds veal for stewing,
  cut into 1-inch cubes
¼ cup flour
1½ teaspoons salt
1 teaspoon pepper
½ cup margarine
3 cups chopped onion
1 cup chopped green pepper

2 cloves garlic, minced
½ teaspoon savory
½ teaspoon oregano
½ teaspoon rosemary
2 cups canned tomatoes
1 cup cooked lima beans
1 cup cooked rice

Roll veal cubes into mixture of flour, salt, and pepper. Brown meat evenly in margarine in heavy skillet. Add onion and green pepper; cook 2 minutes. Add any remaining flour; stir well. Add garlic, savory, oregano, rosemary, and tomatoes. Heat oven to 350° F. Turn veal mixture into 2-quart baking dish. Cover; bake 1 hour. Add beans and rice. Continue baking, covered, 55 minutes longer. Makes 8 servings.

Veal Marengo

1½ pounds lean veal,
  cut into 1-inch cubes
3 tablespoons vegetable oil
1 small onion, finely chopped
1 cup canned tomatoes,
  drained, chopped
1½ teaspoons salt
¼ teaspoon pepper
¼ teaspoon paprika

2½ teaspoons flour
2¼ cups chicken broth
12 small white onions
16 whole button mushrooms
1 package (7 ounces) frozen peas
2 tablespoons chopped parsley
8 wedges of toasted garlic
  French bread

Brown veal in vegetable oil in skillet. Add onion, tomatoes, salt, pepper, and paprika. Stir in flour and chicken broth; blend well. Simmer, covered, 30 minutes. Add onions; simmer 30 minutes longer. Add mushrooms; continue cooking for 25 minutes more, or until meat is tender. Add frozen peas; heat thoroughly. Turn onto serving platter; sprinkle with parsley. Surround with French bread wedges.

Jellied Veal Loaf

A savory loaf just perfect for a buffet supper or informal party—economical, too.

1 veal knuckle, sawed in 3 pieces	8 pimiento-stuffed green olives, sliced
1 pound veal shoulder, cut up	1 tablespoon Worcestershire sauce
1 onion	⅛ teaspoon pepper
1 tablespoon salt	8 spiced peach halves
2 hard-cooked eggs, sliced	8 mounds coleslaw in lettuce cups

Place veal knuckle, meat, 2 teaspoons salt, in large deep kettle, in water to cover. Cook, covered, 2 hours or until meat is tender. Strain veal broth. Chop meat finely. Garnish bottom of a 9 × 5 × 3-inch pan with egg slices and olive slices. Cook veal broth until reduced to 1 cupful. Add chopped veal, remaining 1 teaspoon salt and Worcestershire sauce. Cool thoroughly. Press meat firmly into pan. Chill until set. Unmold onto serving platter and surround with peach halves and coleslaw in lettuce cups. Makes 8 servings.

Veal and Ham Pie Paisano

1½ pounds lean veal	2 sprigs parsley
Veal bones	3 tablespoons flour
Water	2 hard-cooked eggs, cut in pieces
1½ teaspoons salt	Pastry for 9-inch pie shell
¼ teaspoon pepper	
1 medium onion	

Heat oven to 375° F. Place meat and veal bones in heavy, deep kettle. Add water, salt, pepper, onion, and parsley. Bring to boil; reduce heat and simmer, covered, until meat is tender, about 1½ hours. Remove meat, cool, and cut into bite-size pieces. Skim fat off stock; strain and cook until reduced to 2½ cups. Add flour; blend well until smooth and slightly thickened. Add eggs. Turn meat mixture into a 2-quart baking dish. Cover with pastry, fitting it tight to the edges; slash top for steam. Bake 30 minutes. Makes 8 servings.

Veal Risotto

Feather-light cutlets from economical veal shoulder on top of a blanket of delicious rice with a ham flavor.

4 thin veal cutlets
  shoulder or rump
1 onion, chopped
2 tablespoons margarine
½ cup cooked ground ham
2 cups rice

1 cup canned tomatoes
1 cup water
2 chicken bouillon cubes
2 tablespoons grated sharp cheese
2 tablespoons chopped parsley

Pound cutlets with edge of saucer until flat. Sauté onion in margarine; add ham, cook 5 minutes. Add rice, tomatoes, water, and bouillon cubes. Stir; cook 20 minutes or until rice is tender. Add cheese; beat well to form a creamy risotto. Panfry veal cutlets on both sides until lightly browned. Turn rice mixture onto heated serving platter; arrange cutlets on top. Sprinkle with parsley.

Southern Veal Loaf

2 pounds boneless veal neck, ground
¼ pound salt pork, ground
1 cup soft bread crumbs
1 tablespoon Worcestershire sauce
1 teaspoon salt

2 tablespoons ketchup
1 egg
½ cup milk
4 slices bacon

Heat oven to 325° F. Combine veal, salt pork, bread crumbs, Worcestershire sauce, salt, ketchup, egg, and milk; mix thoroughly. Pack into greased 9 × 5 × 3-inch loaf pan. Cover with strips of bacon. Bake 2 hours.

Saltimbocca

This recipe is great for a party buffet and you can double it with ease. Serve it with hot rolls and a tossed green salad.

1 pound veal, cut in thin strips
2 tablespoons margarine
¾ teaspoon salt
⅛ teaspoon pepper
¼ cup water
1 can (10½ ounces)
  chicken rice soup

2 tablespoons chopped pimiento
1 small green pepper, chopped
2 cups medium noodles,
  cooked and drained
1 cup cream-style corn
¾ cup buttered bread crumbs

Heat oven to 350° F. Grease a 1-quart baking dish. Brown veal in margarine on both sides. Season with salt and pepper. Remove meat to platter. Add water in skillet; heat, stirring. Blend soup, pimiento, green pepper, and noodles in skillet; heat 3 minutes. Turn meat into baking dish, pour soup mixture over it. Spoon corn on top. Sprinkle buttered bread crumbs; bake 45 minutes.

Veal Chops with Onion Sauce

4 veal chops
2 tablespoons margarine
1 teaspoon salt
¼ teaspoon pepper
6 onions, sliced
3 tablespoons flour
¼ cup tomato sauce

⅛ teaspoon thyme
⅛ teaspoon marjoram
½ bay leaf
4 bouillon cubes
2 cups water
1 cup wine

Heat oven to 350°F. Brown chops in margarine on both sides. Turn into a 2-quart baking dish. Season with salt and pepper. Brown onion slices in same skillet. Blend in flour and tomato sauce. Add herbs, bouillon cubes, water, and wine. Bring to boil, stirring frequently until well blended. Pour over chops. Bake, covered, 35 minutes.

Rolled Veal Continental

Here's an economical dish, a stuffed breast of veal which may be prepared ahead of time and reheated at serving time.

2½ pounds boned breast of veal
½ pound chopped chuck beef
1½ teaspoons salt
¼ teaspoon pepper
1 egg, slightly beaten
10 green olives, pitted and chopped
¼ cup vegetable oil

3 cloves garlic, peeled
1 medium onion, quartered
1 small carrot, quartered
1 bay leaf
2 tablespoons ketchup
½ cup white wine
1 cup water

Pound veal flat. Combine beef with ½ teaspoon salt, pepper, egg, and olives. Press beef mixture flat over veal to within ½ inch from edges. Roll up veal, tucking in edges; tie with cord. Brown veal in vegetable oil in deep kettle with garlic; discard garlic. Add onion, carrot, bay leaf, ketchup, wine, water, and remaining 1 teaspoon salt. Simmer, covered, 2½ hours or until meat is fork tender. Makes 8 to 10 servings.

Veal and Turkey Amandine

Use leftover turkey to stretch one pound of veal to six generous servings.

1 pound veal cutlet, ¼ inch thick,
   cut into thin strips
¼ cup margarine
¾ teaspoon salt
¼ teaspoon white pepper
½ teaspoon ground ginger
¼ teaspoon mace
1 tablespoon flour
1 cup milk

½ cup light cream
½ cup dry white wine
½ pound fresh mushrooms, sliced
8 green onions, sliced
½ cup sour cream
2 cups cooked turkey, cubed
2 cups green noodles, cooked
   and buttered
¼ cup toasted slivered almonds

Brown meat in 2 tablespoons margarine. Season with salt, pepper, ginger, and mace. Combine flour with 2 tablespoons milk; make a smooth paste and add to meat with remaining milk and cream. Blend well; cook, covered, over low heat 30 minutes, stirring occasionally. Stir in wine. Sauté onions and mushrooms in remaining margarine; add veal mixture and turkey. Heat through; stir in sour cream until heated. Serve over noodles; sprinkle with almonds.

Blanquette De Veau

2 pounds veal shoulder,
   cut into 1¼-inch pieces
4 whole cloves
1 small onion
6 medium carrots, quartered
1 bay leaf
⅛ teaspoon thyme
2 sprigs parsley
½ cup thinly sliced celery
4 peppercorns

1 tablespoon salt
6 tablespoons margarine
12 small white onions
½ pound fresh mushrooms
¼ cup flour
2 egg yolks
2 tablespoons lemon juice
2 cups hot mashed potatoes
2 tablespoons chopped parsley

Place meat in heavy kettle with cloves stuck in onion, carrots, bay leaf, thyme, parsley, celery, peppercorns, and salt. Add water to cover. Simmer 1 hour or until meat is tender. Drain; reserve 3½ cups stock. Discard vegetables and seasonings. Melt ¼ cup margarine in large skillet; add white onions and simmer, covered, over low heat 30 minutes, or until tender. Add to cooked veal. In same skillet sauté mushrooms. Add ½ cup veal stock, and veal-and-onion mixture. Melt remaining 2 tablespoons margarine; stir in flour until smooth. Slowly add 3 cups of remaining reserved stock. Cook over medium heat, stirring constantly until thickened and boiling. Beat egg yolks slightly with lemon juice; slowly stir in ¼ cup of hot sauce; then stir the mixture slowly into remaining hot sauce. Pour over veal mixture; heat thoroughly but do not boil. Arrange ring of mashed potatoes on heated serving platter; spoon veal mixture in center. Sprinkle with parsley. Makes 6 servings.

Veal Consuelo

Tender, juicy veal is the most versatile meat in the world—serve this dish with a tossed green salad with caraway seeds, popovers and coffee gelatin with whipped cream.

¼ cup flour
1 teaspoon salt
¼ teaspoon pepper
½ teaspoon thyme
4 veal chops
1 clove garlic, minced
1 medium onion, minced

3 tablespoons shortening
1 can consommé
¾ cup sherry wine
4 carrots, sliced
4 medium potatoes, halved
8 small white onions

Combine flour, salt, pepper, and thyme. Coat chops well in mixture and pound them with edge of saucer. Sauté garlic and onion in shortening in heavy skillet until soft. Add chops, brown on both sides. Add consommé and wine. Simmer, covered, 40 minutes. Arrange carrots, potatoes, and onions in skillet. Cover; simmer 30 minutes longer or until vegetables are tender.

Spanish Veal

An attractive, hearty main dish, well seasoned with tomatoes and garlic.

1½ pounds boneless veal
   shoulder, cut in 1½-inch cubes
¼ cup vegetable oil
1 teaspoon salt
⅛ teaspoon pepper
1 bay leaf
1 large clove garlic, minced
1 tablespoon minced onion

1 can (1 pound) tomatoes
1 cup water
2 tablespoons flour
¼ cup chicken broth
1 cup cooked green beans
½ cup cooked garbanzos
   (chick peas)

Brown meat in oil on both sides. Stir in salt, pepper, bay leaf, garlic, onion, tomatoes, and water. Simmer, covered, 1½ hours. Combine flour and broth; stir into meat mixture and blend well. Add green beans and garbanzos. Heat thoroughly.

Veal Loaf Allemande

1 pound ground veal
1 pound ground pork
1 can (10½ ounces) chicken soup
1 cup quick-cooking oatmeal
½ teaspoon rosemary
1 egg

1½ teaspoons salt
¼ teaspoon pepper
1 tablespoon onion juice
1 teaspoon paprika
Sauce Allemande (recipe below)

Heat oven to 350° F. Grease a 9 × 5 × 3-inch loaf pan. Combine all ingredients, except paprika and Sauce Allemande; mix well. Turn into loaf pan. Sprinkle with paprika. Bake 1½ hours. Serve with Sauce Allemande. Makes 8 servings.

Sauce Allemande

2 tablespoons margarine
2 tablespoons flour
1 cup milk

¼ teaspoon salt
⅛ teaspoon pepper
½ teaspoon minced onion

Melt margarine in small saucepan over moderate heat. Add flour; blend thoroughly. Slowly add milk. Cook, stirring constantly, until smooth and thickened. Add salt, pepper and onion. Heat thoroughly.

Veal Stew Origan

½ pound dried marrow beans
3 cups water
¼ pound salt pork, thinly sliced
1 pound boneless veal stew meat
1 medium onion, sliced
1 clove garlic, minced
1½ teaspoons paprika

⅛ teaspoon thyme
¼ teaspoon marjoram
⅛ teaspoon pepper
2 large carrots, sliced
1 green pepper, cut in eighths
2 stalks celery, sliced
2 tablespoons chopped parsley

Wash beans, add water, and bring to boil; boil 2 minutes. Remove from heat; let stand 1 hour. Fry salt pork 5 minutes in skillet; add meat, onion, and garlic, and brown lightly. Stir in paprika, thyme, marjoram, and pepper. Add to beans and water. Cover, simmer 1½ hours, or until beans and meat are almost tender. Add carrots, green pepper, and celery; simmer 25 minutes longer or until vegetables are tender. Serve sprinkled with parsley.

Veal Rolls Romanesque

Capture the sunshine of Italy for your table in a succulent dish of veal. Herbs and seasonings can do it for you with ease!

1½ pounds veal round,
  thinly sliced into 6 slices
1 teaspoon salt
¼ teaspoon pepper
1 can (4 ounces) deviled ham
6 slices Swiss cheese
2 tablespoons margarine
1 tablespoon minced onion

1 tablespoon flour
¾ cup consommé
1 teaspoon wine vinegar
½ teaspoon marjoram
3 cups hot buttered noodles
2 tablespoons chopped parsley
½ cup grated Parmesan cheese

Heat oven to 350° F. Sprinkle veal with salt and pepper; pound lightly to flatten. Spread each slice with deviled ham; cover with cheese. Roll up and fasten with wooden picks. Brown lightly in margarine on all sides. Remove to shallow baking dish. Stir onion and flour in drippings. Add consommé, vinegar, and marjoram; stir until boiling. Pour around veal. Cover loosely with aluminum foil. Bake 45 minutes or until tender. Serve over noodles, tossed with parsley and Parmesan cheese. Makes 6 servings.

Cream Veal Goulash with Rice

1¼ pounds breast of veal,
   cut in 1½-inch cubes
1 quart water
½ small onion
¾ teaspoon salt
2 peppercorns
1 whole clove

½ bay leaf
1½ tablespoons margarine
1½ tablespoons flour
¼ cup dry white wine
½ cup heavy cream
1 egg yolk
2 cups hot cooked rice

Combine veal cubes, water, onion, salt, peppercorns, clove, and bay leaf in a large heavy saucepan. Cover and bring to boil. Reduce heat; simmer 1 hour or until meat is tender. Drain meat; reserve broth. Melt margarine; blend in flour. Add 1 cup reserved veal broth. Cook, stirring, until mixture comes to boil and thickens. Stir in wine; boil gently 1 minute. Mix together cream and egg yolk. Stir into hot mixture. Add veal cubes; cook over low heat, stirring, until mixture thickens slightly. Serve over rice.

Veal Cutlet Marjolaine

Veal partners gracefully with curry powder and spiced peaches in this exotic dish.

½ cup flour
2 tablespoons curry powder
¾ teaspoon salt
¼ teaspoon pepper
1 egg, beaten

4 veal chops
2 tablespoons margarine
¼ cup consommé
½ cup chopped sliced peaches

Combine flour with curry powder, salt, and pepper; blend well. Dip veal chops in flour mixture, then in egg, then in flour again. Sauté in margarine in skillet until browned on both sides. Add consommé; cook, covered, over low heat 35 minutes or until tender. Add peaches; heat thoroughly.

Grape-Stuffed Veal

4½ pounds breast of veal
¼ cup chopped onion
½ cup chopped celery
¼ cup margarine
2 cups croutons

½ teaspoon salt
¼ teaspoon pepper
½ teaspoon poultry seasoning
4 tablespoons water
1 cup halved seedless grapes

Have butcher cut a pocket in breast of veal. Heat oven to 325° F. Sauté onion and celery in margarine until soft. Add to croutons. Blend in salt, pepper, poultry seasoning, and water. Add grapes; mix lightly. Fill pocket of meat with stuffing mixture. Close opening with skewers. Place on rack in shallow baking pan. Bake 2¼ hours or until tender and golden brown. Makes 8 servings.

Veal Bean Kettle

2 tablespoons flour	1 cup canned tomatoes
1 teaspoon salt	¼ teaspoon tarragon
⅛ teaspoon pepper	1 cup canned green beans, cut
1 pound veal shoulder,	1 can (4 ounces) sliced mushrooms
cut into 1½-inch cubes	¾ cup whole kernel corn, cooked
1 tablespoon margarine	

Combine flour, salt, and pepper. Coat meat with mixture; brown in margarine in large kettle. Stir in tomatoes and tarragon. Drain liquid from beans and mushrooms into kettle. Bring to boil; cover and simmer 1 to 1¼ hours or until meat is tender. Drain corn and add to meat mixture with beans and mushrooms. Heat thoroughly.

Veal Victoria

Veal is sharing its own delicate lusciousness with aromatic herbs and garden-fresh vegetables.

1½-pound shoulder of veal,	⅛ teaspoon pepper
4 pieces, 4 inches long	¼ cup pimiento strips
3 tablespoons margarine	1 teaspoon grated lemon rind
½ small chopped onion	1 can (17 ounces) peas
2 teaspoons minced parsley	1 tablespoon cornstarch
¼ teaspoon crumbled rosemary	2 tablespoons water
¼ teaspoon garlic salt	1 teaspoon lemon juice
½ teaspoon thyme	

Brown meat in margarine in large skillet. Add onion; sauté until tender. Sprinkle meat with parsley, rosemary, garlic salt, thyme, pepper, pimiento strips, and lemon rind. Drain liquid from peas; add liquid to skillet mixture. Simmer, covered, 30 minutes or until meat is tender. Add peas. Combine cornstarch with water and lemon juice; stir into sauce; heat thoroughly.

Veal À L'Auton

1 pound boneless veal	⅛ teaspoon mace
1¾ cups water	Dash cayenne
2 teaspoons salt	½ teaspoon celery salt
1 medium onion	¼ cup light cream
Celery leaves	3 hard-cooked eggs
6 black peppercorns	2 tablespoons red wine
3 tablespoons flour	2 cups hot, cooked rice

Place meat in large saucepan; pour water over it. Add salt, onion, celery leaves, and peppercorns. Cover; simmer 40 to 50 minutes or until meat is tender. Discard celery leaves, onion, and peppercorns. Cut meat into short strips. Stir flour in pan liquid until smooth. Add mace, cayenne, celery salt, and light cream; cook, stirring constantly, until thickened. Press egg yolks through sieve and cut egg whites lengthwise; add to sauce. Add meat strips. Stir in wine; cook 10 minutes. Serve on rice.

Savory Veal Croquettes

Nutmeg adds a piquant flavor to these veal croquettes; serve them with whipped potatoes and a green salad.

3 tablespoons vegetable oil	Few grains cayenne
Flour	¼ teaspoon nutmeg
1 teaspoon salt	1 teaspoon onion juice
⅛ teaspoon pepper	1 egg
1 cup milk	2 tablespoons water
2 cups cooked veal, finely minced	1 cup dry bread crumbs
⅓ teaspoon celery salt	Shortening

Combine oil, ¼ cup flour, ½ teaspoon salt, pepper, and milk in saucepan. Cook over low heat, stirring constantly until mixture bubbles and is thick. Remove from heat; cool. Combine meat with remaining salt, celery salt, cayenne, nutmeg, and onion juice. Add cooled white sauce; blend well. Chill mixture in refrigerator 2 hours. Shape into small croquettes. Beat egg slightly with water. Roll croquettes in flour, then in egg, then in bread crumbs. Fry in deep fat until browned all over; drain on absorbent paper.

Veal Au Vin

Spring veal, like lamb, is featured at attractive prices during the season, so take advantage of this.

1 pound veal, thinly sliced
¼ cup grated Parmesan cheese
2 tablespoons flour
Dash pepper
1 can (4 ounces) sliced mushrooms, drained

¼ cup margarine
1 can (10½ ounces)
    condensed beef broth
2 tablespoons dry red wine

Pound into veal a mixture of cheese, flour, and pepper, using meat hammer or edge of heavy saucer. Brown mushrooms in margarine in skillet; push to the edge, clearing space in the center to brown meat on both sides. Blend in any remaining flour mixture. Add beef broth and wine. Cook, covered, over low heat 25 minutes or until meat is tender, stirring frequently. Uncover; cook 5 minutes longer.

Mock Chicken Legs Mamee

1 pound ground veal shoulder
1 teaspoon salt
⅛ teaspoon pepper
2 tablespoons chopped parsley
1 tablespoon chopped celery leaves
2 tablespoons melted margarine

¼ teaspoon rosemary
1 egg, slightly beaten
½ cup fine bread crumbs
3 tablespoons butter
1 cup sour cream

Combine veal, salt, pepper, parsley, celery leaves, margarine, rosemary, and egg. Mix lightly. Divide mixture into 4 equal portions. Shape each portion around a wooden skewer to look like a chicken leg. Roll each in bread crumbs, coating all sides. Heat butter in skillet. Fry meat, turning frequently, until well browned, about 15 minutes. Carefully place in center of skillet; cover tightly and cook over low heat for ten minutes. Remove to heated serving platter; keep warm. Add sour cream to drippings in skillet; heat through but do not boil. Pour over meat and serve.

Osso Bucco

Each Italian city has its own version of this delectable dish; this one is from Bergamo.

4 pieces veal shank
1 teaspoon salt
¼ teaspoon pepper
½ cup margarine
1 medium onion, minced
1 carrot, pared and diced
1 celery stalk, sliced
1 garlic clove, minced

2 tablespoons flour
2 canned tomatoes
2 beef bouillon cubes
1½ cups water
¼ cup white wine
½ teaspoon rosemary
½ teaspoon marjoram
1½ tablespoons chopped parsley

Sprinkle veal shank with salt and pepper. Heat ¼ cup margarine in deep heavy skillet; brown veal and set aside. Add onion, carrot, celery, and garlic to skillet; sauté until tender. Add meat. Add remaining margarine, flour, tomatoes, bouillon cubes dissolved in water, wine, herbs, and stir well. Cover; simmer 1½ to 2 hours or until meat is tender. Turn onto serving platter; sprinkle with parsley.

Veal Riblets Audubon

Prepare this ahead of time; bake 2 hours before serving and dinner will be served promptly.

2 tablespoons shortening
3 pounds veal riblets
1½ teaspoons salt
¾ teaspoon pepper
¾ cup chili sauce

¾ cup water
12 small white onions, peeled
4 carrots, thickly sliced
½ pound fresh whole green beans
1 tablespoon chopped parsley

Heat oven to 350° F. Heat shortening in skillet. Brown riblets lightly on both sides. Arrange in shallow baking pan. Sprinkle with salt and pepper. Combine chili sauce and water; pour over meat. Add onions, carrots, and beans. Cover tightly and bake 2 hours or until meat is tender.

Veal Fricassee

A delicious spring meal when veal is plentiful and priced reasonably.

1 pound boneless veal shoulder,
  cut into 1½-inch cubes
1½ tablespoons shortening
¾ teaspoon salt
⅛ teaspoon pepper
¾ cup water

2 medium carrots, cut in half
¼ teaspoon paprika
¼ cup sliced mushrooms
½ cup cooked peas
1½ tablespoons flour
2 cups hot buttered noodles

Brown meat in shortening. Season with salt and pepper. Add water; cover and cook over low heat 30 minutes. Add carrots; cover and cook 30 minutes longer. Add paprika, mushrooms, and peas. Cook 10 minutes or until meat and vegetables are tender. Remove meat and vegetables to heated serving platter; thicken liquid in skillet with flour for gravy. Pour over meat mixture. Serve with noodles.

American-Style Schnitzel

A rich, tasy treatment for veal — colorful with the yellow and red of the cheese and tomato.

4 veal cutlets, ¼ inch thick
⅓ cup flour
2 eggs, slightly beaten
½ cup dry bread crumbs
⅓ cup margarine

4 slices Cheddar cheese
4 slices large tomato
1 teaspoon salt
¼ teaspoon pepper
½ teaspoon basil

Dip meat in flour, then in eggs, and finally in bread crumbs. Sauté in margarine in heavy skillet until light golden brown on both sides. Season with ½ of salt and pepper. Place veal cutlets on baking sheet; arrange a slice of cheese on top of each piece of meat; top with tomato. Season with remaining salt and pepper and basil. Place under broiler and broil 3 to 4 minutes or until tomato is broiled and cheese is bubbly.

LAMB

Lamb is popular throughout the Near East, Europe, and Australia. Some of our most interesting recipes have originated from these countries and lamb appears in practically every cuisine of the world and has adapted itself to the tastes of many lands.

Garlic is one of the most popular flavors associated with lamb. Herbs such as basil, oregano, thyme, dill, sage, rosemary, parsley, and mint are used all over the world. In the Near East, cumin, coriander, cinnamon, and ginger are used profusely along with eggplant, tomatoes, peas, almonds, and pine nuts. Whole lamb barbecued over an open fire is the ideal way to serve a crowd.

Baby lamb is a sheep under three months of age and usually appears in early spring. Sheep, from the age of three to six months, is called spring lamb; up to a year, the meat is referred to simply as lamb; and beyond this age, the flesh becomes mutton.

The meat of the lamb is red and may be served medium rare, medium, or well done. Superfluous fat should be removed from all cuts before cooking as it tends to give a strong flavor to the meat.

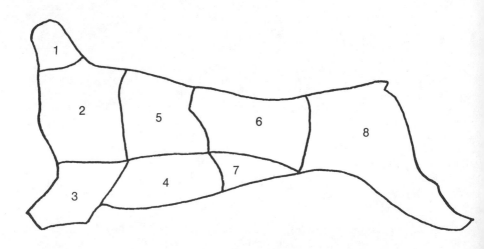

Check the chart to familiarize yourself with the different cuts of lamb.

Inexpensive cuts
1. *Neck:* neck slices
2. *Shoulder:* rolled shoulder, boneless chops, cushion shoulder, blade chops, arm chops
3. *Shank:* stew meat, ground lamb (excellent for patties and meat loaves)
4. *Breast:* stew meat, rolled breast, ground lamb, riblets

Expensive cuts
5. *Back:* crown roast, rib chops
6. *Loin:* loin chops, loin roast, English chops
7. *Saddle:* roasting meat
8. *Leg:* Frenched leg, American leg, sirloin roast

Tips: Cushion shoulder makes a delicious economical meal. It is made by removing the bones from the lamb shoulder so that a pocket is formed. Fill it with a well-seasoned bread or rice stuffing.

Stews are good meat stretchers and lamb makes delicious stews. For economy, use meat from the neck, shoulder, shank, or breast.

Try ground lamb for a different meat loaf.

Savory Lamb Short Ribs

These short ribs lend themselves to family or company feasting served with boiled potatoes sprinkled with paprika, green lima beans, and hot garlic bread.

2 pounds lamb short ribs	¼ cup brown sugar
2 tablespoons melted margarine	2 cups water
2 medium onions, chopped	2 tablespoons vinegar
1 cup celery, sliced	2 tablespoons flour
1 can (6 ounces) tomato paste	½ teaspoon salt

Cook short ribs in margarine in skillet until browned on all sides. Add onions, celery, tomato paste, sugar, and water; blend well. Cover; cook over low heat, stirring occasionally, 55 minutes or until meat is tender. Combine vinegar and flour to make a smooth paste. Gradually add to lamb mixture. Cook, stirring constantly, until thickened. Season with salt.

Cabbage Lamb Duvernois

1 small head cabbage	1 cup uncooked rice
Boiling water	1 teaspoon salt
1 pound ground lamb	½ teaspoon cinnamon
½ cup melted margarine	¼ cup pine nuts
2 eggs	2 tablespoons lemon juice
2 small onions, finely chopped	¼ cup cold water

Place cabbage in large saucepan. Cover with boiling water; let stand 8 minutes until soft enough to separate leaves. Drain; cool slightly. Cut out hard stem end; carefully remove leaves. Combine meat, ¼ cup margarine, 1 beaten egg, onions, rice, salt, cinnamon, and pine nuts; blend well. Place 1 tablespoon of mixture in center of each cabbage leaf; roll leaf around meat and tuck in ends. Place rolls close together in large saucepan pour remaining margarine over top. Weigh rolls down with plate. Cover saucepan tightly; cook over low heat 55 minutes. Remove rolls to heated serving platter. Combine remaining egg, lemon juice, and cold water; beat slightly until blended. Add ¼ cup hot liquid from saucepan; slowly stir in egg mixture until well blended. Pour over cabbage rolls and serve. Makes 8 servings.

Citrus-Glazed Lamb Special

Expecting guests for dinner? If your budget is strained, serve this succulent dish which will delight any gourmet, without challenging your pocketbook.

1 5-pound boned shoulder of	¼ teaspoon pepper
lamb, rolled and tied	¾ cup orange marmalade
2 tablespoons flour	¼ cup lemon juice
1 teaspoon salt	2 cups whipped potatoes

Heat oven to 350° F. Place lamb on rack in shallow roasting pan; bake 1 hour. Combine flour, salt, pepper, marmalade, and lemon juice; blend. Spread on lamb. Bake 2 to 2½ hours longer or until meat is done. Place on wooden plank or heatproof serving platter. Using pastry tube, pipe potatoes around lamb. Brown lightly in broiler. Makes 8 servings.

Spaghetti with Lamb Balls

1 pound ground lamb	1 clove garlic, finely chopped
1 egg, slightly beaten	1 can (1 pound) tomatoes
1 tablespoon salt	1 can (8 ounces) tomato sauce
¼ teaspoon pepper	1 teaspoon oregano
½ teaspoon rosemary	3 quarts boiling water
2 tablespoons vegetable oil	1 package (8 ounces) spaghetti
¼ cup chopped onion	

Combine lamb, egg, ½ teaspoon salt, ⅛ teaspoon pepper, and rosemary; blend and shape into 16 meatballs. Heat oil in skillet; sauté lamb balls, onion, and garlic until balls are browned on all sides. Add tomatoes, tomato sauce, oregano, 1 teaspoon salt, and pepper. Cover; cook over low heat 45 minutes, stirring occasionally. Add remaining salt to rapidly boiling water; gradually add spaghetti. Cook, uncovered, stirring occasionally, until tender; drain. Serve spaghetti with lamb balls and sauce.

Capered Lamb Shoulder Chops

Glamorize shoulder lamb chops with capers. Serve with mashed potatoes, fresh spinach, and an apple-celery salad.

4 shoulder lamb chops, about ½ inch thick	¾ teaspoon salt
	⅛ teaspoon pepper
2 tablespoons margarine	Caper Sauce (recipe below)

Sauté lamb chops in margarine until lightly browned on both sides; season with salt and pepper. Cover; cook 20 minutes or until tender. Turn onto heated serving platter; pour sauce over meat and serve.

Caper Sauce

¼ cup margarine	1 tablespoon prepared mustard
¼ cup mayonnaise	1 tablespoon capers

Combine all ingredients in saucepan; cook over low heat 10 minutes, stirring frequently.

Bulgarian Lamb Stew

1 pound lamb shoulder, cubed	2½ cups stock or bouillon
¾ cup sliced onions	¾ teaspoon salt
1 cup sliced beets	⅛ teaspoon pepper
1 cup cut green beans	1½ cups biscuit mix
2 cups diced tomatoes	½ cup yellow cornmeal
1 cup sliced mushrooms	½ cup milk

Combine lamb and onions in skillet; cook over low heat until meat is browned on all sides. Add beets, green beans, tomatoes, mushrooms, stock or bouillon, salt, and pepper; mix well. Heat oven to 350° F. Turn lamb mixture into a 2-quart casserole. Cover; bake 1 hour or until lamb and beets are tender. Combine biscuit mix with cornmeal. Add milk; mix lightly. Turn out on lightly floured surface and knead gently 10 times. Roll out to ½-inch thickness. Cut into 2½-inch rounds. Arrange biscuits on top of stew. Increase temperature to 400° F. Bake 15 minutes or until biscuits are done.

Lamb Conquistador

A Mexican chili dish adapted to California tastes.

4 tablespoons shortening	2 tablespoons finely chopped celery
1 pound boneless lamb shoulder,	1 can (17 ounces) kidney beans
cut into ½-inch cubes	1 tablespoon flour
1 medium onion, coarsely chopped	1 tablespoon chili powder
1 medium green pepper,	1 can (16 ounces) tomatoes
coarsely chopped	½ teaspoon salt

Heat 2 tablespoons of shortening in large heavy skillet. Add lamb and brown well on all sides. Remove meat from skillet; add remaining 2 tablespoons shortening, onion, green pepper, and celery. Sauté until tender. Drain liquid from beans; mix liquid with flour and chili powder to form smooth paste. Add to skillet with tomatoes, salt, chili mixture, and lamb cubes. Cook over low heat 45 minutes, stirring occasionally. Add beans; cook 10 minutes longer.

Poor Man's Mixed Grill

2 pounds ground lamb
½ teaspoon salt
½ teaspoon garlic salt
½ teaspoon tarragon
½ cup milk
2 large tomatoes, halved
¾ teaspoon onion salt

¼ teaspoon pepper
4 teaspoons prepared mustard
1 teaspoon Worcestershire sauce
4 small zucchini,
   quartered lengthwise
2 tablespoons margarine
4 slices bacon, cut in halves

Preheat broiler 10 minutes. Combine lamb, salt, garlic salt, tarragon, and milk. Blend well. Shape into 8 patties ¾ inch thick. Sprinkle tomato halves with onion salt and pepper. Spread with mustard; sprinkle with Worcestershire sauce. Dot tomatoes and zucchini with butter. Arrange patties, tomatoes, and zucchini on broiler rack. Broil 4 inches from source of heat 5 minutes. Turn patties and zucchini; place bacon pieces over patties. Broil 5 minutes longer. Turn onto heated serving platter and serve at once.

Deviled Lamb Hamburgers

1 pound ground lamb
½ cup finely chopped onion
½ cup finely chopped green pepper
¾ teaspoon salt
⅛ teaspoon pepper

⅞ cup ketchup
1 tablespoon prepared mustard
½ cup shredded sharp cheese
4 hamburger buns, split and toasted
4 sprigs parsley

Combine lamb, onion, and green pepper in a 10-inch skillet. Cook over moderate heat, stirring occasionally, for 15 minutes. Drain off excess fat. Add salt, pepper, ketchup, mustard, and cheese. Cook, stirring frequently, until cheese melts, about 5 minutes. Spoon mixture over toasted buns; garnish with parsley.

Lamb Spareribs Piquant

3 pounds lamb spareribs
1 teaspoon salt
¼ teaspoon pepper
1 teaspoon curry powder
1 cup orange juice
1 teaspoon grated lemon rind
½ cup finely chopped celery

¼ cup finely chopped parsley
1 medium orange, cut
  in ¼-inch slices
1 medium lemon, cut
  in ¼-inch slices
1 can (1 pound 4 ounces)
  sliced pineapple, drained

Put spareribs into a large, heavy skillet. Combine salt, pepper, and curry powder; blend in the orange juice, lemon rind, celery, and parsley. Pour over spareribs. Top with orange, lemon, and pineapple slices. Cover; cook over low heat about 1½ hours, or until tender. Remove spareribs and fruit to heated serving platter. Skim off fat and cook liquid 5 minutes. Pour on meat.

Bigos

A Polish dish featuring leftover lamb with caraway and sauerkraut.

4 strips bacon, diced
1 medium onion, minced
3 cups sauerkraut
½ teaspoon salt
⅛ teaspoon pepper

1 tablespoon caraway seed
2½ cups diced cooked lamb
¼ pound Polish sausage,
  thickly sliced

Cook bacon until limp. Add onion; sauté until golden. Add sauerkraut, salt, pepper, and caraway seed. Heat thoroughly. Add lamb. Cover; simmer over low heat 15 to 20 minutes. Add sausage; cook 15 minutes longer.

Chinese-Style Lamb Chops

Ordinary shoulder lamb chops go an exotic new way in this sweet 'n' sour version spiked with ginger.

4 lamb shoulder chops,
  about 1 inch thick
1 teaspoon shortening
¼ cup vinegar
¼ cup brown sugar
¾ teaspoon salt
⅛ teaspoon pepper

½ teaspoon ground ginger
4 slices orange
4 wedges lemon
1 tablespoon cornstarch
1 tablespoon water
2 cups fluffy hot rice

Brown chops on both sides over low heat in shortening in heavy skillet. Combine vinegar, brown sugar, salt, pepper, and ginger; pour over meat. Top each chop with an orange slice and a lemon wedge. Cover; cook over low heat about 30 minutes, or until chops are tender. Remove to heated serving platter. Pour pan juices into measuring cup; skim off fat and add water to make 1 cup. Return liquid to skillet. Blend cornstarch and 1 tablespoon water; stir into liquid. Cook, stirring constantly until mixture is boiling. Serve over chops on fluffy rice.

Irish Braised Lamb

2 tablespoons vegetable oil
4 shoulder lamb chops,
  about ¾ inch thick
2 cups beef bouillon

2 tablespoons prepared horseradish
¼ cup flour
¼ teaspoon pepper

Heat oil in skillet; cook lamb until browned on both sides. Remove from pan. Reserve drippings. Add bouillon, horseradish, flour, and pepper to drippings; blend. Cook over medium heat, stirring constantly, until thickened. Return lamb to sauce in skillet. Cover; simmer 40 minutes or until meat is tender.

Apple Rice Stuffed Lamb Loaf

¾ cup diced celery
3 tablespoons minced onion
1 tablespoon minced parsley
¼ cup margarine
2 cups cooked rice
1 cup diced, pared apple
1½ teaspoons salt
½ teaspoon pepper

¼ teaspoon savory
1 egg, slightly beaten
¾ cup water
½ cup crisp rice cereal,
  rolled into fine crumbs
1¼ pounds lean ground lamb
1 tablespoon honey

Heat oven to 350° F. Cook celery, onion, and parsley in margarine until celery is tender but not browned. Add rice, apples ½ teaspoon salt, ⅛ teaspoon pepper, and savory; toss lightly. Remove from heat. Combine egg, water, rice cereal crumbs, and remaining salt and pepper. Add lamb; mix thoroughly. Spread half of meat mixture on bottom of 10 × 6 × 2-inch baking pan. Spread stuffing over meat and press down firmly. Cover stuffing with remaining meat mixture; smooth with spatula. Spread honey evenly over the top. Bake 45 minutes or until meat is done. Cut into squares and serve. Makes 8 servings.

Lamb-Macaroni Combo

1 package (14 ounces)
   macaroni-and-cheese dinner
3 cups cooked diced lamb
1 can (8 ounces) tomato sauce
¼ cup chopped
   pimiento-stuffed olives
¼ cup water

½ teaspoon garlic salt
⅛ teaspoon pepper
1 tablespoon grated onion
1 tablespoon Worcestershire sauce
3 tablespoons grated
   Parmesan cheese
3 parsley sprigs

Heat oven to 375° F. Cook macaroni in boiling salted water according to package directions; drain. Combine macaroni and cheese; add lamb, tomato sauce, olives, water, garlic salt, pepper, onion, and Worcestershire sauce; mix well. Turn into 2-quart casserole. Sprinkle with Parmesan cheese. Cover; bake 15 minutes or until thoroughly heated. Garnish with parsley and serve.

Gourmet Lamb Ring

Intriguing flavor and texture distinguish this ring surrounded with peas.

3 cups ground cooked lamb
2 eggs, beaten
1 can (8 ounces) tomato sauce
⅓ cup chopped cashew nuts
⅓ cup diced currants

½ teaspoon salt
⅛ teaspoon ground cloves
⅛ teaspoon cinnamon
⅛ teaspoon allspice
1½ cups buttered peas

Heat oven to 350° F. Combine lamb with eggs and tomato sauce. Combine remaining ingredients, except peas; add to lamb mixture and blend well. Spoon into 4-cup ring mold. Bake 45 to 50 minutes. Unmold onto heated serving platter; surround with hot buttered peas.

Lamb and Okra Skillet Dinner

1 teaspoon salt
⅛ teaspoon pepper
¼ cup all-purpose flour
4 shoulder lamb chops,
   ¾-inch thick
2 tablespoons vegetable oil
2 cloves garlic, chopped

1 medium onion, chopped
1 can (8 ounces) tomato sauce
½ pound fresh okra, or 1 package
   (10 ounces) frozen okra, thawed
1 can (12 ounces) whole kernel corn
½ teaspoon Worcestershire sauce
½ teaspoon celery salt

Mix salt, pepper, and flour together; coat lamb with it. Heat vegetable oil in skillet; cook lamb until browned on both sides. Drain off excess drippings. Add garlic, onion, and tomato sauce. Cook, covered, for 30 minutes over low heat. Add okra; cover and cook 15 minutes longer or until lamb and okra are tender. Add undrained corn, Worcestershire sauce, and celery salt; mix well. Cook 5 minutes or until heated thoroughly.

Stockholm Lamb

The Swedes' idea of combining lamb with dill is truly inspired.

8 lamb shanks	1 bay leaf
Boiling salted water	½ teaspoon dried dill
4 peppercorns	Dill Sauce (recipe below)

Cover lamb shanks with boiling salted water. Add peppercorns, bay leaf, and dill. Cover; simmer 55 minutes or until lamb is tender. Drain; reserve 1½ cups of cooking liquid for sauce. Arrange lamb shanks in heated serving dish; pour Dill Sauce over them.

Dill Sauce

3 tablespoons margarine	2 tablespoons vinegar
3 tablespoons flour	2 teaspoons sugar
1½ cups hot stock	½ teaspoon salt
½ cup milk	1 egg yolk, slightly beaten
2 teaspoons dried dill	

Melt margarine; blend in flour. Combine stock with milk. Gradually stir into flour mixture. Cook over medium heat, stirring constantly until thickened and smooth. Reduce heat; simmer 10 minutes. Add vinegar, dill, sugar, and salt. Pour a little of the hot sauce on egg yolk; return to remaining sauce and blend well. Heat, stirring, for 1 minute. Do not boil. Makes 2 cups.

Lamb Potato Salad

2 cups cubed cooked lamb	½ cup mayonnaise
4 cups diced cooked potatoes	1 teaspoon salt
1 cup sliced celery	¼ teaspoon pepper
8 thin carrot slices	½ teaspoon dry mustard

Combine lamb, potatoes, celery, and carrot slices in bowl. Combine remaining ingredients; pour over lamb mixture and mix lightly. Chill. Serve plain or on crisp salad greens.

Haitian Lamb

The easy-to-carve rolled shoulder lamb becomes regal when glazed flavorfully with a fruity sauce and makes a divine party dish.

1 teaspoon salt
¼ teaspoon pepper
½ teaspoon basil
1 5-pound boned lamb shoulder,
   rolled and tied
1 can (1 pound) purple plums

1 can (1 pound, 4 ounces)
   sliced pineapple
2 tablespoons cornstarch
Red food coloring
⅓ cup red wine or orange juice

Heat oven to 325° F. Combine salt, pepper, and basil; rub over lamb. Place on rack in shallow roasting pan; bake 2 hours. Drain syrup from plums and pineapple; stir into cornstarch in saucepan. Cook, stirring constantly, until thickened and clear. Add a few drops of red food coloring. Drain off lamb drippings; pour 1 cup glaze over lamb; reserve remainder for sauce. Bake meat 35 to 55 minutes longer to desired doneness, basting frequently with drippings from pan. Remove meat to heated serving platter; garnish with the pineapple and plums. Remove string from meat. Stir wine or orange juice and 2 tablespoons of pan drippings into reserved glaze; heat and serve with lamb. Makes 8 servings.

Lamb Casserole with Curried Dumplings

A dish sparked with seasonings topped by light-as-a-feather spiced dumplings.

1 tablespoon shortening
1½ pounds boneless lamb stew
6 cups water
2 beef bouillon cubes
1 bay leaf
4 peppercorns
1½ teaspoons salt
4 medium potatoes

4 medium carrots
4 medium onions
2 cups biscuit mix
1 teaspoon curry powder
⅔ cup evaporated milk
¼ cup flour
½ cup cold water

Heat shortening in large kettle; add lamb and brown well. Add 6 cups water, bouillon cubes, bay leaf, peppercorns, and salt. Bring to simmering point, cover; cook slowly 1½ hours. Add potatoes, carrots and onions; continue cooking 30 minutes longer. Prepare dumplings by blending biscuit mix with curry powder. Add enough water to evaporated milk to measure ¾ cup liquid. Stir into biscuit mixture, blending just enough to dampen dry ingredients. Bring lamb stew to a boil. By tablespoonfuls, drop the dumpling mixture over top of vegetables and meat. Simmer 10 minutes uncovered. Cover; simmer 10 minutes longer. Transfer dumplings to heated serving platter. Make a paste of flour and ½ cup cold water. Slowly add to stew liquid, stirring constantly, until thickened and smooth.

Lamb and Noodle Loaf Paysanne

1 package (8 ounces) wide noodles	¼ teaspoon rosemary
2 cups cooked ground lamb	2 tablespoons pimiento
2 tablespoons grated onion	2 cups milk
2 tablespoons chopped parsley	2 eggs, slightly beaten
1 teaspoon salt	2 green pepper slices
¼ teaspoon pepper	1 can (8 ounces) tomato sauce

Heat oven to 350° F. Cook noodles according to package directions; drain. Combine with lamb, onion, parsley, salt, pepper, and rosemary. Add 1 tablespoon pimiento; mix well. Combine milk and eggs; add to noodle mixture. Pack into greased and floured 9 × 5 × 3-inch loaf pan. Bake 30 minutes or until firm. Unmold on serving platter. Garnish with remaining pimiento and pepper slices. Heat tomato sauce to boiling; serve with loaf.

Lamb Asparagus Rolls

A wonderful way to serve leftover lamb, accompanied by a grapefruit-and-avocado salad, scalloped potatoes and corn sticks.

1 can (8 ounces) tomato sauce	¼ teaspoon salt
1 tablespoon margarine	12 cooked asparagus spears
¼ cup finely chopped onion	4 slices cooked lamb
½ teaspoon garlic salt	

Combine tomato sauce, margarine, garlic salt, onion, and salt; mix well. Arrange asparagus spears on lamb; roll up. Fasten with wooden picks. Arrange on broiler rack. Top with tomato sauce mixture. Broil 3 inches from source of heat, 5 to 7 minutes or until thoroughly heated.

Lamb Curry Tomato Soup

2 tablespoons margarine
1 pound ground lamb
1 cup chopped celery
1 cup chopped onions
2 cans (1 pound each) tomatoes

2 cups water
1½ teaspoons curry powder
½ teaspoon salt
⅛ teaspoon pepper

Melt margarine in deep kettle. Add lamb; cook until lightly browned. Add remaining ingredients. Cover; cook over low heat 30 minutes. Serve plain or with croutons.

Lamb Chops Du Provence

An interesting country dish using breaded lamb chops.

⅓ cup fine dry bread crumbs
½ teaspoon salt
¼ teaspoon pepper
4 shoulder lamb chops,
  cut ¾ inch thick

2 eggs, slightly beaten
½ cup vegetable oil
1 lemon, cut in wedges
1 teaspoon chopped parsley

Combine bread crumbs with salt and pepper. Dip chops in beaten eggs, then in bread crumb mixture. Heat oil in large skillet. Panbroil chops over moderate heat until lightly browned on both sides. Remove to heated serving platter. Garnish with lemon and sprinkle with parsley.

Lamb Louisiana

1 pound lamb neck slices
1 egg
2 tablespoons flour
½ teaspoon salt
¼ teaspoon pepper
½ cup shortening
1 cup bouillon

2½ cups celery chunks
¼ cup sliced onion
1 tablespoon soy sauce
1 tablespoon cornstarch
1 tablespoon molasses
2 cups hot cooked noodles

Coat each piece of meat with beaten mixture of egg, flour, salt, and pepper. Heat shortening in large skillet; brown meat on both sides. Drain off all but 1 tablespoon drippings. Add ⅓ cup bouillon, celery, and onion. Cover tightly; simmer 1½ hours or until meat is tender. Combine soy sauce, cornstarch, molasses, and remaining bouillon. Pour over mixture in skillet; stir. Cover and simmer 10 minutes longer. Serve over noodles.

Creamy Southern Lamb Stew

1½ to 2 pounds lamb neck or
   breast, cut into serving pieces
1 teaspoon salt
¼ teaspoon pepper
2 tablespoons shortening
3½ cups water

4 small onions
4 small carrots, diced
½ cup light cream
1 egg yolk
3 tablespoons flour

Season meat with salt and pepper. Brown in hot shortening, in heavy skillet. Cover with water; simmer 1 hour. Add onions and carrots; cook over low heat until just tender. Combine cream, egg yolk and flour; add to skillet liquid. Cook until mixture is thick and creamy. Serve hot with biscuits or French bread.

Lamb and Cabbage Supreme

In Norway, where this dish originated, it is called Faar ag Kall.

1 pound lamb shoulder,
   cut into serving pieces
1½ teaspoons whole black pepper
1½ teaspoons salt

4 medium carrots
½ small head cabbage
½ cup flour

Place lamb in deep heavy kettle. Add salt, whole pepper, and carrots. Cover with water; simmer 1½ hours. Add cabbage; cook 30 minutes longer. Combine flour with 1 cup water. Add to kettle liquid; stir and cook until thickened.

Bonnie Scotland Stew

1½ pounds lamb shank,
   cut into 2-inch cubes
1 tablespoon shortening
5 cups water
⅓ cup pearl barley

1 onion, sliced
2 tablespoons minced parsley
3 celery tops
1½ teaspoons salt
4 medium potatoes, pared

Brown meat in hot shortening in heavy skillet. Add water, barley, onion, parsley, celery and salt. Cover; cook slowly 1 to 1½ hours or until meat is almost tender. Add potatoes; cook 30 minutes longer.

Cordovan Lamb

The piquant herb flavoring adds a tinge of Old Spain.

1½ pounds lamb shoulder,
  cut in serving pieces
4 slices bacon
¼ cup flour
¾ teaspoon salt
8 small onions
4 small carrots

1½ cup tomato juice
1½ cups diced celery
½ teaspoon sage
¼ teaspoon thyme
1 tablespoon vinegar
¼ cup chopped green pepper
1 tablespoon chopped parsley

Soak lamb in warm water 5 minutes; remove and dry thoroughly. Fry bacon in heavy skillet until lightly browned. Remove and crumble; set aside. Dip lamb in flour and salt mixture; brown with onions in bacon drippings. Cook slowly 10 minutes. Add carrots; pour tomato juice and stir. Add remaining ingredients. Cover; cook slowly 1 hour or until meat is tender.

Persian Lamb Curry

½ cup chopped green pepper
½ cup chopped onion
½ cup chopped celery
1 tablespoon chopped parsley
1 large clove garlic, minced
¼ cup margarine

1 pound lamb cubes
2 teaspoons curry powder
1 can (10½ ounces) condensed
  cream of mushroom soup
1 cup water
Rice Joubal (recipe below)

Sauté green pepper, onion, celery, parsley, and garlic in margarine until tender; push to side of skillet. Add lamb and curry powder; brown well on all sides. Add soup blended with water. Cover; simmer 1 hour or until tender, stirring occasionally. Serve over Rice Joubal.

Rice Joubal

1½ cups uncooked rice
1 tablespoon vegetable oil
¼ teaspoon allspice

2 tablespoons chopped peanuts
3 tablespoons raisins

Brown rice in oil; then prepared boiled rice according to package directions. About 15 minutes before rice is done, stir in remaining ingredients.

Roast Lamb Shoulder

3½ pounds lamb shoulder,
   boned and rolled
1 teaspoon salt

¼ teaspoon pepper
1 teaspoon rosemary

Heat oven to 350° F. Place roast on rack in open roasting pan. Season with salt, pepper, and rosemary. Cook meat, allowing 25 to 35 minutes per pound, 170°-180° on meat thermometer. Makes 4 servings with leftovers.

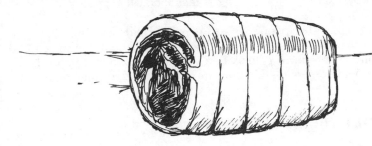

Lamb Smetana

A Russian favorite adapted to American tastes.

4 lamb shanks, halved
2 tablespoons flour
¼ cup vegetable oil
2 teaspoons salt
⅛ teaspoon pepper
½ cup water

½ cup minced onion
1 can (3 ounces) chopped mushrooms
1 can (8 ounces) tomato sauce
¼ cup tomato purée
1 cup sour cream
1 tablespoon chopped parsley

Coat lamb shanks with flour. Brown in heated vegetable oil on all sides in deep heavy kettle. Pour off all fat. Sprinkle salt and pepper over meat. Add water and onion. Cover, simmer 30 minutes. Add mushroom liquid; cover and simmer 45 minutes longer or until tender, turning meat occasionally. Add mushrooms, tomato sauce and purée. Stir in sour cream. Simmer, covered, about 10 minutes or until thoroughly heated. Turn onto serving platter; sprinkle with parsley.

Texan Breast of Lamb

A zippy barbecue sauce makes this dish company fare.

2 lamb breasts, about ¾ pound each
1½ teaspoons salt
¼ teaspoon pepper
2 tablespoons shortening
1 medium onion, chopped
2 tablespoons vinegar
2 tablespoons brown sugar

¼ cup lemon juice
1 cup ketchup
1 cup water
3 tablespoons Worcestershire sauce
Dash soy sauce
Dash cayenne pepper
⅛ teaspoon white pepper

Sprinkle lamb with ½ teaspoon salt and pepper. Heat shortening in deep heavy skillet; brown meat on all sides and set aside. Sauté onion in remaining fat until golden; return meat to skillet. Combine remaining ingredients; pour over lamb. Simmer, covered, 1 hour or until tender, turning meat once.

Savory Lamb Shoulder Chops

Lamb enhancers are many — try this dish with Minted Peas.

4 lamb shoulder chops,
   cut ½ inch thick
1 teaspoon margarine
1 tablespoon vinegar
2 tablespoons water

1 teaspoon salt
¼ teaspoon pepper
½ teaspoon garlic salt
1 teaspoon paprika

Brown lamb chops in margarine in heavy skillet, turning them over once. Combine remaining ingredients. Pour over chops. Cover; simmer 25 to 30 minutes, turning once during cooking.

Lamb Meat Loaf Surprise

Downright delicious and any cut of lamb may be used.

6 tablespoons minced onion
2 tablespoons margarine
1½ pounds ground lamb
¾ cup bread crumbs
2¼ teaspoon salt

⅛ teaspoon pepper
2 tablespoons chopped green pepper
1 tablespoon minced parsley
1 egg
½ cup milk

Heat oven to 350° F. Lightly grease 9 × 5 × 3-inch loaf pan. Sauté onion in margarine until lightly browned. Combine with remaining ingredients; mix well. Fill loaf pan with mixture. Bake 1 hour. Unmold on platter. If desired, spread top of loaf with marmalade. Serve with carrots and white turnips. Makes 6 servings.

Jordan Lamb

Lamb combined with rice and cauliflower makes a meal in one dish with a subtle spicy flavor.

1 pound cubed lean lamb	3 cups boiling water
1 tablespoon margarine	1½ teaspoons salt
1 large onion, sliced	1½ teaspoons allspice
1 small head cauliflower, sliced	2 cups rice
½ cup vegetable oil	1 small green pepper, sliced

Brown lamb in margarine in heavy skillet; remove and keep warm. Sauté onion and cauliflower in vegetable oil in same skillet. Add lamb. Pour water over it. Add salt and allspice. Heat to boiling. Add rice slowly so that all the rice is covered with water. Add more water, if necessary. Bring to a boil; cook 5 minutes. Reduce heat and simmer, covered, about 20 minutes or until rice is tender and almost all of the water is absorbed. Turn onto hot serving platter. Garnish with green pepper.

Lamb Kabobs Armenian

1½ pounds boneless lamb shoulder	4 slices bacon
½ cup French dressing	1 teaspoon salt
1 clove garlic, halved	¼ teaspoon pepper
½ pound button mushrooms	Hot fluffy rice

Trim lamb and cut into 1-inch cubes. Pour French dressing over meat; add garlic. Let stand 1 hour. Wash mushroom caps. Cut bacon into 1-inch squares. Alternate lamb, bacon, and mushrooms on metal skewers. Season with salt and pepper. Broil slowly 15 minutes, 3 inches from source of heat. Turn to brown evenly. Serve with rice.

Svetlana Lamb

1 pound lamb shoulder,
  cut into 1-inch cubes
4 slices bacon cut into
  1-inch pieces

8 small onions
Red Cabbage (recipe below)

Alternate lamb, bacon, and onions on 4 metal skewers. Broil 15 minutes, 3 inches from source of heat, turning to brown evenly. Serve hot on Red Cabbage.

Red Cabbage

2 tablespoons chopped onion
3 tablespoons bacon drippings
4 cups shredded red cabbage
1 tablespoon sugar

½ teaspoon salt
⅛ teaspoon pepper
¼ cup vinegar
¼ cup water

Sauté onion in drippings until tender. Add remaining ingredients. Cook, covered, 25 minutes or until cabbage is just tender, stirring occasionally.

Lamb Curry Bombay

Use pickle relish or orange marmalade in place of chutney for more economy.

1 pound lamb shoulder
  cut into 1-inch cubes
¾ teaspoon salt
¼ teaspoon pepper
½ teaspoon paprika
2 tablespoons shortening
1 cup diced celery

½ cup sliced onion
2 tablespoons chopped parsley
1½ cups water
1 teaspoon, or more, curry powder
2 tablespoons flour
¼ cup chutney
2 cups hot cooked rice

Season lamb with mixture of salt, pepper, and paprika. Brown in hot shortening in heavy skillet. Add celery, onion, and parsley. Pour 1 cup water. Cover; simmer 1 hour. Mix curry powder and flour with remaining ½ cup water. Stir into lamb. Cook slowly 10 minutes longer. Stir in chutney. Serve hot over rice.

Lamb Riblets À L'Orange

1 pound lamb riblets	½ cup orange juice
¾ teaspoon salt	1 teaspoon grated orange rind
¼ teaspoon pepper	1 teaspoon sugar
2 tablespoons flour	½ cup water
1 tablespoon shortening	2 cups cooked lima beans

Season lamb with salt and pepper. Roll in flour, saving 1 teaspoon. Brown in hot shortening in heavy skillet. Pour off excess fat. Add orange juice. Cover; simmer 1 hour. Blend orange rind, sugar, 1 teaspoon flour and water until smooth. Stir into gravy. Cook 5 minutes. Serve hot with lima beans.

Barbecued Breast of Lamb

Good indoors or outdoors.

2 pounds breast of lamb, cut into 4 pieces	½ cup chili sauce
2 teaspoons salt	¼ teaspoon red pepper
1 medium onion, sliced	1 tablespoon vinegar
	½ cup water

Heat oven to 350° F. Season lamb with salt. Brown in heavy skillet; turn into 1½-quart baking pan. Pour off drippings from skillet. Add remaining ingredients; heat 3 minutes. Pour over lamb. Bake 1½ hours, or until sauce is almost absorbed.

Sopron Lamb Goulash

From the plains of Hungary comes this delightful lamb-and-bean dish.

1 pound lamb neck, cut into pieces	2 tablespoons shortening
1½ teaspoons salt	2½ cups canned tomatoes
⅛ teaspoon pepper	1 medium green pepper, diced
¾ teaspoon paprika	2½ cups canned red beans
2 tablespoons flour	

Season lamb pieces with mixture of salt, pepper, and paprika. Roll in flour. Brown slowly in hot shortening in heavy skillet. Add tomatoes and green pepper. Cover; cook slowly 1½ to 2 hours. Add beans; heat thoroughly.

Moussaka

A Near Eastern dish which has many variations.

1 pound ground lean lamb
¾ teaspoon salt
¼ teaspoon pepper
1 medium eggplant, peeled
  and cut into thin slices

1 can (16 ounces) tomatoes
1 tablespoon chopped parsley
½ cup fine dry bread crumbs
½ cup grated Parmesan cheese

Heat oven to 400° F. Season lamb with salt and pepper. Arrange a layer of lamb in bottom of a shallow baking dish. Add a layer of eggplant and ⅓ of the tomatoes. Repeat layers until all ingredients are used. Sprinkle parsley and dry bread crumbs, then cheese. Bake 30 to 35 minutes.

Lamb Stroganoff

A quick way to make this perennial favorite which you may serve over cooked rice or with parsley potatoes.

1 pound boneless lamb shoulder,
  thinly sliced to ¼-inch strips
3 tablespoons flour
¾ teaspoon salt
¼ teaspoon pepper
¼ cup margarine

1 clove garlic, finely chopped
½ cup chopped onions
1 pound mushrooms, sliced
1 can (10½ ounces) condensed
  cream of celery soup
1 cup sour cream

Coat lamb with mixture of flour, salt, and pepper. Melt margarine in large skillet. Add lamb, garlic, and onions and cook until meat is lightly browned on all sides. Add mushrooms and soup; cook, covered, over low heat 20 minutes, stirring occasionally. Add sour cream; mix well. Heat but do not boil.

PORK

Pork is a thrifty meat and is not only highly palatable, but highly nutritious as well. Pork is one of our richest meat sources of vitamin B_1 (thiamine), and also provides us with important quantities of riboflavin and niacin—two other members of the vitamin B group. And like all meat, pork is an excellent protein food.

Modern pork is far less fat and has fewer calories per serving than pork produced a decade ago. At its best, it is pink, tender, and firm, and the fat is white and firm. One of its advantages is that, unlike beef, any part of the animal is tender enough to be roasted, and this is the reason it is not graded by U.S.D.A. as other meats are, although it requires longer cooking than beef. Pork should be cooked thoroughly and no pink should show in any part of the meat.

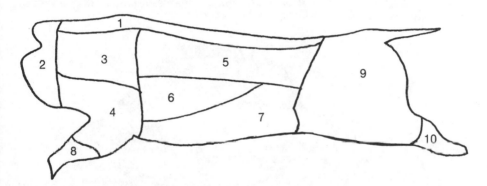

Pork is a thrifty meat and offers a variety of flavorful cuts fresh and smoked.

Inexpensive cuts
1. *Lard*
2. *Jowl:* bacon square
3. *Boston Butt:* smoked boneless butt, blade roast steak
4. *Shoulder:* picnic (fresh and smoked), cushion picnic, arm steaks, hocks
5. *Loin:* roasts, chops
6. *Spareribs*
7. *Side:* bacon (fresh, salt-cured or smoked)
8. *Forefoot*
10. *Hind Foot*

Expensive Cuts
9.   *Ham:* fresh or smoked, hocks

Ham is the cured and smoked hind leg of pork and is available in several styles. Look to the label on the ham to determine whether it is fully cooked or the cook-before-serving kind. Fully cooked ham can be served cold without further cooking or, if you prefer, it may be reheated; simply follow directions on the label.

Tips: Save money by cooking pork properly. Best way to cook pork steaks and chops is by braising. Slow cooking with moist heat brings out their good flavor. Rapid cooking increases shrinkage and causes meat to become dry.

Ham may be baked whole, half, or in portions. Ham slices that are 1 to 2 inches thick may be broiled or baked. Small shank ends may be cooked in water and used in soup.

Poor Man's Crown Roast

When pork is plentiful on the market it is the best buy of all.

1½ pounds pork ribs	3 cups soft bread crumbs
1 teaspoon salt	⅛ teaspoon pepper
½ cup chopped onion	1 teaspoon celery salt
3 tablespoons margarine	1 teaspoon poultry seasoning

Heat oven to 350° F. Rub ribs with salt. Sew ends of ribs together, or tie them to resemble a crown. Combine remaining ingredients; mix well. Place stuffing inside hollow formed by ribs and baked 2½ to 3 hours or until tender. To serve, place on heated serving platter and remove string.

Barbecued Spareribs Superb

Whether baked in the kitchen oven or cooked on the backyard grill this dish lives up to its name in every way.

1 cup chopped onion	2 teaspoons chili powder
1 clove garlic, minced	1 tablespoon prepared mustard
2 tablespoons vegetable oil	¼ teaspoon allspice
1 can (8 ounces) tomato sauce	¼ teaspoon pepper
½ cup water	1 tablespoon brown sugar
3 tablespoons vinegar	2 sides (about 3½ pounds) spareribs
1 tablespoon Worcestershire sauce	4 ripe olives, cut into pieces

Sauté onion and garlic in oil about 5 minutes. Stir in remaining ingredients, except spareribs and olives; heat to boil. Cut spareribs into serving pieces; place in shallow pan and pour barbecue mixture over all. Marinate several hours or overnight. Heat oven to 300° F. Drain ribs; reserve sauce. Place meat in shallow baking pan. Bake 1 hour. Cook sauce over low heat 5 minutes. Baste ribs occasionally with sauce and bake 30 minutes longer. Cook remaining sauce until thickened. Add olives to sauce. Place ribs under broiler until crisp and brown. Serve with sauce. Makes 6 servings.

For Outdoor Grilling
Marinate ribs and drain as above. Place ribs on grill over low fire. Baste and turn frequently until tender, crisp and brown. While ribs are barbecuing, cook sauce on back of grill until thickened; add olives. Serve hot with ribs.

Barbecued Spareribs

¼ cup chopped onion	¼ cup Worcestershire sauce
¼ cup margarine	¼ cup vinegar
¼ cup lemon juice	3½ pounds spareribs
¼ cup ketchup	

Heat oven to 350° F. Sauté onion in margarine until golden. Add lemon juice, ketchup, Worcestershire sauce, and vinegar; blend well. Bring to boil; simmer 5 minutes. Bake spareribs 45 minutes or until browned. Pour off excess fat. Pour barbecue sauce over spareribs. Bake 1 hour or until meat is tender, basting frequently with sauce in the pan. Makes 6 servings.

Sape Babi

Skewered pork, Indonesian style, is a specialty served on hot rice tossed with sesame seed.

1 cup salted peanuts,
  pounded to a paste
2 tablespoons coriander
2 cloves garlic, minced
1 teaspoon crushed red pepper
1 cup sliced onions,
  boiled and mashed
¼ cup lemon juice

2 tablespoons brown sugar
¼ cup soy sauce
½ teaspoon pepper
½ cup melted margarine
½ cup bouillon
1½ pounds lean pork,
  cut into 1-inch cubes

Combine peanuts, coriander, garlic, red pepper, onions, lemon juice, brown sugar, soy sauce, and pepper; blend mixture to a fine purée. Place in saucepan; bring to boil. Stir in margarine and bouillon. Remove from heat; cool. Pour over pork cubes in shallow pan; marinate 8 hours. Thread pork on skewers and broil slowly, turning frequently to brown and cook on all sides. Cook 30 minutes. Heat marinade. Serve with pork, plain or over sesame rice.

Pork Tostados

Quick and easy is the Mexican salad-sandwich, known as a tostado.

1 small head iceberg lettuce
8 tortillas, canned or frozen
¼ cup vegetable oil
1 medium onion, finely chopped
1 can (1 pound) kidney beans, drained
½ teaspoon salt
⅛ teaspoon pepper

2 tablespoons grated Cheddar
  cheese
1 small tomato, sliced
1½ cups cooked, ground,
  leftover pork
1 small avocado, peeled and sliced
Texas Sauce (recipe below)

Core lettuce; wash in cold water and drain well. Shred with sharp knife. Fry each tortilla in hot oil 3 seconds; drain on absorbent towel. Drain off all but 2 tablespoons oil; sauté onion until tender. Add beans, salt, and pepper; mash to a thick paste. Mound onto plate; sprinkle with cheese and garnish with tomato and avocado. Let each person make 2 tostados by layering each tortilla with bean spread, lettuce, meat, and Texas Sauce.

Texas Sauce

3 tablespoons margarine
1 clove minced garlic
3 tablespoons flour
1½ teaspoons chili powder

1 teaspoon salt
¼ teaspoon cumin
1¼ cups water

Melt margarine in saucepan; sauté garlic until soft. Stir in flour, chili powder, salt, and cumin. Slowly add water, stirring constantly. Cook over low heat, stirring, until thickened.

Oriental Pork Roast

4 pounds loin of pork
4 teaspoons sugar
1 teaspoon salt
1½ tablespoons honey
1 tablespoon soy sauce

1 cup chicken broth
3 tablespoons vinegar
¼ cup water
½ teaspoon savory

Place meat in shallow pan. Combine sugar, salt, honey, soy sauce, and broth; blend well. Pour over meat; let stand 2 hours, turning it occasionally. Heat oven to 350° F. Place meat in roasting pan; bake 2½ to 3 hours. Baste frequently with sugar mixture. Combine remaining ingredients; from time to time use 2 tablespoons of vinegar mixture and baste alternately with sweet mixture to prevent sugar from scorching and to add sweet-sour flavor. Makes 8 servings.

Pork and Cabbage Katoush

1 pound pork shoulder
    cut into 1-inch cubes
1 tablespoon chopped onion
2 teaspoons salt

1 quart water
3 cups shredded cabbage
⅛ teaspoon pepper

Sauté pork in its own fat with onion. Add 1 teaspoon salt and water. Simmer, covered, 45 minutes or until pork is almost tender. Arrange cabbage over pork. Sprinkle with remaining 1 teaspoon salt and pepper. Cover skillet; cook 15 minutes longer or until cabbage is tender.

Surprise Drumsticks

These should make a hit with the younger crowd.

½ pound ground pork shoulder	2 tablespoons ketchup
1 cup fine dry bread crumbs	4 frankfurters
½ teaspoon salt	1 egg, beaten
⅛ teaspoon pepper	1½ teaspoons water
2 tablespoons milk	1 tablespoon vegetable oil

Combine pork, ¼ cup bread crumbs, salt, pepper, milk, and ketchup; mix well. Cut frankfurters lengthwise into two pieces. Divide pork mixture into 8 equal portions; shape each portion around piece of frankfurter to form drumstick. Combine egg and water. Dip drumstick into egg; then roll in remaining bread crumbs. Sauté drumsticks in vegetable oil over low heat, about 15 minutes, turning to brown evenly on all sides.

Stuffed Pork New Orleans

A very dress-up dish to serve at a special dinner.

1 5- to 6-pound fresh pork shoulder	2 tablespoons melted margarine
½ package (8 ounces) ready-mix bread stuffing	1 tablespoon finely chopped onion
	½ cup hot water
2 tablespoons sugar	¼ cup fresh chopped cranberries
½ teaspoon salt	½ cup chopped apple
¼ teaspoon poultry seasoning	¼ cup raisins
	Cranberry Glaze (recipe below)

Have bone removed from pork shoulder, leaving a pocket for stuffing. Heat oven to 325° F. Combine bread stuffing, sugar, salt, and poultry seasoning. Pour margarine in small skillet; sauté onion until soft. Add margarine and onion, water, and fruits to bread stuffing mixture. Pack stuffing lightly into pocket in meat. Bring edges of opening together and fasten with metal skewers, lacing them with string. Place meat on rack in shallow baking pan. Bake 35 to 40 minutes per pound. After meat has cooked 1 hour, remove from oven and peel off hard rind. Return to oven. Continue cooking, basting frequently with Cranberry Glaze. Makes 8 servings.

Cranberry Glaze

1 cup fresh cranberries
¼ cup water

½ cup corn syrup

Combine all ingredients in saucepan. Cook over moderate heat until cranberries are soft, about 5 minutes.

Smoked Pork Collins

A flavorful dish from Colorado, and thrifty, too.

¾ pound dried red kidney beans
Water
1 (1¾ to 2 pounds)
   smoked pork shoulder
1¼ teaspoons salt
⅛ teaspoon pepper

1 bay leaf
¼ cup chopped celery
½ cup chopped onion
1 small (¾ to 1 pound) head of
   cabbage, coarsely shredded
½ teaspoon celery salt

Wash beans; place in large heavy kettle. Add enough water to just cover beans. Bring to a boil; cook 2 minutes. Remove from heat and let stand 1 hour. Add pork shoulder, salt, pepper, bay leaf, celery, and onion. Pour 2½ cups water over all. Bring to a boil. Reduce heat and simmer, covered, 1 hour. Add cabbage and celery salt; simmer 20 to 25 more minutes or until cabbage is crisp tender. Remove meat to a board; peel off outside casing and cut in thin slices. Serve with beans and cabbage mixture.

Pork Cathay

This oriental dish features a sweet and pungent flavor which is irresistible to young and old.

2 tablespoons flour
¼ teaspoon salt
⅛ teaspoon pepper
1 egg
½ cup vegetable oil
1 teaspoon onion salt
1 clove garlic, finely chopped
1 pound lean boneless pork,
　cut into ½-inch cubes
1 chicken bouillon cube

1 cup boiling water
1 cup pineapple cubes, drained
3 medium green peppers, cubed
2½ tablespoons cornstarch
2 teaspoons soy sauce
½ cup vinegar
½ cup sugar
¼ cup slivered almonds
1 can (5½ ounces) crisp
　Chinese noodles

Combine flour, salt, and pepper; add to egg and beat with fork until blended. Heat oil in large, heavy skillet. Add onion salt and garlic. Dip each piece of pork in egg mixture and drop into hot oil. Cook 10 minutes, or until meat is browned all over. Pour off all but 1 tablespoon of oil. Dissolve chicken bouillon cube in boiling water. Add ⅓ cup of bouillon, along with the pineapple and green peppers, to the meat mixture. Cover; cook over low heat 10 minutes. Blend together cornstarch, soy sauce, vinegar, sugar, and remaining bouillon. Add to meat mixture. Cook, stirring constantly, until clear and thickened, about 5 minutes. Add almonds. Serve over noodles.

Stuffed Loin of Pork Supreme

Easy for the host to carve, filled with a juicy fruit stuffing.

1 4-pound loin of pork
1 teaspoon salt
¼ teaspoon pepper
½ teaspoon sage
3 teaspoons Worcestershire sauce

2 cups stuffing mix
2 tablespoons melted margarine
½ cup water
½ cup chopped unpared apples
½ cup chopped pitted prunes

Have butcher saw off backbone of roast to allow easier carving, and cut meat away from the rib bones to form a pocket. Sprinkle meat with salt, pepper, sage, and 1 teaspoon Worcestershire sauce; rub well into the meat. Combine stuffing mix with margarine, water, and remaining 2 teaspoons Worcestershire sauce. Add apples and prunes; blend lightly. Fill meat pocket with stuffing; skewer opening and tie with string. Bake 2½ hours or until meat thermometer registers 185°. Makes 8 servings.

Smoked Pork with Peaches

The meat is cooked in water, which can be done ahead of time, then finished in the oven when ready to serve.

1 3-pound boneless smoked pork shoulder butt	Dash cloves
½ cup brown sugar	8 peach halves
⅛ teaspoon nutmeg	½ cup sweet pickle relish

Place meat in large pan; cover with water. Simmer, covered, 1½ hours. Drain. Heat oven to 400° F. Place meat on rack in shallow baking pan. Slice diagonally almost all the way through. Sprinkle with brown sugar and spices. Bake 30 minutes. Turn onto heated serving platter. Heat peach halves in syrup 2 minutes. Place around meat; fill with pickle relish. Makes 8 servings.

Spiced Fresh Ham

1 fresh ham (about 5 pounds)	1½ teaspoons whole allspice
1½ cups water	1 bay leaf
1 teaspoon salt	1 tablespoon slivered lemon rind
¾ teaspoon thyme	2 tablespoons lemon juice
1 teaspoon sage	1 medium onion, chopped
¼ teaspoon marjoram	1 large carrot, diced
1 teaspoon whole cloves	

Trim some fat from ham and fry in skillet; discard. Brown meat in drippings on all sides. Pour off fat. Place meat on rack in deep kettle. Add remaining ingredients; simmer, covered, 4 hours or until meat is tender, basting occasionally with liquid in kettle, adding more water if necessary. Makes 10 servings.

Pork and Cabbage Navarro

Fresh pork is oven braised in a peppy sauce and served with creamy horseradish.

1 large onion, sliced
1 tablespoon marjoram
1 fresh boned pork picnic
shoulder (about 5 pounds)
¾ cup bottled barbecue sauce

¾ cup water
1 small cabbage, cut into eighths
1 tablespoon caraway seeds
Creamy Horseradish Sauce
(recipe below)

Heat oven to 350° F. Season onion slices with marjoram; stuff into pocket of boned meat, tie with string and score top rind and fat. Place in large heavy baking pan; pour mixture of barbecue sauce and water over; cover tightly. Bake 3½ to 4 hours, or until meat is tender when pierced with fork. Remove from oven; heat to boiling on top of range. Add cabbage wedges; cover and steam 10 to 12 minutes or until cabbage is just tender. Arrange meat and cabbage on heated serving platter; sprinkle cabbage with caraway seeds and serve with Creamy Horseradish Sauce. Makes 8 servings.

Creamy Horseradish Sauce

1 cup sour cream
1 tablespoon prepared horseradish
1 tablespoon lemon juice
2 teaspoons prepared mustard

½ teaspoon salt
½ teaspoon sugar
¼ teaspoon paprika

Combine sour cream with horseradish. Blend lemon juice with mustard; add to sour cream mixture. Add salt and sugar; blend well. Sprinkle with paprika. Makes 1 cup.

Pork Tenderloin Oahu

Pork tenderloin is a good buy because it is all meat with no waste. This fruited version is extra delicious.

1 pork tenderloin, about 2 pounds
¼ cup flour
1 cup orange juice
½ cup crushed pinapple

½ teaspoon salt
¼ teaspoon allspice
1 cup sour cream

Heat oven to 350° F. Split tenderloin lengthwise almost in two. Open out flat. Cut into 4 hinged pieces. Flour meat on both sides and brown in skillet. Combine orange juice, pineapple, salt, and allspice. Pour over browned meat. Bake 45 minutes or until fork tender. Turn meat once during cooking. Remove meat to heated platter. Add sour cream to sauce in skillet. Stir and cook until heated through. Pour over meat and serve.

Cranberried Pork Chops

Cranberries and oranges add tangy flavor to this dish.

4 thick pork chops
½ teaspoon salt
¼ teaspoon pepper
2 large oranges
2 tablespoons brown sugar

5 slices diced white bread
⅓ cup chopped fresh cranberries
¼ cup chopped celery
3 tablespoons water

Heat oven to 350° F. Trim all but thin layer of fat from chops; sprinkle with salt and pepper. Heat fat trimmings in large skillet; remove. Brown pork chops in drippings; arrange in single layer in shallow baking dish. Cut 4 equal slices from middle of oranges; squeeze juice from remaining pieces and add water, if necessary, to make ½ cup liquid. Stir in brown sugar; pour over chops. Bake 45 minutes, basting occasionally. Mix diced bread, cranberries, celery, salt, and water in small bowl. Divide evenly into mounds on orange slices; set on top of chops. Spoon juices from pan over. Bake 20 minutes longer or until meat is fork tender.

Breaded and Baked Pork Chops

A homey dish with a fruity flavor — serve with sweet potatoes and an asparagus salad.

1¼ teaspoons salt
1¼ teaspoons pepper
1 egg
2 tablespoons water
Dash onion salt
4 pork shoulder chops

¾ cup dry bread crumbs
½ cup margarine
2 large cooking apples, quartered
⅓ cup raisins
1 bouillon cube
½ cup boiling water

Heat oven to 325° F. Combine salt, pepper, egg, water, and onion salt; beat slightly. Dip chops in egg mixture; coat with bread crumbs. Melt ¼ cup margarine in skillet; brown chops on both sides. Place in shallow baking pan. Toss apples and raisins over chops; dot with remaining ¼ cup margarine. Dissolve bouillon cube in boiling water; pour over fruit and chops. Bake 1 hour, basting occasionally.

German Pork Chops

6 pork chops
1 can (1 pound 11 ounces)
   sauerkraut, drained
1 tablespoon minced onion

¼ cup brown sugar
¼ cup dry red wine
2 apples, cut in eighths
4 frankfurters, finely chopped

Remove excess fat from chops; fry fat in heavy skillet and discard. Brown chops in remaining hot fat on both sides. Combine the other ingredients; mix well. Remove chops from skillet; add sauerkraut mixture, pile chops on top. Cover; cook slowly 45 to 50 minutes or until chops are tender. Makes 6 servings.

Pork Chops À L'Orange

Pork is the second most important meat in family meals, following beef. When it is on the plentiful-foods list and inexpensive, serve it often.

1 onion, sliced
1 tablespoon vegetable oil
6 pork chops
2 teaspoons salt
¼ cup water
1 cup orange juice

½ teaspoon grated orange rind
1 teaspoon cornstarch
1½ pounds drained sauerkraut
¼ teaspoon caraway seeds
2 oranges, sectioned

In large skillet sauté onion in oil until tender. Add pork chops; sprinkle with salt. Brown lightly on both sides. Add water; cover and cook over low heat 1 hour or until tender. Remove chops to heated platter. Add orange juice and ¼ teaspoon orange rind to skillet; blend well with drippings. Mix cornstarch with a little water; stir into skillet. Bring just to boil, stirring constantly. Pour over chops. Combine sauerkraut with caraway seeds. Cover, cook 15 minutes, tossing occasionally. Add orange sections and remaining ¼ teaspoon rind. Cover; heat 10 minutes. Serve with pork chops. Makes 6 servings.

New Orleans Pork Skillet

6 pork shoulder chops, ½ inch thick	1½ teaspoons salt
	⅛ teaspoon pepper
1 cup sliced onion	1 teaspoon sugar
2½ cups canned tomatoes	1 tablespoon flour
¼ cup diced green pepper	2 tablespoons water
½ cup diced celery	½ cup chopped peanuts
½ teaspoon chili powder	

Brown pork in skillet on both sides. Add onion; sauté until lightly browned. Add tomatoes, green pepper, celery, chili powder, salt, pepper, and sugar. Cover; cook slowly 1 hour. Make smooth paste of flour and water. Stir in tomato mixture. Cook, stirring, until thickened. Add peanuts. Cover; simmer 5 minutes longer. Makes 6 servings.

Pork Chops Valencia

Delicious way with onions and peppers.

4 pork chops	1½ cups tomato purée
Dash pepper	⅛ teaspoon oregano
4 onion slices	⅛ teaspoon basil
4 green pepper rings	¼ teaspoon thyme

Brown chops on both sides in skillet. Heat oven to 350° F. Place chops in shallow baking pan; sprinkle with pepper. Place a slice of onion and a green pepper ring on each chop. Combine remaining ingredients; pour over meat. Cover. Bake 45 minutes or until tender.

Arancini Siciliani

These stuffed rice balls may be served as an appetizer cold, or hot as a main dish.

1 cup rice
1 cup vegetable oil
¼ pound ground ham
¼ pound ground beef
1 small onion, minced
½ cup chopped mushrooms
2 tablespoons tomato paste

½ cup margarine
⅓ cup grated Parmesan cheese
2 egg yolks
1 egg, beaten
1 cup bread crumbs
Vegetable oil

Cook rice according to package directions. Heat 1 cup oil in small skillet; sauté ham, beef, onion, and mushrooms. Stir in tomato paste; simmer 20 minutes. Blend warm rice with margarine, cheese, and egg yolks; chill mixture 1 hour. Place 1½ tablespoons of rice mixture in palm of hand; make a dent with back of spoon; fill with 1 teaspoon meat mixture. Top with an additional 1½ tablespoons rice; shape into a large ball. Roll in egg, then in bread crumbs. Chill. Fry in vegetable oil until golden brown. Makes 6 servings.

Ham-Bake Amsterdam

A low-cost treat that is party-good.

1 cup diced cooked ham
2 tablespoons chopped onion
⅛ teaspoon tarragon
2 tablespoons margarine
1 can (10½ ounces)
   condensed cream of chicken soup
½ cup water

1½ cups cooked noodles
½ cup cooked and sliced green
   beans
2 tablespoons fine dry bread crumbs
½ small clove garlic, minced
¼ teaspoon paprika

Heat oven to 350° F. Butter a 1-quart baking dish. Sauté ham, onion, and tarragon in 1 tablespoon margarine until ham is browned and onion is tender. Stir in soup, water, noodles and green beans. Turn into baking dish. Lightly brown crumbs, garlic, and paprika in remaining tablespoon margarine; sprinkle over top of ham mixture. Bake 30 minutes or until hot and bubbly.

Ham in Cider Sauce

An elegant way to stretch leftover ham, good enough for unexpected company when recipe is doubled.

2½ cups mashed, cooked, sweet potatoes	¾ teaspoon salt
5 tablespoons milk	Dash pepper
2 tablespoons margarine	2 cups cooked ham, cubed or sliced
	Cider Sauce (recipe below)

Heat oven to 350° F. Combine sweet potatoes with milk, margarine, salt, and pepper; blend well. Spoon around edge of shallow 1-quart baking dish. Arrange ham in center. Pour Cider Sauce over ham. Bake 20 minutes.

Cider Sauce

¾ cup cider	2 tablespoons brown sugar
2 tablespoons seedless raisins	¼ teaspoon salt
1¾ teaspoons cornstarch	1½ teaspoons lemon juice
½ teaspoon dry mustard	

Cook cider and raisins over low heat for 10 minutes. Combine remaining ingredients; blend until smooth. Stir into cider mixture. Cook, stirring constantly, until thick and clear.

Ham Soufflé Sandor

A high-style quick dish made with leftover ham—serve buttered green beans and marinated tomatoes with it.

½ cup mayonnaise	1 cup coarsely chopped cooked ham
¼ cup flour	2 tablespoons chopped parsley
¼ teaspoon salt	¼ teaspoon minced onion
⅛ teaspoon pepper	4 egg whites
¼ cup milk	Swiss Cheese Sauce (recipe below)

Heat oven to 325° F. Grease a 1-quart baking or soufflé dish. Mix mayonnaise, flour, salt, and pepper; slowly stir in milk and blend well. Stir in ham, parsley, and onion. Beat egg whites until stiff. Gently fold in ham mixture until well blended. Pour into baking dish. Bake 40 to 45 minutes or until puffed and golden. Serve at once with Swiss Cheese Sauce.

Swiss Cheese Sauce

½ pound sliced process
  Swiss cheese
½ cup milk

¼ teaspoon Worcestershire sauce
3 drops Tabasco
2 tablespoons chopped pimiento

Heat cheese and milk in top of double boiler until cheese is melted. Stir in Worcestershire sauce, Tabasco, and pimiento. If sauce seems too thick, thin with a little hot milk.

Ham Hock Dinner

2 pounds smoked ham hocks
Water
4 medium carrots
4 medium onions

4 medium potatoes
1 small head (about ½ pound)
  cabbage, quartered

Cover ham hocks with water in deep kettle. Cover; simmer 2 hours. When meat has cooked 1½ hours, remove skins from hocks. Return hocks to kettle. Add carrots, onions, and potatoes. Cook 15 minutes. Add cabbage; cook 15 minutes longer or until meat and vegetables are tender.

Ham Cakes with Jelly Sauce

4 cups soft bread crumbs
1½ cups milk
½ teaspoon dry mustard
¼ teaspoon curry powder
1 egg, slightly beaten

2 cups small bits of cooked
  leftover ham
2 tablespoons shortening
¼ cup currant jelly
1 tablespoon warm water

Combine bread crumbs, milk, mustard, and curry powder in saucepan. Cook, stirring frequently, until thickened. Beat in egg. Stir in ham and blend. Heat shortening in skillet. Drop ham mixture by tablespoonfuls; cook until brown. Turn and brown other side. Beat together jelly with water. Serve ham cakes hot; spoon jelly sauce over top.

Glazed Stuffed Ham Rolls

Roll 'em up for the family table or double the quantity for company fare.

2 tablespoons margarine
2 tablespoons finely chopped onion
2 tablespoon chopped celery
1 cup cooked rice
¼ cup seedless raisins
⅛ teaspoon salt

⅛ teaspoon nutmeg
4 slices, 5 × 4 × ⅛-inch,
   boiled boned ham
1 tablespoon brown sugar
1½ teaspoons water

Melt 1 tablespoon margarine in skillet over low heat; add onion and celery and cook until tender, about 5 minutes. Remove from heat; add rice, raisins, salt, and nutmeg; mix well and let stand. Heat oven to 350° F. Spread about 2 tablespoons of rice mixture on each ham slice; roll up, fasten with wooden picks. Place in greased baking pan. Combine remaining 1 tablespoon margarine with brown sugar and water in small saucepan; cook over low heat 3 minutes. Pour over ham rolls. Bake 15 to 20 minutes.

Ham Aspic Élégante

This special luncheon dish is summery and delicious as well as a budget saver to serve your bridge party.

1 cup finely chopped dill pickle
1 cup finely chopped celery
¼ cup minced onion
1 tablespoon finely chopped parsley
3 cups cooked ground ham
2 teaspoons prepared mustard
3 tablespoons prepared horseradish,
   drained

1 cup mayonnaise
2 envelopes unflavored gelatin
½ cup cold water
½ cup boiling water
Lettuce greens
Radish roses

Combine dill pickle, celery, onion, parsley, and ham. Mix thoroughly mustard, horseradish, and mayonnaise; blend into ham mixture. Soften gelatin in cold water; dissolve in boiling water. Add to ham mixture. Turn into 5-cup mold. Chill until set. Unmold on lettuce greens; garnish with radish roses. Makes 8 servings.

Ham-and-Veal Meat Loaf

½ pound ham, ground
2 pounds boned veal shoulder, ground
3 tablespoons minced parsley
2 teaspoons grated onion
1½ cups soft bread crumbs
½ cup evaporated milk

1 egg
1 teaspoon salt
⅛ teaspoon pepper
1 can (9 ounces) pineapple
　slices, drained
¼ cup brown sugar

Heat oven to 350° F. Combine ham, veal, parsley, onion, bread crumbs, milk, egg, salt, and pepper; mix well. Arrange pineapple slices in a design in bottom of greased 9 × 5 × 3-inch loaf pan. Sprinkle with brown sugar. Pack meat mixture in pan. Cover with aluminum foil. Bake 30 minutes. Remove foil. Continue baking 1 hour longer. Makes 8 servings.

Apricot-Glazed Ham Patties

1½ pounds ground cooked ham
½ cup soft bread crumbs
½ cup milk
2 eggs
¼ cup chopped onion
¼ cup crumbled blue cheese

1 tablespoon Worcestershire sauce
2 teaspoons prepared mustard
¼ teaspoon sage
¼ teaspoon pepper
½ cup apricot preserves
2 teaspoons vinegar

Heat oven to 350° F. Combine ham with bread crumbs, milk, eggs, onion, cheese, Worcestershire sauce, 1 teaspoon prepared mustard, sage, and pepper. Shape in 6 patties. Place in shallow baking dish; bake 30 minutes. Combine preserves, vinegar, and remaining 1 teaspoon prepared mustard. Brush on ham patties. Bake 10 minutes longer. Makes 6 servings.

Ham Cantonese

3 tablespoons vegetable oil
1½ cups cubed cooked ham
½ cup thin onion slices
1 cup thin celery slices
1 cup water
1 can (1 pound) mixed Chinese
　vegetables, drained
1 teaspoon salt

⅛ teaspoon pepper
½ teaspoon sugar
1 tablespoon soy sauce
3 tablespoons flour
1 can (3 ounces) mushrooms,
　drained
⅓ cup slivered almonds

Heat oil in skillet; add ham, onion, and celery slices and cook 5 minutes, stirring often. Add water; cook, covered, 8 minutes. Add Chinese vegetables, salt, pepper, sugar, and soy sauce; heat to boil. Remove from heat. Blend flour with 3 tablespoons liquid from drained vegetables to make smooth paste; stir into meat mixture. Cook, stirring constantly, until thickened. Add mushrooms and almonds. Heat and serve.

Orange Ham Cakes

Take advantage of special supermarket offers on smoked ham which can give you a variety of flavorful dishes.

3 cups ground cooked ham	¼ teaspoon salt
½ pound ground beef	¾ cup evaporated milk
1 egg, beaten	8 slices peeled orange
¾ cup crushed corn flakes	1 can (8 ounces) tomato sauce
1 teaspoon dry mustard	2 tablespoons brown sugar

Heat oven to 375° F. Combine ham, beef, egg, corn flakes, mustard, salt, and evaporated milk. Shape into 8 balls. Place a slice of orange in bottom of each of 8 custard cups. Combine tomato sauce and brown sugar; blend well. Drizzle over each orange slice some of the tomato mixture. Place a meat ball into each baking dish. Bake 50 minutes. When done, invert meat cakes onto a heated serving platter with orange slices on top. Makes 8 servings.

Ham and Lentil Bake

2 cups dried lentils	½ teaspoon thyme
2 cups leftover ham in large chunks	½ teaspoon marjoram
1 onion, chopped	½ teaspoon pepper
2 bay leaves	6 carrots, cut in chunks
1 quart water	1 can (8 ounces) tomato sauce

Combine lentils, ham, onion, bay leaves and water in large saucepan; bring to boil. Simmer, covered, 30 minutes. Drain lentils and ham. Combine with remaining ingredients. Heat oven to 350° F. Pour ham mixture into 2-quart baking dish. Bake, covered, 1½ hours. Remove cover; bake 15 minutes longer. Makes 6 servings.

VARIETY MEATS

Don't overlook the variety meats—liver, heart, kidneys, sausage, and the ready-to-eat meats which come in so many flavors, textures, colors, and shapes. Some are highly spiced, others are bland. Ready-to-eat meats may also be served hot in easy, delicious, money-saving recipes as you will see when you read this chapter.

Although these meats are seldom on special sale, they are attractive and economical because they are all meat.

Sausage meat is made of pork meat, finely chopped and seasoned. It may be sold in bulk, in casings, or in cloth bags.

And don't forget the frankfurter — it is an old standby and an all-time favorite and as American as the Fourth of July.

Tips:

How to Prepare a Heart. Beef, pork, lamb, and veal hearts are all excellent foods. This variety meat should be washed and the hard parts removed. Since heart is a less tender meat, it requires long, slow cooking in moisture.

To cook in liquid: Cover heart with water to which 1 teaspoon of salt for each quart of water has been added. Cover tightly and cook slowly until tender. Beef hearts require about 3 to 3½ hours, and pork, lamb, and veal hearts, about 2½ hours.

To braise: Brown the heart on all sides in a small amount of shortening or drippings. Add a small amount of liquid (about ⅛ cup). Season with salt and pepper. Cover tightly. Cook at a low temperature on top of the range or a 300° F. oven, 3 to 3½ hours for beef hearts and 2 to 2½ hours for pork, lamb and veal hearts. Hearts may be stuffed before braising.

Baked Stuffed Heart

1 beef heart
Bread Stuffing (recipe below)
¼ cup flour
1 teaspoon salt

⅛ teaspoon pepper
2 tablespoons shortening
¼ cup water

Heat oven to 300° F. Wash heart thoroughly; remove hard parts. Fill with Bread Stuffing; skewer opening. Dredge heart in combined flour, salt, and pepper mixture. Brown on all sides in shortening in baking pan. Cover tightly; bake 3 to 3½ hours or until tender, adding more water if necessary. Makes 8 servings.

Bread Stuffing

2 cups soft bread crumbs
½ teaspoon salt
⅛ teaspoon pepper
1 teaspoon sage
2 tablespoons chopped onion

1 tablespoon chopped parsley
¼ cup chopped celery
1 egg, beaten
Water

Combine bread crumbs, salt, pepper, sage, onion, parsley, celery, egg, and enough water to make a slightly moist stuffing.

Heart Andalouse

A delicious and unusual all-in-one casserole.

1 small (about 1 pound) veal heart
1 cup water
1 teaspoon salt
1 can (10½ ounces)
  condensed tomato soup
1 tablespoon Worcestershire sauce

¼ cup flour
½ cup milk
¼ pound grated Cheddar cheese
2 cups hot cooked rice
1½ cups hot cooked peas

Wash heart; remove hard parts and cut into ¾-inch cubes. Place in deep kettle. Add water and salt. Simmer, covered, 1½ hours. Add tomato soup and Worcestershire sauce. Combine flour and milk into a smooth paste; add to heart mixture. Add cheese; heat thoroughly until melted. Serve over rice and peas.

Heart Lyonnaise

2 small (about ½ pound each)
  veal hearts
3 tablespoons flour
¼ cup bacon drippings
1 teaspoon salt

¼ teaspoon pepper
½ cup thinly sliced onion
1 cup diced carrots
1 cup canned tomatoes

Wash heart; remove hard parts and slice across grain. Dredge in flour. Brown in bacon drippings. Season with salt and pepper. Add onion; sauté until lightly browned. Add carrots and tomatoes. Cover; cook over slow heat 1½ to 2½ hours or until tender.

Fricassee of Liver Delight

1 medium onion, thinly sliced
5 tablespoons margarine
½ pound calf liver,
    cut into strips
1 can (10½ ounces) condensed
    cream of mushroom soup
3 tablespoons milk

1 can (3 ounces) chopped
    mushrooms with liquid
4 stuffed green olives, chopped
¼ teaspoon thyme
2 tablespoons chopped parsley
2 cups hot cooked rice

Sauté onion in 3 tablespoons margarine until almost tender. Add liver; sauté just 5 minutes. Add soup, milk, 3 tablespoons mushroom liquid, and olives; heat, stirring frequently. Drain mushrooms; lightly sauté in remaining margarine. Toss with thyme, parsley, and rice; turn onto heated platter. Top with liver mixture and serve at once.

Liver Loaf Alaska

Dress it up with a mashed-potato topping for a festive touch or serve it with Creole Sauce (p. 54).

½ pound liver, parboiled
2 tablespoons onion
¼ cup chopped celery
¼ cup chopped green pepper
½ pound sausage meat
½ cup dry bread crumbs
1 egg
1 teaspoon Worcestershire sauce
½ teaspoon salt

⅛ teaspoon pepper
¼ teaspoon dry mustard
1 tablespoon chopped parsley
¼ teaspoon marjoram
¼ teaspoon basil
2½ cups seasoned mashed
    potatoes
2 tablespoons mayonnaise
1 tablespoon heavy cream

Heat oven to 350° F. Grease a 9 × 5 × 3-inch loaf pan; line with wax paper. Grind up liver with onion. Sauté celery and green pepper with sausage meat for 5 minutes, breaking up meat with fork. Combine with liver mixture, bread crumbs, egg. and seasonings; mix thoroughly. Press into prepared loaf pan. Bake 1 hour. Turn out onto heatproof platter; remove wax paper. Frost top and sides with potatoes. Combine mayonnaise and cream; brush potato covering. Increase oven temperature to 450° F. Bake 5 minutes or until lightly browned.

Liver Patties Vinto

Transform a pound of nutritious liver into delicate-tasting delicious patties.

1 pound liver (beef or lamb)	⅛ teaspoon pepper
½ cup onion, chopped	2 tablespoons milk
½ cup fine cracker or bread crumbs	2 eggs slightly beaten
1 teaspoon salt	3 tablespoons shortening

Remove membrane from liver; grind coarsely. Mix with onions, crumbs, salt, pepper, milk, and eggs. Heat shortening in skillet. Drop liver mixture by tablespoonfuls. Fry until nicely browned on both sides, about 2 minutes. Makes 16 patties.

Roman Kidneys

Nutritionally, kidneys are a fine source of iron, thiamin and riboflavin, and a treasure of good taste and interesting texture.

1 pound kidneys (lamb, pork, veal, or beef)	1 teaspoon Worcestershire sauce
½ cup chopped onion	½ teaspoon salt
3 tablespoons shortening	⅛ teaspoon pepper
½ cup thinly sliced celery	¼ teaspoon garlic salt
1 can (8 ounces) tomato sauce	¼ teaspoon basil
	2 cups cooked rice

Remove membrane from kidneys. Split lamb or pork kidneys in half; cut veal or beef kidneys into ½-inch slices. Remove hard white portion. Brown kidney pieces and onion in shortening. Add remaining ingredients, except rice. Cover tightly; cook over low heat 45 minutes to 1 hour or until tender. Serve over cooked rice.

Braised Oxtail

Thrifty Europeans who relish delicious dishes consider oxtail the most savory of meats.

1 oxtail, cut in pieces
2 tablespoons shortening
1 medium onion, coarsely chopped
1 can (1 pound 4 ounces) tomatoes
½ cup water
1 teaspoon salt

½ teaspoon sugar
⅛ teaspoon pepper
1 bay leaf
3 whole cloves
4 carrots, cut into chunks
4 stalks celery, cut into chunks

Brown meat in shortening in heavy skillet. Add onion; cook 5 minutes until limp. Add tomatoes and water. Season with salt, sugar, and pepper. Add bay leaf and cloves. Cook to a boil. Cover; reduce heat and cook 2½ hours. Add carrots and celery. Cook 30 minutes longer.

Pepper and Sausage Patties Louise

2 large green peppers
1 large onion, minced
¼ cup margarine
4 slices white bread, crumbed
½ teaspoon oregano
¼ teaspoon thyme
¼ teaspoon rosemary

2 tablespoons chopped celery
½ teaspoon salt
⅛ teaspoon pepper
1 egg, beaten
2 cans (8 ounces each)
   tomato sauce
8 sausage patties, well browned

Heat oven to 400° F. Halve peppers lengthwise; remove seeds. Cook, covered, in boiling salted water, 5 minutes. Drain pepper halves and remove to shallow baking dish. Sauté onion in margarine until tender. Add bread, herbs, celery, salt, and pepper. Remove from heat; add egg and toss to blend. Heap mixture in pepper halves and pour tomato sauce over. Bake 20 minutes. Arrange cooked sausage patties on heated platter with stuffed peppers, pour pan drippings over and serve.

Sausage Macaroni Casserole

Give a lift to appetites with this casserole which stretches one pound of sausage to four hearty servings.

1 pound sausage meat	3½ cups cooked elbow macaroni
½ cup chopped green pepper	1 cup cheese cubes
½ cup onion	1 teaspoon salt
2 tablespoons flour	¼ teaspoon pepper
2½ cups canned tomatoes	

Heat oven to 350° F. Shape sausage meat into 8 patties; fry slowly until half cooked, about 5 minutes. Remove from skillet. Add pepper and onion; sauté until lightly browned. Stir flour into fat. Add tomatoes; cook, stirring constantly, until thickened. Add macaroni, cheese, salt, and pepper; blend well. In 1½-quart baking dish place half the macaroni, then lay 4 sausage patties on top. Add remaining macaroni and top with remaining sausage patties. Bake 30 minutes.

Grandma's Jambalaya

Sausage links and luncheon meat add flavor to this thrifty casserole.

1 pound fresh pork sausage links	1 clove garlic, minced
¾ cup coarsely chopped onion	1 bay leaf
¼ cup coarsely chopped celery	1 teaspoon salt
¼ cup chopped green pepper	¼ teaspoon chili powder
1 can (1 pound 12 ounces) tomatoes	4 slices canned luncheon meat,
¾ cup water	cut into strips
1¼ cups rice	1 tablespoon chopped parsley
1 beef bouillon cube	

Brown sausage links in skillet, turning frequently. Remove and set aside. Remove all but ¼ cup sausage fat from skillet. Sauté onion, celery, and green pepper until tender, turning occasionally. Add tomatoes, water, rice, bouillon cube, garlic, bay leaf, salt, chili powder, and sausage. Cover; cook 30 to 35 minutes, stirring occasionally, until rice is tender. Stir in luncheon meat; heat thoroughly. Garnish with parsley. Makes 6 to 8 servings.

Eggplant Genovese

Serve this delicious dish with mashed potatoes and a green salad.

2 medium eggplants,
    cut in half lengthwise
Boiling water
1 pound bulk fresh pork sausage
1 large onion, chopped
1 clove garlic, minced
½ cup diced celery
3 tablespoons chopped green pepper
1 tablespoon chopped parsley

1 can (1 pound) tomatoes
¼ teaspoon basil
¾ teaspoon salt
⅛ teaspoon pepper
½ teaspoon sugar
¼ cup dry bread crumbs
3 tablespoons grated Parmesan
    cheese

Heat oven to 375° F. Grease an oblong baking dish. Parboil eggplant in salted water 10 minutes or until just tender. Remove and let cool. Scoop out pulp leaving a shell ½ inch thick. Brown sausage in skillet; drain on absorbent paper, and crumble. Remove all but 2 tablespoons fat from skillet; sauté onion, garlic, celery, green pepper, and parsley until limp. Chop eggplant pulp; add to skillet mixture. Stir in tomatoes, basil, salt, pepper, and sugar; simmer 4 minutes. Add sausage; simmer 5 minutes longer. Pile lightly in eggplant shells in baking dish. Top with combined bread crumbs and cheese. Bake 45 minutes. Serve hot.

Bologna Puff

6 ounces bologna, cut in strips
2 tablespoons margarine
1 large onion, sliced
1 can (1 pound 13 ounces)
    tomatoes, drained
1 package (10 ounces) frozen peas

¾ teaspoon salt
½ teaspoon oregano
⅛ teaspoon pepper
1 envelope instant mashed potatoes
½ cup grated sharp Cheddar cheese

Heat oven to 350° F. Sauté bologna strips in margarine in skillet, about 3 minutes. Add onion, separated into rings; sauté 3 minutes longer. Add tomatoes, peas, salt, oregano, and pepper; bring to boil. Reduce heat; simmer 5 minutes. Turn into 1½-quart baking dish. Prepare mashed potatoes according to package directions; spoon around edge of bologna mixture. Sprinkle with cheese. Bake 25 to 30 minutes or until potatoes are lightly browned.

Chula Vista Casserole

1 tablespoon vegetable oil
¼ cup coarsely chopped onion
¼ cup coarsely chopped green pepper
1 cup canned tomatoes
½ cup cooked corn
¾ cup cooked lima beans
4 pitted ripe olives, sliced
¼ pound sliced bologna, cubed
1 teaspoon chili powder

½ cup yellow cornmeal
1 tablespoon flour
1½ teaspoons sugar
½ teaspoon salt
1 teaspoon baking powder
1 egg, slightly beaten
¼ cup tomato juice
1 tablespoon melted margarine

Heat oven to 425° F. Heat vegetable oil in skillet. Add onion and green pepper; sauté until tender. Add tomatoes, corn, lima beans, olives, bologna, and chili powder. Cover; cook 10 minutes over low heat, stirring occasionally. Turn into 1-quart casserole. Combine cornmeal with flour, sugar, salt, and baking powder. Mix egg with tomato juice and margarine; stir into cornmeal mixture and blend well. Spoon over bologna mixture. Bake 20 to 25 minutes or until lightly browned.

Luncheon Loaf Ananas

Here's a rich, robust meat dish that won't get you in a dither of budgeting.

2 tablespoons margarine
3 tablespoons brown sugar
2 teaspoons cornstarch

1 cup crushed pineapple
1 can (12 ounces) luncheon meat
4 cooked sweet potatoes, peeled

Heat oven to 375° F. Melt margarine over low heat in small shallow baking pan. Combine brown sugar, cornstarch, pineapple, and margarine; mix well. Place luncheon meat in center of baking pan. Slice potatoes lengthwise and arrange around meat. Spoon pineapple mixture over meat and potatoes. Bake 30 to 35 minutes, basting twice with pan drippings during last half of the baking period.

Pinchpenny Kabobs

2 tablespoons margarine
½ cup finely chopped onion
1 cup chili sauce
2 tablespoons vinegar
2 teaspoons sugar
1 teaspoon celery seed
¼ pound sliced cooked salami
¼ pound sliced luncheon meat

¼ pound sliced peppered beef loaf
¼ pound sliced bologna
½ pound small mushrooms
½ large cucumber, sliced
16 cherry tomatoes
1 can (8 ounces) whole
   carrots, drained
4 small white potatoes, cooked

Heat margarine in skillet; add onion and sauté until tender. Add chili sauce, vinegar, sugar, and celery seed; simmer 5 minutes. Remove from heat; set aside. Prepare kabobs using long skewers and alternating remaining ingredients until all are used. Broil until lightly browned on all sides, turning and basting frequently with the sauce. Serve hot with remaining sauce.

Macaroni Delight

A party loaf to delight your guests and stretch your food dollars.

1 package lemon-flavored gelatin
1½ cups hot water
¼ cup sour cream
¼ cup salad dressing
2 teaspoons prepared mustard
Dash Tabasco
1 teaspoon salt
4 cups cold cooked
   elbow macaroni

1 cup shredded process
   American cheese
2 tablespoons finely
   chopped green pepper
2 tablespoons finely
   chopped pimiento
8 slices luncheon meat
2 medium tomatoes, cut in wedges
8 cucumber slices

Dissolve gelatin in hot water in large bowl; refrigerate until slightly thickened. Combine sour cream, salad dressing, mustard, Tabasco, and salt; add to gelatin and mix well. Stir in macaroni, cheese, green pepper, and pimiento. Spoon ⅓ of macaroni mixture into a 9 × 5 × 3-inch loaf pan. Top with 4 slices of luncheon meat. Repeat layers once again; cover meat with remaining macaroni mixture. Chill until firm. Unmold on serving platter; garnish with tomatoes and cucumber slices. Cut into slices to serve. Makes 8 to 10 servings.

Choucroute

One of the most popular Continental dishes, this inexpensive sauerkraut-and-frankfurter dish is served in the best restaurants of Europe.

¼ pound bacon slices,
cut into short, thin strips
3 medium onions, sliced
1 can (1 pound 11 ounces) sauerkraut

8 frankfurters, halved
4 cooked small new potatoes
1 teaspoon chopped parsley

In large deep skillet brown bacon; drain on absorbent paper. Remove all but 2 tablespoons of bacon drippings. Sauté onions until tender. Add sauerkraut. Cover; cook until thoroughly heated. Add bacon, frankfurters, and potatoes. Cover; simmer 15 minutes. Turn onto serving plate; sprinkle with parsley.

Frankfurter Corn Cake

4 frankfurters
1 cup yellow cornmeal
1 teaspoon baking powder
½ teaspoon baking soda
¾ teaspoon salt

1 cup sour milk or buttermilk
1 egg
3 tablespoons melted shortening
Celery Sauce (recipe below)

Heat oven to 425° F. Grease well a 9-inch pie plate. Slice frankfurters in rounds about ⅜-inch thick. Mix together cornmeal, baking powder, baking soda, and salt. Add sour milk and egg to shortening; blend with dry ingredients and mix well. Stir in frankfurters. Pour into pie plate. Bake 30 minutes. Cut in wedges and serve with Celery Sauce.

Celery Sauce

1 can (10½ ounces) condensed
cream of celery soup
1 cup milk

2 tablespoons minced parsley
⅛ teaspoon pepper

Combine soup with milk in saucepan; blend well. Bring to boil over low heat. Add parsley and pepper and stir.

Frankfurter-Kraut Stuffed Buns

Any time is a good time for an informal patio supper. Serve these frankfurter specialties in a basket with relishes and corn chips.

8 frankfurters
8 bacon slices
1 can (16 ounces) sauerkraut, drained

1 medium apple, pared,
  cored, chopped
2 tablespoons margarine
8 toasted frankfurter buns

Wrap each frankfurter with a bacon slice; secure with wooden pick. Pan-broil until bacon is crisp, turning occasionally. Remove frankfurters to heated platter; keep warm. Remove wooden picks. Melt margarine in skillet; add drained sauerkraut and apple. Cook slowly until heated through, stirring occasionally. Place 3 to 4 tablespoons sauerkraut-apple mixture in each bun; top with bacon-wrapped frankfurter.

Oahu Frank and Bean Casserole

An all-American favorite with a new twist.

¼ cup chopped onion
1 tablespoon margarine
2 cans (1 pound each) pork
  and beans in tomato sauce
¼ cup ketchup
2 tablespoons prepared mustard

8 frankfurters
4 pineapple slices, cut in half
¼ cup brown sugar
Dash nutmeg
1 tablespoon pineapple syrup

Sauté onion in margarine until tender. Add pork and beans, ketchup, and 1 tablespoon mustard; bring to boil. Heat oven to 375° F. Pour pork-and-beans mixture into a 2-quart baking dish. Arrange frankfurters over beans in herringbone design. Place pineapple slices in center to overlap. Blend sugar, nutmeg, remaining mustard, and pineapple syrup. Spread over frankfurters and pineapple slices. Bake 20 to 25 minutes or until thoroughly heated.

Frankfurter Stew with Dumplings

½ pound frankfurters,
  cut into 1-inch pieces
1½ cups sliced onions
3 tablespoons margarine
1 cup ketchup
3 cups water
2 teaspoons Worcestershire sauce
1½ teaspoons salt

⅛ teaspoon pepper
3 cups cubed potatoes
1½ cups sliced cooked carrots
2 tablespoons minced parsley
2 tablespoons flour
¼ cup cold water
2 cups packaged biscuit mix

Sauté frankfurters and onions in margarine in large skillet until lightly browned. Combine ketchup with water, Worcestershire sauce, salt, and pepper; add to frankfurters and onions. Bring to a boil. Add potatoes, carrots, and parsley; cook, covered, 30 minutes or until vegetables are tender. Combine flour with ¼ cup water; add to vegetables; simmer 5 minutes, stirring constantly, until thickened. Prepare dumplings according to package directions. Drop by spoonfuls onto hot stew. Cook, uncovered, over low heat 10 minutes. Cover; cook 10 minutes longer. Makes 6 servings.

Hawaiian Franks

¼ cup chopped onion
¼ cup green pepper strips
1 tablespoon vegetable oil
1 tablespoon flour
4 pineapple slices, halved
  and drained, reserving
½ cup pineapply syrup
¼ cup water
1 beef bouillon cube

2 tablespoons brown sugar
½ teaspoon salt
¼ teaspoon pepper
1 teaspoon soy sauce
½ teaspoon ground ginger
2 cups drained sauerkraut
1 pound frankfurters,
  cut in 2-inch pieces

Heat oven to 350° F. Sauté onion and green pepper in vegetable oil until crisp tender. Stir in flour. Gradually blend in pineapple syrup and water. Stir in beef bouillon cube, sugar, salt, pepper, soy sauce, and ginger. Bring to a boil, stirring constantly. Arrange layers of sauerkraut and halved pineapple slices around sides of large 2-quart casserole. Pile frankfurters in center. Pour sauce over all. Bake 30 minutes.

Spicy Franks and Sauerkraut

1 cup sliced celery
½ cup sliced onion
½ cup julienned green pepper
2 tablespoons vegetable oil
1 pound frankfurters,
    diagonally sliced
2 cups diced fresh tomatoes

2 cups drained sauerkraut
1 bay leaf
1 teaspoon oregano
½ teaspoon salt
⅛ teaspoon pepper
1 cup beef bouillon

Sauté celery, onion, and green pepper in oil in large skillet until tender; remove. In same skillet quickly brown frankfurter slices; remove. In same skillet, cook tomatoes 1 minute. Add sauerkraut, seasonings, and beef bouillon. Add onion mixture and frankfurter slices. Cover; simmer 10 minutes, stirring occasionally.

Tangy Frank Ricerole

The zesty sauce gives rice a barbecue flavor.

2 tablespoons prepared mustard
2 cups tomato sauce
½ cup dark corn syrup
⅓ cup vinegar
⅓ cup minced onion
2 tablespoons Worcestershire sauce

½ teaspoon celery seed
½ teaspoon pepper
2 tablespoons chili sauce
8 frankfurters, sliced diagonally
2 cups hot cooked rice
1 tablespoon chopped parsley

Blend mustard and ¼ cup tomato sauce in saucepan; heat 1 minute. Add remaining tomato sauce with corn syrup, vinegar, onion, Worcestershire sauce, celery seed, pepper, and chili sauce. Cook over medium heat, stirring frequently, until mixture comes to a boil. Reduce heat; simmer 25 minutes. Add franks; cook 8 minutes longer or until thoroughly heated. Serve over rice; sprinkle with parsley.

Poor Man's Boiled Dinner

A hearty meal to serve with boiled potatoes and rye bread.

1 small head cabbage (about
    1½ pounds), cut into wedges
8 frankfurters
Boiling water
¾ teaspoon salt

1 tablespoon margarine
1 tablespoon flour
¾ cup milk
1½ tablespoons prepared mustard

Place cabbage in deep, heavy kettle; top with frankfurters. Add enough boiling water and salt to just cover cabbage. Cover; boil 10 minutes or until cabbage is crisp tender. Drain; remove cabbage wedges and frankfurters to heated serving platter and keep warm. Melt margarine in saucepan; stir in flour until smooth. Slowly add milk, stirring constantly, until smooth. Stir in mustard; continue cooking, stirring constantly, until thickened. Spoon sauce over cabbage and frankfurters.

Hearty Bean Casserole

A dandy meal to beat the day-before-payday blues. Serve with celery and carrot sticks, heated French bread chunks and canned fruit.

2 medium carrots, diced	1 teaspoon salt
Boiling salted water	⅛ teaspoon pepper
2 tablespoons margarine	1 cup milk
2 tablespoons minced onion	1 can (1 pound) baked beans
2 tablespoons minced green pepper	in tomato sauce
2 tablespoons flour	4 frankfurters, chopped

Cook carrots in 1 inch boiling salted water, covered, until tender; drain, reserving liquid. Melt margarine in saucepan; sauté onion and green pepper until tender. Add flour, salt, and pepper; blend well. Add enough water to carrot liquid to make 1 cup; combine with milk and stir into flour mixture. Heat over medium heat until thickened, stirring constantly. Add carrots, beans, and chopped frankfurters; heat thoroughly and serve.

Western Chow Mein

If your budget cannot cope with chicken or shrimp replace these with frankfurters which add a special flavor of their own.

2 tablespoons vegetable oil	2 tablespoons cornstarch
8 frankfurters, thinly sliced	2 teaspoons soy sauce
½ cup chicken bouillon	¼ cup water
¾ teaspoon salt	2 cups hot cooked rice
3 cups sliced onions	2 cups chow-mein noodles

Heat oil in large skillet; sauté frankfurters until browned, stirring frequently. Add chicken bouillon, salt and onions. Cover; cook 10 minutes, stirring occasionally. Blend cornstarch with soy sauce and water until smooth. Add to frankfurter mixture; cook, stirring, until thickened. Serve with rice and noodles.

German Boiled Dinner

A boon to the budgeting and busy homemaker are the spicy meats which require so little time to prepare.

4 knockwursts
4 cups boiling water
2 beef bouillon cubes
¾ teaspoon salt
4 small potatoes, pared
   and halved

4 carrots, cut in pieces
4 white turnips, pared
   and quartered
1 head (1 pound) green cabbage,
   cut in 4 wedges
Horseradish

Place knockwursts in boiling water; cover and let stand 12 minutes. Remove knockwursts; cover and keep warm. Add bouillon cubes and salt to water; heat until cubes dissolve. Add vegetables. Cover; bring to boil. Simmer 20 minutes. Drain and serve with knockwursts and horseradish.

Pennsylvania Dutch Supper

A hearty and economical dish which dates back to Colonial days.

1 can (No. 2½) sauerkraut, drained
¼ cup margarine
¼ cup heavy cream
3 tablespoons minced onion
1 teaspoon caraway seeds
¼ pound thinly sliced hard
   salami, halved

4 knockwursts
1 cup packaged biscuit mix
1 teaspoon dry mustard
2 tablespoons butter
2 tablespoons chopped parsley

Place drained sauerkraut in heavy skillet; dot with margarine. Pour cream over all; sprinkle with onion and caraway seeds. Heat through but do not boil. Add salami slices and mix into sauerkraut. Lay knockwursts on top. Cover, heat until bubbling. Prepare biscuit mix for dumplings according to package directions. Arrange by spoonfuls on top of bubbling sauerkraut. Cover; cook 10 minutes. Uncover; cook 10 minutes longer or until done. Blend mustard with butter. As soon as dumplings are done, turn sauerkraut mixture onto serving platter with dumplings on top. Dot with mustard butter; sprinkle with parsley.

POULTRY: SOMETHING TO CROW ABOUT!

Chicken has always been a favorite, for either a simple family meal, a dressed-up "Chicken every Sunday" or an elaborate banquet. It's at home in every part of the world and equally welcomed by the peasant and the gourmet.

Chickens are sold whole, in halves, quarters, or by the piece, and they are government inspected for wholesomeness and graded for quality.

They are available in the following classifications:

Broiler-Fryers: young, tender chickens up to 3½ pounds. They are good for frying, broiling and barbecuing.

Roasters: young, tender chickens 3½ to 5 pounds. Ideal for roasting, rotisserie cooking, and barbecuing.

Capons: young, tender chickens 5 to 9 pounds. A de luxe product especially desirable for roasting.

Caponettes: plump, tender chickens 3 to 6 pounds. Good for roasting, frying, broiling, barbecuing, rotisserie cooking.

Stewing Chickens: mature, less tender hens, 3 to 7 pounds; good for soups, stews, casseroles and other slow-cooked dishes.

Turkeys: are sold in just about the same manner as chickens. They are identified as Roasters and Fryers, Hen Turkeys, and Tom Turkeys.

Chicken Fritters

2 eggs, separated
2 cups chopped cooked chicken
½ cup minced celery and leaves
1 teaspoon grated onion

¼ cup flour
½ teaspoon salt
Vegetable oil
1 cup hot chicken gravy

Combine egg yolks with chicken, celery, onion, flour, and salt; mix well. Beat egg whites until stiff. Fold in chicken mixture. Drop by tablespoonfuls into heated oil. Brown on both sides. Serve with hot chicken gravy. Makes 8 fritters.

Chicken Riviera

The flavor of rosemary and lemon adds a new dimension to chicken.

1 2½ - to 3-pound broiler, cut up
½ cup flour
1½ teaspoons salt
¼ teaspoon pepper
Vegetable oil
1 clove garlic, minced

2 cups chicken broth
¼ teaspoon rosemary
3 sliced carrots
3 lemon slices
2 tablespoons chopped parsley

Shake chicken pieces in paper bag with flour, salt, and pepper. Heat oil in heavy skillet. Add chicken, brown on all sides; remove. Drain off all but 2 tablespoons oil. Add garlic, broth, and rosemary, stir well. Replace chicken in skillet; top with carrots, lemon slices, and parsley. Simmer, covered, 30 minutes or until chicken is tender.

Chicken Parmesan

1 2½ - to 3-pound broiler
   cut in serving pieces
½ cup flour
¼ cup grated Parmesan cheese

1½ teaspoons salt
⅛ teaspoon pepper
⅛ teaspoon paprika
Vegetable oil

Wash and dry chicken. Combine flour, cheese, salt, pepper, and paprika. Roll chicken pieces in flour mixture. Have oil heated in deep fryer or kettle. Fry chicken 15 to 20 minutes, or until tender and golden brown. Drain.

Southern Chicken Pie

⅓ cup chicken fat
½ cup flour
3 cups chicken broth
½ cup milk
½ cup light cream
1 tablespoon minced onion

½ teaspoon ground ginger
¾ teaspoon salt
¾ teaspoon pepper
4 cups cooked chicken,
   cut in large cubes
1 9-inch round pastry

Heat oven to 425° F. Blend chicken fat and flour in saucepan over low heat until bubbly. Add broth, milk, and cream, and cook, stirring constantly, until thickened and smooth. Add onion, ginger, salt, and pepper. Place chicken in 2-quart shallow casserole. Pour in hot gravy. Roll pastry to fit casserole. Cut openings for steam vent. Adjust edge, and flute. Bake 25 to 35 minutes or until top is brown and sauce bubbly. Makes 6 servings.

Fried Chicken, Border Style

When you're racking your brain for "something different," try two favorite chicken ideas—the taste of chicken with barbecue sauce and the tempting eye-appeal of fried chicken.

1 2½- to 3-pound broiler
   cut in serving pieces
1 cup flour
1 teaspoon poultry seasoning
1 teaspoon salt
1 teaspoon paprika
1 teaspoon chili powder

1 tablespoon prepared mustard
2 tablespoons chili sauce
2 tablespoons vinegar
⅛ teaspoon Tabasco
1 egg, slightly beaten
½ cup evaporated milk
½ cup margarine

Wash and dry chicken. Combine flour, poultry seasoning, salt, paprika, and chili powder. Blend together mustard, chili sauce, vinegar, and Tabasco; stir in egg and evaporated milk and mix well. Roll chicken in flour mixture, then dip into vinegar mixture, and roll in flour mixture again. Let stand 10 minutes. Heat oven to 350° F. Melt margarine in shallow baking pan. Place chicken, skin side down, in pan. Bake 25 minutes; turn and bake 20 minutes longer or until chicken is tender.

Chicken Chop Suey

2 cups cubed cooked chicken
2 tablespoons.margarine
2 cups thinly sliced celery
1½ cups thinly sliced onions
⅛ teaspoon pepper
2 cups chicken broth
2¼ cups canned mixed Chinese
   vegetables, drained

1 can (4 ounces) mushroom
   caps, drained
2 tablespoons cornstarch
3 tablespoons soy sauce
2 cups cooked rice
2 tablespoons toasted
   slivered almonds

Brown chicken cubes lightly in margarine; add celery, onions, pepper, and broth. Cook, covered, 10 minutes or until vegetables are just tender. Add drained Chinese vegetables and mushrooms; heat to boil. Combine cornstarch with soy sauce; add to hot mixture, stirring constantly, until slightly thickened. Simmer 2 minutes. Serve chop suey over hot rice. Garnish with almonds. Makes 6 servings.

Chicken in Casserole

This all-in-one casserole cooks in 1 hour—use a heat-proof baking dish and bring it right to the table.

1 2½ - to 3-pound broiler
1 teaspoon salt
¼ teaspoon pepper
2 cups Savory Stuffing
  (recipe below)
¼ cup margarine

½ cup bouillon
4 medium potatoes, pared,
  quartered
½ pound fresh peas
6 carrots, scraped, sliced

Heat oven to 375° F. Wash and dry chicken. Sprinkle cavity with ½ teaspoon of salt, and pepper. Stuff with Savory Stuffing; tie legs together. Brown on all sides in margarine in deep baking pan. Add bouillon and potatoes. Bake, covered, 30 minutes. Add peas and carrots and remaining ½ teaspoon salt. Cover. Bake 30 minutes longer.

Savory Stuffing

1 package (8 ounces) prepared
  stuffing mix
¼ cup chopped onion

1½ cups diced celery with leaves
Butter
Liquid per directions in mix

Combine stuffing mix with onion and celery. In saucepan melt butter called for in package directions. Stir in stuffing mix; cook 5 minutes but do not brown. Add liquid called for in package directions; heat 2 minutes.

Skillet Cherry Chicken

1 cup cherry preserves
2 tablespoons lemon juice
4 whole cloves
¼ teaspoon salt
¼ teaspoon allspice

¼ teaspoon mace
½ cup flour
1 2½ - to 3-pound broiler,
  cut up
¼ cup vegetable oil

Blend preserves, lemon juice, cloves, salt, allspice, and mace; set aside. Place flour in paper bag. Add 2 or 3 pieces of chicken at a time and shake to coat. Brown chicken in oil in skillet, turning once. Cover; cook 15 minutes. Drain off fat; add cherry sauce. Cover, simmer 15 minutes longer. Turn and simmer 15 minutes more or until tender.

Molokai Chicken

Add a touch of the exotic to your next oven-fried chicken. It's beautifully crisp outside, moist and tender inside.

¼ cup sesame seeds
⅔ cup fine cracker crumbs
1 2½ - to 3-pound broiler, cut up

⅓ cup evaporated milk
½ cup margarine, melted

Heat oven to 350° F. Place sesame seeds in shallow baking pan; heat in oven 10 minutes, stirring once or twice. Combine cracker crumbs with sesame seeds. Dip chicken pieces in evaporated milk, then roll in cracker mixture. Pour margarine into a shallow baking pan. Dip skin side of chicken pieces in margarine; turn over and arrange skin side up in baking dish. Bake 1½ hours or until done. Remove to warm serving platter.

Chick 'N' Chip Bake

1 large eggplant
Salted water
3 tablespoons chopped green onion
3 tablespoons chopped parsley
1 ¾ cup finely crushed potato chips
1 cup cooked cubed chicken
6 tablespoons margarine
½ teaspoon salt

5 tablespoons flour
2 cups milk
¼ cup heavy cream
1 tablespoon finely chopped onion
⅛ teaspoon pepper
1 chicken bouillon cube
6 tablespoons grated
   Parmesan cheese

Cut eggplant in half, lengthwise; parboil in salted water 12 minutes. Cool slightly. Scoop out pulp of eggplant, leaving about ½-inch shell. Chop pulp fine. Combine with green onion, parsley, 1 cup crushed potato chips, and chicken. Heat oven to 375° F. Spoon chicken mixture into eggplant shells. Sprinkle top with remaining potato chips. Dot with 1 tablespoon margarine. Bake 20 minutes. Sauté onion in remaining 4 tablespoons margarine until just tender. Stir in pepper, salt, and flour. Gradually add milk and bouillon cube. Cook, stirring constantly, until thickened and bouillon cube has dissolved. Blend in 3 tablespoons Parmesan cheese. Divide baked eggplant into 4 portions by cutting each shell in two. Place in ovenproof serving dishes on cookie sheet. Spoon cheese sauce over individual eggplant servings. Beat heavy cream until stiff. Fold in remaining cheese sauce. Spoon on top of each eggplant. Sprinkle remaining 3 tablespoons cheese over all. Place under broiler 5 to 6 inches from source of heat. Broil 3 to 5 minutes until puffy and brown.

Alta Vista Chicken

Multi-flavored canned fruit cocktail in the sauce adds much to the eating satisfaction of this dish.

2 (2 pounds each) broiler quartered
3 tablespoons vegetable oil
1 teaspoon salt
¼ teaspoon pepper
¼ cup chopped green onion
⅛ teaspoon garlic powder

1 teaspoon dry mustard
1 can (1 pound 14 ounces) fruit
   cocktail, drain and reserve syrup
¼ cup lemon juice
Dash Tabasco
2 tablespoons margarine

Brush chicken all over with oil; sprinkle with salt and pepper. Broil, turning often to brown evenly. In large saucepan combine onion, garlic powder, mustard, drained syrup from fruit cocktail, and 1 teaspoon lemon juice; stir. Boil until syrup mixture is reduced to about ½ cup. Add fruit cocktail, remaining lemon juice, Tabasco, and margarine. Stir; heat thoroughly. Brush chicken with sauce during last few minutes of broiling. Serve sauce with chicken. Makes 8 servings.

Chicken Cranberry Mousse

A party-bright, colorful, main-dish chicken salad.

2 tablespoons unflavored gelatin
1½ cups water
1 can (1 pound) whole
   cranberry sauce
½ cup chopped nuts
3 tablespoons lemon juice
1 chicken bouillon cube

½ cup instant powdered cream
1½ cups finely diced
   cooked chicken
¼ cup finely chopped celery
¼ cup finely chopped
   stuffed olives
Lettuce greens

Sprinkle 1 tablespoon gelatin on ½ cup water to soften. Place over low heat; stir until gelatin is dissolved. Combine cranberry sauce, nuts, and 2 tablespoons lemon juice; add dissolved gelatin and stir until blended. Pour into 8 individual molds and chill until firm. Sprinkle remaining 1 tablespoon gelatin on 1 cup water to soften. Place over low heat; add chicken bouillon cube and stir until gelatin and bouillon cube are dissolved. Bring to boil. Place mixture in bowl; add instant powdered cream; stir until dissolved. Place bowl in freezing compartment 45 to 50 minutes or until gelatin is set.

Beat at high speed with electric or rotary beater 3 to 5 minutes or until peaks form. Fold in remaining ingredients; spoon into molds on top of cranberry layer. Chill until firm. Unmold on lettuce greens in serving plate. Makes 8 servings.

Chicken Wing Wongs

These make ideal appetizers or, served on a bed of hot fluffy rice, a delicious dinner dish.

3 pounds broiler chicken wings, about 18	⅛ teaspoon pepper
	½ teaspoon oregano
½ cup flour	¾ cup buttermilk
½ cup grated Parmesan cheese	2 cups hot fluffy rice
1 teaspoon salt	Shortening
1 teaspoon paprika	

Cut wings in half; use drumstick half for frying and use remaining half to make soup for another meal. Blend together flour, cheese, salt, paprika, pepper, and oregano. Dip chicken pieces in buttermilk; roll in dry ingredients. Heat oil or shortening in deep fryer. Fry chicken pieces 5 minutes. Drain on absorbent paper. Serve over rice.

Savory Chicken Bake

2 eggs, beaten	⅛ teaspoon pepper
½ cup milk	¼ teaspoon celery salt
2 cups soft bread crumbs	1½ cups diced cooked chicken
1 medium onion, chopped	½ cup mayonnaise
2 tablespoons chopped parsley	½ cup sour cream
¼ teaspoon thyme	½ teaspoon prepared mustard
¾ teaspoon salt	3 tablespoons minced parsley

Heat oven to 350° F. Combine eggs and milk; soak bread crumbs 3 minutes. Add onion, chopped parsley, thyme, salt, pepper, celery salt, and chicken; mix well. Turn into 1½-quart baking dish. Bake 45 minutes or until firm. Let stand 4 minutes. Loosen edges with spatula. Place serving platter on top of baking dish; invert both; lift off baking dish. Combine remaining ingredients in saucepan; blend. Heat, stirring constantly. Pour sauce over chicken loaf. Makes 4 servings.

Hot Chicken Pie Parisienne

An unusual dish to delight your luncheon guests—the French version features an elegant almond pastry shell.

4 cups diced cooked chicken	¼ teaspoon Tabasco
1 teaspoon salt	1 9-inch baked pastry shell
1 cup mayonnaise	3 tablespoons melted margarine
2 tablespoons lemon juice	2 cups finely cubed bread crumbs
1 teaspoon dry mustard	1 cup grated American cheese
1 teaspoon Worcestershire sauce	

Heat oven to 350° F. Sprinkle chicken with salt. Combine mayonnaise, lemon juice, dry mustard, Worcestershire sauce and Tabasco. Add to chicken; toss to blend. Turn into baked pastry shell. Combine margarine and bread crumbs; sprinkle over chicken. Sprinkle with cheese. Bake 30 to 35 minutes or until heated through. Cut in wedges. Makes 8 servings.

Island Skillet Chicken

A vividly colorful sweet-and-sour Hawaiian dinner with a combination of fresh vegetables and pineapple.

1 pound fresh green beans	1½ cups cherry tomatoes
1 cup sliced celery	1 can (1 pound 4 ounces) pineapple
1 medium green pepper, sliced	spears, drain and reserve juice
in ⅓-inch strips	1 ripe banana
½ cup water	Oriental Sauce (recipe below)
1 teaspoon salt	1½ cups buttered narrow
8 slices cooked chicken	noodles, cooked

Wash beans and snap off ends, leaving beans whole. Bring water and salt to boil in large skillet; place beans, celery, and green pepper side by side in skillet. Cook 5 minutes. Cover skillet; reduce heat and simmer 20 to 25 minutes or until beans are crisp tender. Push beans into a pie-shaped wedge in skillet; arrange sliced chicken in wedge next to beans; arrange green pepper and celery into a wedge next to chicken; arrange a wedge of cherry tomatoes next to green pepper and celery; drain pineapple, reserving juice for sauce, and arrange pineapple spears in a wedge, topped by sliced banana. Pour Oriental Sauce over all; bring to boil. Reduce heat; simmer, covered, 15 minutes or until heated through. Serve with hot buttered noodles.

Oriental Sauce

3 tablespoons cornstarch
¾ cup cold water
2 chicken bouillon cubes
¾ cup brown sugar

3 tablespoons light molasses
⅓ cup vinegar
Reserved pineapple juice

Blend cornstarch and water in saucepan to make thin paste. Add remaining ingredients; blend. Bring to boil, stirring constantly. Boil 1 minute or until sauce is thick and clear.

Chicken-and-Split-Pea Squares

¾ cup quick-cooking split peas
1 small bay leaf
2 bouillon cubes
2 cups water
⅔ cup finely diced carrots
1 cup thinly sliced celery
1½ cups coarsely chopped
    cooked chicken

3 tablespoons minced onion
½ cup tapioca
1 teaspoon salt
⅛ teaspoon pepper
½ cup milk
4 strips bacon

Combine peas, bay leaf, bouillon cubes, and water in saucepan. Cover; cook over low heat 30 minutes, stirring occasionally. Add carrots and celery. Cook, covered, 15 minutes longer or until vegetables are tender. Remove bay leaf. Measure 2 cups of peas mixture. Heat oven to 450° F. Grease an 8-inch square pan. Combine split pea mixture with remaining ingredients, except bacon; mix well. Turn into baking pan. Place bacon strips on top. Bake 35 minutes or until browned, tipping pan occasionally to spread melted bacon fat. Cut into squares and serve hot.

Chicken Montmorency

An elegant party dish and nobody will guess that it is economical.

1 can (1 pound) pitted red sour
   cherries, water pack
1 3½-pound frying chicken, cut up
1 teaspoon salt
¼ teaspoon pepper
¼ teaspoon paprika
3 tablespoons margarine

1 tablespoon flour
1 teaspoon sugar
⅛ teaspoon allspice
⅛ teaspoon cinnamon
1 can (9 ounces) crushed pineapple
1 chicken bouillon cube
¼ teaspoon red food coloring

Drain cherries; reserve liquid. Wash and dry chicken pieces; sprinkle with salt, pepper, and paprika. Brown chicken in margarine in skillet; remove and keep warm. Add flour, sugar, and spices to drippings; blend well. Gradually add cherry liquid. Add remaining ingredients; stir well. Add chicken. Cover; bring to boil. Reduce heat; simmer 40 minutes or until chicken is tender. Add drained cherries last 5 minutes of cooking time.

Chicken Rissoles Victor

6 eggs, separated
½ cup flour
½ teaspoon salt
1 teaspoon baking powder
½ cup chopped pimientos
½ cup chopped mushrooms
½ green pepper, chopped

1¼ cups cooked chicken,
   finely diced
1 tablespoon sherry wine
1 tablespoon melted margarine
Vegetable oil
Mushroom Sauce (p. 77)

Beat egg whites until they form peaks. Slowly add flour, salt, and baking powder, beating constantly, until stiff. Combine pimientos, mushrooms, green pepper, and chicken; mix well. Beat egg yolks with wine and margarine. Combine with egg-white mixture; fold in chicken mixture and blend well. Drop by tablespoonfuls into deep hot oil and fry until golden brown. Serve with Mushroom Sauce.

Chicken Grazzia

2 pounds chicken parts
¼ cup margarine
1 can (10½ ounces) condensed
   cream of mushroom soup

⅛ teaspoon thyme
⅛ teaspoon rosemary
⅓ cup water
12 small white onions

Brown chicken in margarine in large skillet. Stir in soup, thyme, rosemary, and water; bring to boiling. Cover; reduce heat and simmer 5 minutes. Add onions; simmer 40 minutes longer or until chicken is tender, stirring often.

Chicken Orientale

Use your prettiest heat-and-serve skillet and bring it right to your dining room table.

1 chicken fryer (2 to 2½ pounds) cut up	1 clove garlic, crushed
½ cup margarine	1 cup uncooked rice
¾ teaspoon salt	3½ cups canned tomatoes
⅛ teaspoon pepper	2½ cups canned lima beans, undrained
1 cup cubed cooked ham	¼ cup pimiento, chopped
1 large onion, sliced	3 hard-cooked eggs

Brown chicken in margarine and season with salt and pepper. Remove from skillet. Add ham, onion, and garlic; sauté 3 minutes. Add rice, tomatoes, lima beans, and pimiento; stir. Add chicken pieces. Cover; cook over low heat 30 to 40 minutes or until chicken is tender. Garnish with eggs.

Spiced Chicken Mindan

Sesame seeds blend with spices to make this tender chicken dish especially appetizing.

2 (1½ pounds each) frying chickens, quartered	1 clove garlic, minced
½ cup sesame seeds	½ teaspoon ginger
⅓ cup vegetable oil	⅛ teaspoon cloves
¼ cup minced onion	⅛ teaspoon chili powder
1½ teaspoons salt	1 tablespoon cornstarch
½ teaspoon cardamom	1 cup water
	2 cups hot fluffy rice

Heat oven to 350° F. Place chicken pieces, skin side down, in shallow baking dish. Mix remaining ingredients, except cornstarch, water, and rice; blend well. Brush some of spice mixture on chicken. Bake 30 minutes, basting frequently with remaining spice mixture. Turn skin side up; continue baking and basting 30 minutes longer. Put under broiler and lightly brown. Remove chicken to heated serving platter. Surround with rice. Blend cornstarch with water; stir into pan drippings. Cook, stirring, until thickened. Pour over chicken and rice.

Polish Stuffed Chicken

1 roasting chicken, about 4 pounds
Stuffing
Vegetable oil
1 teaspoon salt
¼ teaspoon pepper
¾ cup water

4 medium potatoes, pared
4 carrots, cut in pieces
4 small white onions
¼ pound whole green beans
1 cup frozen lima beans

Fill chicken with your favorite stuffing; sew up openings. Tie legs together. Brown on all sides in small amount of oil in heavy kettle. Pour off fat. Return chicken to kettle; season with salt and pepper. Add water, cover and simmer 1 hour. Add vegetables. Simmer, covered, 45 minutes longer or until chicken and vegetables are tender.

Chicken Tandor

Chicken Tandor or Tandoori is a favorite in Pakistan.

1 2½-pound broiler
3 cloves garlic, minced
1 onion, chopped
¼ teaspoon chili peppers, ground
¼ teasppon ground cloves
¾ teaspoon salt

¼ teaspoon pepper
1 cardamom seed, ground
¼ teaspoon ground ginger
¼ cup ground almonds
2 tablespoons melted margarine
1 tablespoon water

Heat oven to 350° F. Carefully remove all of the skin from the whole chicken. Prick all over with fork. Combine garlic, onion, chili peppers, cloves, salt, pepper, cardamom seed, ginger, almonds, and margarine; blend into a paste. Spread over the chicken and rub a little on the inside. Place in roasting pan. Bake 1½ hours or until tender.

Chicken South of the Border

1 pound dry kidney beans	1 large onion, chopped
4 to 4½ pounds stewing chicken	1 clove garlic, minced
1 tablespoon salt	1 small green pepper, chopped
¼ teaspoon pepper	1 can (8 ounces) tomato sauce
¼ teaspoon cayenne	3 teaspoons chili powder
¼ cup flour	1 bay leaf
¼ pound margarine	¼ teaspoon thyme

Cover kidney beans with cold water; soak overnight. Drain; add enough cold water to cover beans. Cook over moderate heat 1½ hours or until tender. Drain; reserve 1½ cups bean stock. Cut chicken in serving pieces; sprinkle with salt, pepper, cayenne, and coat lightly with flour. Melt margarine in heavy kettle; add chicken pieces and fry until golden all over. Remove to platter. Sauté onion, garlic and green pepper in kettle until soft. Stir in tomato sauce, chili powder, bay leaf, and thyme. Add chicken. Pour in reserved 1½ cups bean stock and 2 cups water. Cook, covered, over low heat 1 to 1½ hours, stirring occasionally, or until chicken is tender. Add drained beans; cook 15 minutes longer, uncovered. Makes 8 servings.

Deviled Chicken Longo

Crisp golden brown chicken in a rich sauce.

1 2½- to 3-pound frying chicken, cut up	⅓ cup bacon drippings
	1 can (10½ ounces) cream
2 tablespoons dry mustard	of mushroom soup
Water	1 soup can milk
¼ cup flour	1 can (10½ ounces) condensed
½ teaspoon salt	tomato soup
¼ teaspoon pepper	

Wash and dry chicken parts. Mix mustard with enough water to make a thick paste. Spread chicken pieces liberally with paste. Combine flour, salt, and pepper and dredge chicken with mixture. Fry in bacon drippings until crisp and golden brown, turning once. Remove chicken from skillet. Add remaining ingredients; mix well. Return chicken to skillet. Simmer, covered, 30 minutes or until tender.

Chicken Stroganoff

1 frying chicken (about 2½ pounds),
  cut up
½ cup flour
¾ teaspoon salt
⅛ teaspoon pepper
1¼ teaspoons paprika
¼ cup margarine
¼ cup water

2 tablespoons chopped pimiento
1 can (4 ounces) button mushrooms
¼ cup chopped green pepper
1 can (10½ ounces) condensed
  cream of mushroom soup
1 cup sour cream
2 cups parsley-buttered cooked rice

Place chicken pieces in paper bag with mixture of flour, salt, pepper, and paprika; shake thoroughly until well coated. Melt margarine in large skillet. Add chicken; cook until brown. Add water and cook, covered, until tender, about 30 minutes. Remove chicken to heated serving platter; keep warm. Add pimiento, mushrooms, green pepper, and soup to skillet; stir. Cook 5 minutes. Add sour cream; heat thoroughly but do not boil. Arrange chicken in center of platter with a border of rice; pour sour cream sauce over chicken.

Chicken Montmarte

A blending of different flavors makes this chicken gourmet fare.

½ teaspoon salt
1 teaspoon paprika
¼ teaspoon pepper
1 frying chicken (about 3 pounds),
  quartered
3 tablespoons margarine
¼ cup chopped onion

½ cup dry white wine
1 cup sliced fresh mushrooms
1 can (10½ ounces) condensed
  cream of chicken soup
⅛ teaspoon Tabasco
¼ cup currant jelly

Combine salt, paprika, and pepper; sprinkle on chicken. Melt 2 tablespoons margarine in skillet; brown chicken on both sides. Add onion and ¼ cup wine. Cook, covered, over low heat until tender, about 30 minutes. Sauté mushrooms in remaining 1 tablespoon margarine; add to chicken. Combine remaining ingredients; blend well. Pour over chicken. Cover; heat thoroughly.

Chicken Wingding

If you never thought of chicken wings as the meat entrée, try this recipe. They're good to eat and very modest in cost.

2½ pounds chicken wings, about 16
¼ cup flour
1 medium onion, chopped
¼ cup vegetable oil
2 cans (10½ ounces each) tomato soup
2 soup cans water

1 teaspoon salt
¼ teaspoon chili powder
⅛ teaspoon pepper
⅛ teaspoon basil
⅛ teaspoon thyme
Toasted split corn bread (your own or made from a mix)

Shake chicken wings in paper bag with flour to coat well. Brown a few at a time, with onion in oil in large heavy skillet. Stir in soup, water and seasonings. Simmer, covered, 40 to 45 minutes or until tender. Arrange on heated serving platter with toasted split corn bread. Spoon sauce over all.

Crusty Chicken Americana

A crisp brown crust makes this tender chicken appetizing with an Old World flavor.

1½ cups finely crushed potato chips
1 teaspoon salt
¼ teaspoon pepper
½ teaspoon curry powder
⅛ teaspoon ginger

1 3-pound frying chicken, cut up
2 eggs, beaten
¼ cup milk
½ cup butter or margarine, melted

Heat oven to 375° F. Mix potato chips, salt, pepper, curry powder, and ginger. Wash and dry chicken pieces. Combine eggs and milk. Pour butter or margarine in shallow baking dish. Dip chicken pieces in chips, then in egg mixture, then in chips again. Put pieces side by side in butter in dish. Bake 45 minutes.

Turkey-Ham Cranberry Ring

After the holiday is over, combine leftover turkey and ham into a delectable surprise.

1 can (1 pound) jellied cranberry sauce	3 tablespoons orange juice
1 envelope unflavored gelatin	Dash salt
¼ cup cold water	Lettuce greens
1 tablespoon lemon juice	Turkey-Ham Combo (recipe below)

Whip cranberry sauce with rotary beater until smooth. Sprinkle gelatin over mixture of water, lemon, and orange juice. Let stand 5 minutes; dissolve over hot water. Add gelatin mixture and salt to cranberry sauce. Stir until thoroughly blended. Pour into lightly buttered 1-quart mold. Chill until firm. Unmold on lettuce greens. Fill center with Turkey-Ham Combo.

Turkey-Ham Combo

1 cup diced cooked turkey	½ teaspoon salt
¾ cup diced cooked ham	⅛ teaspoon pepper
2½ tablespoons sour cream	1 tablespoon capers
1½ tablespoons mayonnaise	

Combine all ingredients; mix well. Chill thoroughly.

Chicken and Noodles Cacciatore

Thrifty, delicious and well worth the time it takes to prepare it.

1 4- to 5-pound stewing chicken	3½ cups canned tomatoes
3 cups water	8 stuffed olives
Stalk of celery	1 can (3 ounces) sliced mushrooms
1 slice onion	½ cup green pepper, cut in strips
1½ tablespoons salt	⅛ teaspoon pepper
2 tablespoons vegetable oil	¼ teaspoon basil
¼ cup chopped onion	1 package (1 pound) wide noodles
1 clove garlic, minced	

Wash chicken and place in large deep kettle with water, celery, and ¾ teaspoon salt; cover tightly and simmer 3 to 4 hours until tender. Cool. Remove meat and cut in large serving pieces; reserve broth. Heat vegetable oil in large skillet; sauté chopped onion and garlic until soft. Add tomatoes, olives, mushrooms, green pepper, ¼ teaspoon salt, pepper, and basil. Continue cooking over low heat 20 minutes. Skim fat from chicken broth; measure broth and add enough water to make 5 cups; pour into large saucepan. Bring to a boil; add remaining 2½ teaspoons salt, and noodles. Bring to a boil; cook 10 to 15 minutes or until tender. Drain; place in shallow 2-quart baking dish. Heat oven to 350° F. Arrange chicken on noodles; pour sauce over all. Bake 20 minutes. Makes 8 servings.

Fran's Chicken Fricassee

Take advantage of the excellent stocks of poultry on the market and serve chicken often. This popular dish is complemented with a green vegetable, a crisp salad and hot biscuits.

1 2½ - to 3-pound chicken,
   cut into serving pieces
2 tablespoons margarine
1 cup chicken stock or water
1 teaspoon salt

¼ teaspoon pepper
1 bay leaf
1 tablespoon flour
½ cup milk

Brown chicken in margarine in skillet. Pour chicken stock or water over it. Season with salt, pepper, and bay leaf. Cover; simmer until tender, about 55 minutes. Remove chicken to heated serving platter. Strain liquid. Mix flour with water to form paste. Stir into liquid with milk. Cook, over medium heat stirring constantly, until thickened and smooth. Pour over chicken and serve.

Iloilo Chicken

1 chicken for stewing
   (2 to 2½ pounds), cut in pieces
2 tablespoons margarine
2 tablespoons chopped onions
1 cup canned tomatoes
½ cup water
1½ teaspoons salt

⅛ teaspoon pepper
Dash cayenne pepper
½ teaspoon Worcestershire sauce
1 cup fresh lima beans
1 cup fresh corn, cut from cob
1 tablespoon flour
¼ cup tomato juice

Brown chicken in margarine in heavy skillet; remove. Add onions; sauté until lightly browned. Add chicken, tomatoes, water, salt, pepper, and cayenne. Simmer, covered, 1 to 1½ hours, or until chicken is nearly tender. Add Worcestershire sauce and lima beans; continue cooking 20 minutes. Add corn. Blend flour with tomato juice; add to stew, stirring vigorously until thickened. Cook 5 minutes.

Viennese Chicken

To achieve elegance with ease, use chicken, the friendly stand-by of family cookery, for this elegant dish—and it's also economical.

2 2- to 2½-pound broilers, quartered	¼ teaspoon thyme
1½ teaspoons salt	2 tablespoons flour
¼ teaspoon pepper	1½ cups chicken broth
½ cup margarine	Almond Pilaf (recipe below)
½ teaspoon tarragon	

Sprinkle chicken pieces with salt and pepper. Melt margarine in large heavy skillet; stir in herbs. Add chicken and brown on both sides, about 25 to 30 minutes. Remove chicken; keep warm. Blend flour into drippings. Add broth; cook, stirring constantly, until mixture thickens and comes to a boil. To serve, mound Almond Pilaf in center of heated serving platter; arrange chicken pieces around it. Serve with sauce. Makes 8 servings.

Almond Pilaf

¼ cup margarine	1½ cups diced celery
½ cup slivered almonds	3 bouillon cubes
1 can (6 ounces) sliced mushrooms,	½ teaspoon salt
reserve liquid	1½ cups rice
Water	

Melt margarine in heavy saucepan. Add almonds and sauté until lightly browned. Drain mushrooms; add enough water to mushroom liquid to make 3 cups. Add to skillet with celery, bouillon cubes, and salt; bring to boil. Cover; reduce heat and add rice slowly. Simmer 14 minutes. Fluff with fork; add mushrooms. Cover; let stand 10 minutes.

FISH: A BUDGET-SMART CATCH

Most homemakers pass up fish because they don't know how to prepare it. Before frozen fish came into being, only the people living on the coast or near lakes were able to find it, and the rich, who considered it a luxury because it was scarce, included it on their menus as a delicacy. Most of us took our marine bill of fare for granted and usually prepared it one way—fried.

But there is nothing casual about American seafood specialties. From the Pilgrims on, traditional seafood cookery has been handed down from generation to generation along with the treasured tureens and precious recipes from the Old World and, today, homemakers are rediscovering this food. The popularity of fish is universal.

Fish are not only delicious but nutritious as well. An average serving of fish or shellfish provides nearly all the animal protein you need each day to help build and repair body tissue. In addition, fish are valuable sources of minerals and also supply essential vitamins.

For economy, versatility and convenience nothing beats a can of tuna or salmon and, although the flavor, texture and appearance of the fish and shellfish vary according to their species, the fundamental rules for cooking seafoods are few and easy to follow, be it baking, broiling, frying, poaching, or sautéing, and the results are really gratifying.

Broiled Salmon Steaks

1 pound salmon steaks	⅛ teaspoon pepper
2 tablespoons margarine	2 egg yolks, slightly beaten
½ cup diced cucumber	5 tablespoons vegetable oil
1 tablespoon chopped onion	5 tablespoons milk
¼ cup lemon juice	1 tablespoon flour
2 tablespoons chopped pimiento	¾ teaspoon dry mustard
1 teaspoon salt	1½ teaspoons sugar

Place salmon steaks on baking sheet; dot with margarine. Broil until lightly browned; turn and broil on other side. Remove to heated serving platter; keep warm. Combine cucumber, onion, lemon juice, pimiento, salt, and pepper in top of double boiler; beat until well blended. Cook over boiling water 10 minutes or until cucumber is blanched. Add egg yolks and oil; stir until well blended. Add remaining ingredients; cook, stirring constantly until thickened. Pour over salmon steaks.

Cod Steaks Au Champignons

4 fresh codfish steaks,
   ¾ inch thick
1 small onion, chopped
¼ pound mushrooms, chopped
6 tablespoons boiling water
3 tablespoons margarine

3 tablespoons flour
2 cups milk
1 teaspoon salt
¼ teaspoon pepper
½ teaspoon paprika

Heat oven to 350° F. Grease a shallow baking dish. Place steaks in dish. Sauté onion and mushrooms in margarine until soft; add water and stir. Combine flour with milk. Add to onion mixture. Heat to boiling, stirring constantly, until smooth and thickened. Add salt and pepper. Pour over fish. Sprinkle with paprika. Bake 30 to 35 minutes or until tender.

Codfish Rabbit

A can of codfish goes a long way these days; seasoned and cooked, it's a gourmet's dish.

1 can (11½ ounces) ready-cooked
   salt codfish
1½ tablespoons margarine
1½ tablespoons flour
¼ teaspoon minced onion
Dash cayenne pepper

1½ cups milk
1 cup grated process
   American cheese
1 egg, beaten
4 slices white bread, toasted
4 sprigs parsley

Drain codfish. Melt butter in double boiler; stir in flour, onion, and cayenne. Add milk; cook, stirring constantly, until thickened. Add cheese and codfish; cook until cheese melts. Stir in egg; cook 5 minutes longer. Serve on toast; garnish with parsley.

Carp Chowder Deluxe

2 medium onions, finely chopped
2 tablespoons chopped parsley
2 tablespoons shortening
2 tablespoons flour
3 cups milk

2 cups flaked, cooked whitefish,
   carp, or haddock
2 cups diced, cooked potatoes
1½ teaspoons salt
¼ teaspoon pepper

Sauté onions and parsley in shortening in skillet until tender. Remove from heat; blend in flour. Slowly stir in milk. Cook, stirring constantly, until smooth and thickened. Add fish, potatoes, salt, and pepper; heat thoroughly.

Red Snapper with Shrimp Stuffing

If the high cost of shrimp deprives you of its use, plan to have a small amount to use for stuffing a fish—it will be delicious and different.

1 red snapper (3 to 4 pounds),
   dressed
1¾ teaspoons salt
¼ cup chopped celery
2 tablespoons chopped onion
2 tablespoons bacon drippings,
   melted

3 slices cooked crisp bacon,
   crumbled
1 cup soft bread crumbs
½ cup chopped cooked shrimp
1 egg, slightly beaten
⅛ teaspoon pepper

Heat oven to 350° F. Rub 1 teaspoon salt inside and outside of fish. Sauté celery and onion in 1 tablespoon bacon drippings until soft. Add remaining ¾ teaspoon salt and remaining ingredients; mix well. Stuff fish with shrimp mixture. Fasten together with skewers. Brush with bacon drippings. Place in shallow baking pan. Bake 40 minutes or until fish flakes easily when tested with a fork. Makes 6 to 8 servings.

Baked Fish Espagnole

4 2-inch slices whitefish
¾ teaspoon salt
⅛ teaspoon pepper
⅛ teaspoon paprika
⅛ teaspoon mace
1½ teaspoons vegetable oil
1 medium onion, thinly sliced
1 tablespoon pimiento

4 thick slices tomato
2 tablespoons chopped green onion
¾ cup thinly sliced fresh
   mushrooms
3 tablespoons white wine
¾ cup dry bread crumbs
5 tablespoons margarine

Heat oven to 350° F. Sprinkle fish slices with mixture of salt, pepper, paprika, and mace. Spread bottom of 1½-quart baking dish with oil. Place onion slices and pimiento in bottom of baking dish. Arrange fish slices on top. Cover each piece of fish with a tomato slice; sprinkle with green onion. Scatter mushrooms and pour wine over all. Brown bread crumbs in margarine; sprinkle over top of fish. Bake 30 to 35 minutes or until fish is tender.

Shrimp Casserole Vita

6 hard-cooked eggs
1 cup cooked shrimp,
  cut in half lengthwise
1 package (10 ounces) frozen
  mixed vegetables
1 cup chopped celery
¼ cup chopped onion

¼ cup margarine
¼ cup flour
2 cups milk
¾ teaspoon salt
⅛ teaspoon pepper
1 cup shredded process
  American cheese

Heat oven to 350° F. Butter a shallow 1½-quart baking pan. Cut eggs in half lengthwise; arrange in pan. Add shrimp. Cook vegetables with celery according to package directions; drain. Combine with onion. Melt margarine in saucepan; add flour and blend. Add milk; cook, stirring constantly, until thickened and smooth. Add half the cheese and stir over low heat until melted. Add vegetables, salt, and pepper. Pour over eggs and shrimp. Sprinkle with remaining cheese. Bake 20 to 25 minutes or until heated through and top is lightly browned. Makes 6 servings.

Ring-A-Tuna

An ideal buffet dish for company or a Sunday supper family treat.

½ package (8 ounces) egg noodles
2 eggs, slightly beaten
1 cup milk
¾ cup grated sharp Cheddar cheese
1¼ teaspoons salt
½ teaspoon Worcestershire sauce
¼ teaspoon pepper
¼ teaspoon Tabasco

1 cup Medium Cream Sauce
  (recipe below)
1 can (7 ounces) flaked tuna
¼ cup minced onion
¾ teaspoon margarine
1½ teaspoons minced pimiento
1 cup cooked peas

Cook egg noodles according to package directions; drain and set aside. Combine eggs with milk, cheese, ¾ teaspoon salt, and half the Worcestershire sauce, pepper, and Tabasco. Add noodles to milk mixture; mix well. Pour into greased ring mold. Let stand in refrigerator 15 minutes. Heat oven to 350° F. Set ring mold in pan of hot water. Bake 40 to 45 minutes or until set. Combine Cream Sauce with ½ teaspoon salt and remaining Worcestershire sauce, pepper, and Tabasco. Fold in tuna. Sauté onion in margarine until tender. Add to tuna mixture with pimiento and peas; simmer 10 minutes until heated through. Unmold noodle ring onto heated serving platter and fill center with tuna sauce.

Medium Cream Sauce

3 tablespoons margarine   1 cup milk
3 tablespoons flour

   Melt margarine in saucepan. Slowly, blend in flour. Add milk, a little at a time, stirring constantly until thickened to a medium consistency.

Tuna and Cheese Trianon

1 can (10½ ounces) cream   1 teaspoon cold water
   of mushroom soup   Dash cayenne pepper
¼ cup milk   4 baked patty shells
8 ounces pasteurized process   1 can (7 ounces) tuna
   cheese spread   ¾ cup cooked peas
½ teaspoon dry mustard

   Combine soup, milk, and cheese spread in saucepan; cook over low heat until cheese melts, stirring occasionally. Mix mustard with cold water; add to saucepan. Add cayenne. Drain tuna; flake with fork. Add to cheese sauce. Mix lightly and continue cooking over low heat. Place patty shells on serving plate. Stir peas into tuna mixture; heat thoroughly. Fill each shell with tuna mixture. Serve immediately.

Tuna Fish Pie

   Golden cheese strips are crisscrossed to form a latticed crust.

2 tablespoons margarine   1½ teaspoons minced onion
¼ cup flour   1 cup cooked peas
1 cup hot milk   1 cup cooked carrots
1 cup vegetable stock   1 can (7 ounces) tuna
1 teaspoon salt   Cheese Strips (recipe below)
⅛ teaspoon pepper

   Heat oven to 375° F. Melt margarine in top of double boiler. Add flour; blend. Add milk and vegetable stock gradually, stirring until smooth. Add salt, pepper, and onion; continue cooking, stirring occasionally, until thickened. Add peas, carrots, and tuna fish. Turn into 1½-quart baking dish. Arrange Cheese Strips on top in crosscross or lattice fashion. Bake 30 minutes.

Cheese Strips

1 cup flour	2 to 3 tablespoons shortening
1¼ teaspoons double-acting	5 tablespoons milk
baking powder	½ cup grated process
½ scant teaspoon salt	American cheese

Combine flour, baking powder and salt. Cut in shortening until mixture looks like coarse meal, using pastry blender and starting with 2 tablespoons shortening, adding more, if necessary. Add milk, mixing until a soft dough is formed. Add cheese; blend. Turn dough onto lightly floured board and knead half a minute. Roll or pat ½ inch thick. Cut into 1-inch strips.

Tuna Balane

For this inexpensive feast, serve lima beans with the tuna croquettes, a tossed green salad, and a chocolate pudding

1 cup dry bread crumbs	1 cup shredded carrots
½ cup milk	½ teaspoon salt
1 can (7 ounces) tuna	⅛ teaspoon pepper
1 tablespoon minced onion	Green Island Sauce (recipe below)
½ cup finely chopped celery	

Soften bread crumbs in milk. Add tuna fish, onion, celery, carrots, salt, and pepper; mix well. Refrigerate 2 hours. Heat oven to 400° F. Shape tuna mixture into 8 small croquettes; place on greased shallow baking pan. Bake 20 minutes. Serve with sauce.

Green Island Sauce

2 tablespoons margarine
2 tablespoons flour
½ teaspoon salt

⅛ teaspoon pepper
1 cup milk
¼ cup chopped parsley

Melt margarine in saucepan; add flour, salt, and pepper. Stir until well blended and bubbly. Remove from heat. Gradually stir in milk; return to heat. Cook, stirring constantly, until smooth and thickened. Add parsley; stir. Makes 1 cup.

Oceania Fish Bake

¼ cup chopped onion
2 tablespoons margarine
1 can (10½ ounces)
　condensed cream of celery soup
½ cup milk
1 cup shredded sharp Cheddar

2 cups cooked macaroni
1 can (7 ounces) tuna,
　drained and flaked
2 tablespoons buttered bread
　crumbs

Heat oven to 350° F. Sauté onion in margarine until tender. Stir in soup, milk, ¾ cup cheese, macaroni, and fish. Pour into a 1½-quart casserole. Top with bread crumbs; sprinkle remaining cheese. Bake 25 to 30 minutes or until lightly browned and bubbling.

Deep-Sea Timbales

Applause will ring the louder when you serve an accompaniment of buttered peas and onions, creamed carrots, and canned peaches.

1 egg, well beaten
1 can (7 ounces) chunk-style tuna
¼ teaspoon salt
⅛ teaspoon pepper
⅛ teaspoon celery salt
½ teaspoon paprika

½ teaspoon Worcestershire sauce
1½ teaspoons lemon juice
¾ cup milk
½ cup uncooked quick-cooking
　rolled oats

Heat oven to 350° F. Grease 4 custard cups. Combine all ingredients; mix well. Turn into custard cups. Bake 50 to 55 minutes or until firm to touch. Unmold; serve plain or with hot tomato sauce.

Curried Fillets

3 tablespoons margarine
2 tablespoons onion, chopped
½ teaspoon salt
⅛ teaspoon pepper
¾ teaspoon curry powder
½ cup white wine

1½ pounds flounder fillets
4 large whole mushrooms
1½ tablespoons flour
5 tablespoons milk
4 large slices tomato

Heat oven to 350° F. Melt 1½ tablespoons margarine in skillet; add onion, salt, pepper, curry, and 2 tablespoons wine. Cook fish in wine mixture 2 minutes; gently transfer to shallow 2-quart baking dish. Pour skillet drippings over fish. Melt remaining 1½ tablespoons margarine; sauté mushrooms, remove and set aside. Add flour to skillet drippings, stirring until blended. Gradually stir in milk and remaining wine; cook, stirring constantly until slightly thickened. Pour over fish; top with tomato slices and mushrooms. Bake 20 minutes.

Fish Puff Pacifico

A special fish with a heavenly soufflé sauce to boost your reputation and your budget.

4 cups cooked rice
1 cup grated Cheddar cheese
¼ cup milk
1 egg, separated; reserve white
2 tablespoons chopped parsley
1 tablespoon grated onion
1 pound cod fillets,
    cut into 4 servings

4 cups hot water
2 slices lemon
1 slice onion
¼ teaspoon pepper
1 bay leaf
Soufflé Sauce (recipe below)

Heat oven to 350° F. Grease a 2-quart baking dish. Combine rice, cheese, milk, 1 egg yolk, parsley, and onion, in baking dish; press mixture lightly to sides and bottom to line dish. Cover; bake 15 minutes. Lower fish into hot water seasoned with lemon, onion, pepper, and bay leaf. Cover; simmer 10 minutes or until fish flakes easily. Lift out with slotted spoon; drain well. Arrange fish in center of baking dish. Increase oven temperature to 475° F. Top fish with Soufflé Sauce; bake 10 minutes or until puffed and golden.

Soufflé Sauce
1 egg white
¼ cup mayonnaise
1 tablespoon sweet pickle relish
1 tablespoon chopped parsley

2 teaspoons lemon juice
¼ teaspoon salt
Dash cayenne

Beat egg white until stiff. Combine all ingredients; fold into egg white.

Fish Turbans

Try this thrifty meat-skipper recipe for a change of pace.

1 package frozen flounder
  fillets or 4 fresh fillets
6 slices bread, crumbled
¼ cup diced celery
¼ cup chopped green pepper

2 tablespoons minced onion
1 teaspoon salt
⅛ teaspoon pepper
½ cup mayonnaise
3 tablespoons milk

Heat oven to 425° F. Butter muffin tins. Cut 3 fillets lengthwise in half and trim to line sides of pans. Finely cut remaining fish; combine with remaining ingredients. Fill centers of fish-lined muffin tins with mixture. Bake 20 to 25 minutes. Carefully turn onto heated serving platter. Makes 6 servings.

Tsi Suang's Fish

1 package (12 ounces) frozen
  fish fillets, thawed
1 egg, beaten
1 tablespoon flour
2 tablespoons vegetable oil
¼ cup ketchup
2 tablespoons sugar

2 tablespoons vinegar
½ teaspoon salt
⅛ teaspoon pepper
¼ cup minced onion
¾ cup chopped celery
2 cups hot cooked rice

Separate fillets and cut into serving pieces. Combine egg with flour; coat fillets with mixture. Sauté on both sides in hot oil until browned. Combine ketchup, sugar, vinegar, salt, and pepper; mix well. Pour over cooked fish; bring to a boil. Add onion and celery; simmer 2 to 3 minutes. Serve over rice.

Flounder Fillets Almondine

A little fish goes a long way toward eating pleasure when you use this savory stuffing to augment the portions.

1½ pounds flounder fillets,
   fresh or frozen
½ cup margarine
¼ cup chopped onion
4 cups soft bread crumbs
¼ cup blanched almonds, slivered

2 tablespoons lemon juice
1 teaspoon salt
⅛ teaspoon pepper
2 tablespoons softened butter
½ teaspoon paprika

Heat oven to 375° F. Let fillets thaw. Melt margarine in saucepan. Sauté onion until tender. Add bread crumbs, almonds, lemon juice, salt, and pepper. Place half the fillets close together in greased 1½-quart baking dish. Cover with stuffing, then with remaining fillets. Spread top of fish with softened butter; sprinkle with paprika. Bake 15 minutes or until fish flakes easily with a fork.

Dilly Onion Sole

¼ cup melted margarine
1 tablespoon minced onion
1 teaspoon dill weed
2 tablespoons chopped parsley
2 tablespoons lemon juice

1 teaspoon paprika
½ teaspoon salt
1 pound white fish fillets
4 lemon wedges

Heat oven to 325° F. Grease a shallow baking dish. Combine margarine, onion, dill weed, parsley, lemon juice, paprika, and salt; mix well. Place fish in baking dish; spoon on sauce. Bake 20 minutes or until fish is tender, basting occasionally. Serve with lemon wedges.

Batter-Baked Fillets

⅔ cup pancake mix
¾ teaspoon salt
1 egg, slightly beaten
1½ teaspoons vegetable oil
¾ cup milk
Dash Tabasco

2 tablespoons melted margarine
2 cups crushed shredded corn
   cereal
2 packages (12 ounces each)
   frozen fish fillets, thawed

Heat oven to 400° F. Combine pancake mix and salt in bowl. Mix together egg, oil, milk, and Tabasco; add to dry ingredients and beat until smooth. Combine margarine and cereal in flat pan. Dip fillets in pancake mix then roll in cereal mixture. Bake on ungreased cookie sheet 15 minutes. Turn; bake 10 minutes longer or until crumbs are lightly browned. Makes 6 servings.

Fishburgers Acapulco

Serve these in hamburger buns or as an entrée topped with tomato sauce.

1 pound fish fillets
1 medium green pepper, chopped
3 medium onions, chopped
2 cups soft bread crumbs

¾ teaspoon salt
¼ teaspoon pepper
3 tablespoons shortening

Bone fish; put through food chopper or chop finely with knife. Combine with green pepper, onions, bread crumbs, salt, and pepper; mix well. Shape into patties about 4 inches in diameter. Brown on both sides in shortening in skillet over moderate heat 10 to 15 minutes. Makes 8 patties.

Florida Fish Mousse

1½ cups water
1 medium onion, sliced
¾ teaspoon Tabasco
2 teaspoons salt
1½ pounds fillets of
    fish (sole or flounder)
1 envelope unflavored gelatin

6 tablespoons (½ can) frozen
    grapefruit juice concentrate
½ cup mayonnaise
1 cup heavy cream, whipped
Salad greens
Grapefruit sections

Combine water, onion, ¼ teaspoon Tabasco, and 1 teaspoon salt in large skillet. Add fish fillets; bring to a boil. Reduce heat; simmer, covered, 6 to 8 minutes, or until fish flakes easily with a fork. Remove fish from liquid; cool. Strain stock; measure ¾ cup and cool. Flake fish as finely as possible, removing any bones. Sprinkle gelatin on cooled stock in saucepan; stir over medium heat until dissolved. Stir in remaining ½ teaspoon Tabasco, 1 teaspoon salt, grapefruit juice concentrate, and mayonnaise; beat until smooth. Chill until slightly thickened. Stir in flaked fish. Gently fold in whipped cream. Turn into 1½-quart mold; chill until firm. Unmold on salad greens; garnish with grapefruit sections. Makes 8 servings.

Bedeviled Fillets

Fish dishes need fixings—and the tangy flavors of this dish make an elegant seafood creation.

1 teaspoon minced parsley	2 teaspoons curry powder
1 tablespoon Worcestershire sauce	1 tablespoon flour
1 teaspoon celery salt	½ teaspoon salt
1½ cups tomato juice	⅛ teaspoon cayenne
1 pound fish fillets	1 teaspoon thyme
3 tablespoons margarine	¼ cup soft bread crumbs
1 cup chopped onions	

Combine parsley, Worcestershire sauce, celery salt, and tomato juice in saucepan; bring to boil. Reduce heat; add fish and simmer 10 to 15 minutes or until tender. Remove and flake fish with fork, saving tomato juice mixture. Heat oven to 425° F. Melt margarine in skillet; add onions and sauté until soft. Add curry powder and flour and cook, stirring constantly, over low heat until bubbly. Remove from heat; gradually add hot tomato juice mixture, salt, cayenne, and thyme. Return to heat; cook until thickened, stirring constantly. Add flaked fish; mix well. Turn into 4 individual baking dishes. Sprinkle with bread crumbs. Bake 10 to 15 minutes or until lightly browned.

Kedgeree

This traditional Indian dish has as many variations as there are states in India.

½ cup rice	½ teaspoon pickling spice
½ teaspoon salt	2 teaspoons curry powder
1 cup water	½ teaspoon Worcestershire sauce
2 cups frozen fish fillets,	1 hard-cooked egg, chopped
cut up	1 hard-cooked egg, sliced
½ teaspoon onion flakes	1 tablespoon chopped parsley

Place rice, salt and water in 1-quart saucepan; bring to a vigorous boil. Reduce heat; simmer, covered, 14 minutes. Remove from heat; let covered rice stand. Heat oven to 400° F. Butter a 1-quart baking dish. Place fish, onion flakes, and pickling spice in saucepan; cover with water; bring to boil. Reduce heat; simmer 12 minutes or until fish flakes easily with fork. Remove fish; flake, add to rice and add curry powder. Blend in Worcestershire sauce and chopped egg. Turn into baking dish. Cover; bake 10 minutes. Serve garnished with hard-cooked egg slices and chopped parsley.

Broiled Fillets Florentine

1 package (7 ounces) frozen
   chopped spinach
¼ cup minced onion
2 tablespoons margarine
1 pound fresh haddock fillets
   or thawed frozen fillets

1 teaspoon lemon juice
1 tablespoon butter
¼ cup milk
1 cup process Cheddar cheese,
   grated

Cook spinach according to package directions; drain well. Sauté onion in margarine; add to spinach and mix. Arrange fillets side by side in greased shallow baking dish. Sprinkle with lemon juice; dot with butter. Broil 2 inches below heat 8 to 10 minutes or until fish flakes easily with fork, without turning. Heat milk in top of double boiler; stir in cheese until melted and smooth sauce is formed. Arrange spinach over fish; pour sauce over all. Broil until golden brown.

Magic with Meatless Dishes

Budget shot to pieces? And no meat left in the larder? Don't be upset, for gourmets the world over have used meatless main dishes, now and then, as a basis for some of their most famed recipes.

In a category by themselves these *spécialités de la maison* emerge as triumphant entrées. The wise homemaker, when serving a meatless main dish, simply shrugs her shoulders and explains that a change of diet now and then is very good for everyone. And truly it is.

Eggs, in combination with other foods, are enormously versatile; cheese, one of the oldest foods known, makes an elegant main dish; and the many forms of pasta, teamed up with tomato sauce, cheese, and vegetables can make a solo appearance which will guarantee to satisfy the heartiest of appetites.

Puffy Omelet with Spanish Sauce

6 eggs, separated
½ teaspoon salt
⅛ teaspoon pepper
Dash cayenne

6 tablespoons hot water
1½ tablespoons margarine
4 sprigs of parsley
Spanish Sauce (recipe below)

Heat oven to 350° F. Prepare Sauce. Beat egg whites until stiff. In separate bowl, cream egg yolks until thick and fluffy. Add salt, pepper, cayenne, and hot water; mix well. Fold egg-yolk mixture into beaten egg whites. In heavy frying pan heat margarine; pour in egg mixture and spread evenly over bottom of pan. Cook over low heat until delicately browned on bottom. Place pan in oven for 10 minutes or until omelet springs back when lightly pressed. Pour hot Spanish Sauce over half of omelet; fold over other half. Turn omelet onto heated serving platter; garnish with parsley.

Spanish Sauce

3 tablespoons margarine
¼ cup chopped green pepper
¼ chopped onion
1 cup canned tomatoes

¼ cup chopped celery
¼ cup chopped mushrooms
½ teaspoon salt
⅛ teaspoon pepper

Heat margarine in heavy skillet; add green pepper and onion and sauté until soft. Add remaining ingredients; cook over low heat 10 minutes.

Eggs Ensenada

3 bacon slices
2 tablespoons margarine
¼ cup finely chopped green pepper
6 eggs
1 teaspoon salt

½ teaspoon chili powder
1 can (1 pound) tomatoes,
   drained and chopped
¼ cup finely chopped ripe olives

Sauté bacon until crisp; remove to absorbent paper. Crumble. Discard bacon drippings. Heat margarine in skillet; sauté green pepper until tender, about 5 minutes. Beat eggs in small bowl with salt and chili powder; pour over green pepper in skillet. Cook, stirring occasionally, until eggs are partially set, about 3 minutes. Add tomatoes and olives; cook, stirring, until eggs are set, 3 minutes longer. Top with bacon and serve.

Egg Croquettes Malfel

1 can (10½ ounces) condensed
    cream of celery soup
8 hard-cooked eggs, finely chopped
¾ cup fine dry bread crumbs
2 tablespoons minced parsley
2 tablespoons minced onion

1 tablespoon minced celery
½ teaspoon salt
⅛ teaspoon pepper
2 tablespoons shortening
⅓ cup milk
½ teaspoon thyme

Mix 3 tablespoons soup with eggs, ¼ cup bread crumbs, parsley, onion, celery, salt, and pepper; chill 1 hour. Form into 8 croquettes. Roll in remaining bread crumbs. Fry croquettes slowly in shortening until browned on all sides. Combine remaining soup with milk and thyme; heat. Serve as sauce over croquettes.

Curried Egg Divine

6 eggs, at room temperature
¼ cup shortening
¼ cup flour
1¼ teaspoons curry powder

1 teaspoon salt
4 cups milk
3 cups cooked rice
2 tablespoons fine bread crumbs

Heat oven to 350° F. Grease a 12-inch shallow baking pan. Have eggs at room temperature. Melt shortening in skillet; blend in flour, curry powder, and salt. Slowly add milk, stirring constantly; cook until thickened and smooth. Pile cooked rice in baking pan. Make 6 depressions in the surface of the rice. Break egg into each depression. Pour curry sauce over eggs and rice. Sprinkle with bread crumbs. Bake 25 minutes or until eggs are set. Makes 6 servings.

Spinach and Eggs Garnis

A nourishing dish made quickly with fresh spinach and macaroni.

2 pounds spinach
Water
3 cups cooked macaroni

1 cup white sauce
6 poached eggs
6 slices process American cheese

Remove stems from spinach and cook in very little water until just tender. Drain; chop fine. Combine macaroni and white sauce; heat thoroughly. Heat oven to 375° F. Divide macaroni equally into 6 individual baking casseroles. Top with spinach. Place 1 poached egg on top of spinach; cover with cheese. Bake 6 to 8 minutes or until cheese is bubbly. Makes 6 servings.

Country Omelet

A hearty dish, good also for supper or brunch.

2 cups cooked, diced, potatoes	2 tablespoons light cream
3 slices diced bacon	¾ teaspoon salt
¼ cup minced onion	¼ teaspoon pepper
4 eggs, separated	1 tablespoon chopped parsley

Brown potatoes, bacon, and onion in skillet. Remove and set aside to cool. Beat egg yolks slightly; add milk, salt, pepper and chopped parsley. Blend into potato mixture. Beat egg whites until stiff; fold into egg yolk mixture. Heat skillet on high heat. If there is not enough grease left from frying the bacon, add 1 or 2 tablespoons of shortening to skillet. Pour in egg mixture. Reduce heat; cook over low heat until lightly browned on the bottom, about 15 minutes. Brown top slowly under broiler. Serve immediately.

Eggs Divan

Eggs are one of the best foods the homemaker can serve her family. When the price is reasonable, plan to serve a meatless treat such as this dish.

1 package (10 ounces) frozen broccoli	⅛ teaspoon pepper
6 hard-cooked eggs	1 envelope cheese sauce mix
3 tablespoons mayonnaise	1 cup milk
1 teaspoon prepared mustard	1 tablespoon margarine
1 teaspoon vinegar	¼ teaspoon paprika
¼ teaspoon onion salt	

Cook broccoli until just tender according to package directions; drain well. Heat oven to 375° F. Cut cooked eggs in half, crosswise. Remove yolks; force through a sieve. Add mayonnaise, mustard, vinegar, onion salt, and pepper. Refill centers of egg whites. Arrange broccoli pieces in shallow baking pan. Place eggs, stuffed ends up, on broccoli pieces. Prepare cheese sauce mix, using 1 cup milk as envelope directs. Add margarine. Spoon sauce over eggs and broccoli. Sprinkle with paprika. Bake 24 minutes or until bubbly hot.

Continental Pancakes

In France the specialty of the day is a vanilla flavored pancake. They make the crêpes paper-thin so they can be folded or rolled. Try this for brunch or lunch.

3 tablespoons margarine
1½ cups milk
1½ teaspoons vanilla
3 eggs, well beaten
¾ cup flour

1½ teaspoons baking powder
¾ teaspoon salt
Cottage Cheese Filling
    (recipe below)
2 tablespoons marmalade

Combine margarine and milk; heat to scalding. Cool slightly. Add vanilla and beat milk mixture into eggs. Combine flour, baking powder and salt. Gradually beat into egg mixture. Using only enough batter to cover bottom, pour into a 5-inch, lightly greased, hot skillet. Tilt skillet to spread evenly. Cook 1 minute or until browned underneath. Loosen from bottom of skillet with spatula. Flip to cook other side. Spread with Cottage Cheese Filling. Roll up pancakes and stack them on heated serving platter. Spoon marmalade over top. Makes 2 dozen pancakes.

Cottage Cheese Filling

2 cups cottage cheese
⅓ cup sour cream
3 tablespoons sugar

1 teaspoon vanilla
Dash salt

Combine all ingredients; mix well.

Gnocchi

½ pound cottage cheese
½ cup melted margarine
¾ cup grated Parmesan cheese
½ cup flour

3 egg yolks
½ teaspoon salt
Pinch nutmeg
Boiling salted water

Press cottage cheese through fine sieve into a bowl; add ¼ cup margarine, ¼ cup Parmesan cheese, flour, egg yolks, salt, and nutmeg. Mix well. Bring large kettle of salted water to a gentle boil. Drop gnocchi mixture into the water by teaspoonfuls, or force through pastry bag fitted with plain tip, snipping with scissors into 1-inch pieces. Cook 5 to 6 minutes; remove gnocchi with slotted spoon. Drain on absorbent paper. Heat oven to 350° F.

Turn gnocchi into 1-quart shallow baking dish. Pour remaining margarine over top; sprinkle with remaining Parmesan cheese. Bake 10 minutes, then brown 3 minutes under broiler. Makes 6 servings.

Spaghetti Loaf

An appetizing meatless main dish takes on a delicate richness with cheese and eggs.

2 cups spaghetti, broken
   in 2-inch pieces
1 clove garlic
Salted boiling water
½ pound process American cheese
1⅔ cups (1 tall can)
   evaporated milk

2 eggs, well beaten
¾ teaspoon salt
¼ cup finely chopped parsley
1 tablespoon grated onion

Heat oven to 350° F. Grease a 9 × 5 × 3-inch loaf pan. Cook spaghetti and garlic in salted boiling water until tender. Drain; discard garlic. Melt cheese in evaporated milk in top of double boiler. Add 3 tablespoons hot mixture to eggs; blend well and return to cheese sauce, stirring constantly until well blended. Add salt, parsley, and onion. Remove from heat. Add cooked spaghetti; mix well. Turn into loaf pan. Bake 1 hour.

Southern Peanut Loaf

Some days, you *can* win. If you find that your budget has been over-stretched and you're looking for high protein meat substitutes, try this delicious meatless loaf.

1¼ cups crunchy peanut butter
1½ cups cooked lima beans
¼ cup onion, finely chopped
½ teaspoon basil
1 teaspoon salt
¼ teaspoon pepper
1¼ cups soft bread crumbs

1½ cups grated process
   American cheese
1½ cups milk
2 tablespoons chopped parsley
4 eggs, well beaten
1½ cups tomato sauce, heated

Heat oven to 350° F. Grease a 9 × 5 × 3-inch loaf pan. Combine all ingredients, except tomato sauce; mix well. Turn into loaf pan. Bake 40 to 45 minutes. Unmold on platter; serve hot with tomato sauce. Makes 8 servings.

Blue Cheese Garlic Bread

¼ cup blue cheese
¼ cup margarine

½ clove garlic, minced
1 loaf French bread

Heat oven to 400° F. Mix together cheese and margarine; blend well. Add garlic. Slice bread diagonally, not quite through bottom crust. Spread one side of each slice with mixture. Heat in oven 10 to 15 minutes or until hot and crusty. Serve with cottage cheese and a tossed green salad for a quick and economical meal.

Fresh Garden Loaf

1 pound spinach
½ pound green beans
½ pound shelled walnuts
1 large onion, quartered
2 carrots, cut in pieces
1 celery stalk, cut in pieces
1 cup soft bread crumbs
1 can (15½ ounces) baked beans

3 eggs, slightly beaten
1 tablespoon vegetable oil
2 teaspoons salt
¼ teaspoon pepper
¼ teaspoon paprika
½ teaspoon Worcestershire sauce
½ cup crushed potato chips
½ cup water

Heat oven to 350° F. Grease a shallow baking pan. Wash green vegetables; put through food grinder or chop together with nuts, onion, carrots, celery, and crumbs; mash beans and blend into vegetable mixture. Add eggs, oil, and seasonings; blend well. Shape into an 8-inch loaf; place in baking pan. Sprinkle with potato chip crumbs. Bake 1 hour or until loaf is firm, adding ½ cup water by tablespoonfuls while loaf is cooking. Makes 6 servings.

Rice Griddle Cakes

1½ cups flour
3 teaspoons baking powder
1½ teaspoons salt
2 tablespoons sugar
3 eggs, beaten
2 cups milk

3 tablespoons melted margarine
1½ cups cooked rice
1 jar (16 ounces) process
   cheese spread
8 pitted black olives, chopped

Combine flour, baking powder, salt, and sugar. Combine eggs and milk; add to flour mixture. Stir until smooth. Add margarine and rice; mix well. Cook on hot, lightly greased griddle about ⅛ cup mixture per pancake. Heat cheese spread; blend in chopped olives. Serve as sauce over griddle cakes. Makes 18 cakes, about 6 servings.

Chow Yong Medley

½ cup margarine
1 cup thinly sliced onions
1 cup diced celery
½ cup thinly sliced cucumbers
1 pound sliced mushrooms
4 cups coarsely chopped
  Chinese cabbage

1 teaspoon cornstarch
½ teaspoon salt
2 tablespoons cold water
2 cups cooked rice
1 teaspoon sugar
1½ teaspoons soy sauce
1 can (6 ounces) chow mein noodles

Melt margarine in large saucepan; add onions, celery, cucumbers, mushrooms, and cabbage. Cook 5 to 7 minutes or until just tender, tossing constantly with fork. Combine cornstarch, salt, and water; mix well into vegetables. Add rice; cook over low heat until thoroughly heated, tossing constantly. Add sugar and soy sauce; simmer 3 minutes. Serve over chow mein noodles. Makes 6 servings.

Stuffed Pepper Boats

A quick, economical and delicious dish without meat.

2 large peppers, cut lengthwise
1¼ cups cooked rice
½ pound process American
  cheese, cubed

1 can (10½ ounces) cream
  of tomato soup

Heat oven to 350° F. Cut peppers; remove seeds and parboil 5 minutes. Drain. Combine rice, cheese, and ½ of tomato soup. Fill peppers with rice mixture. Place peppers in shallow baking pan. Pour remaining ½ of tomato soup around pepper boats. Bake 30 minutes.

Spaghettini Loaf

⅓ pound spaghettini
Boiling salted water
2 tablespoons margarine
3 eggs
1 cup milk
1 cup grated process Cheddar cheese
1¼ cups coarse cracker crumbs
1 teaspoon minced onion

1 medium green pepper, chopped
2 pimientos, sliced
1 tablespoon minced parsley
¾ teaspoon salt
1 tablespoon sesame seeds
2 stuffed green olives, halved
1½ cups hot tomato sauce

Break spaghettini into 3-inch pieces and cook in rapidly boiling water according to package directions; drain. Melt margarine in 9 × 5 × 3-inch loaf pan. Heat oven to 350° F. Beat eggs until light and fluffy; add spaghettini and remaining ingredients, except stuffed green olives and tomato sauce; mix well. Turn mixture into loaf pan. Bake 45 minutes. Turn onto heated serving platter. Serve with tomato sauce and garnish with olives.

Green Bean Tetrazzini

1 pound package spaghetti
1 pound fresh, cooked,
    sliced green beans
1 can (10½ ounces) condensed
    cream of mushroom soup

1 cup milk
½ cup blanched, slivered almonds
¾ cup grated Parmesan cheese
2 tablespoons margarine
½ teaspoon paprika

Break spaghetti into 3-inch lengths and cook according to package directions. Heat oven to 350° F. Grease a 2-quart shallow baking dish. Combine spaghetti, beans, mushroom soup, milk, almonds, and ½ cup cheese. Turn into baking dish; sprinkle with remaining cheese. Dot with margarine and sprinkle with paprika. Bake 25 minutes or until bubbly and lightly browned.

Macaroni and Cheese Supreme

1 package (8 ounces) elbow macaroni
¼ cup margarine
¼ cup flour
1 cup tomato juice
1 cup evaporated milk
1½ cups grated sharp Cheddar cheese

½ teaspoon salt
¼ teaspoon white pepper
2 strips crisp bacon, crumbled
½ cup ready-to-eat cereal flakes
1 tablespoon bacon fat

Cook macaroni according to package directions; drain and turn into shallow baking dish. Melt margarine in saucepan over low heat; blend in flour. Gradually add tomato juice and evaporated milk, stirring constantly; cook until well blended. Add cheese, salt, and pepper; stir over very low heat until cheese melts; pour sauce over macaroni. Heat oven to 375° F. Combine bacon, cereal flakes, and bacon fat; sprinkle over top. Bake 25 to 30 minutes.

Macaroni Patties

New idea for leftover macaroni to use with pot roast.

½ cup shortening
5 tablespoons flour
1 cup milk
1 teaspoon salt
1 cup grated Cheddar cheese
1½ cups cooked macaroni

1 tablespoon chopped parsley
1 teaspoon minced onion
1¼ cups fine dry bread crumbs
1 egg
1 tablespoon water
¾ cup hot tomato sauce

Melt ¼ cup shortening in saucepan; blend in flour. Add milk and salt; stir until smooth and thickened. Remove from heat. Add cheese; stir until cheese is melted. Add macaroni, parsley, and onion. Turn into well-greased 9-inch square pan. Chill until firm. Cut into patties. Dip in bread crumbs, then in beaten egg which has been diluted with water, then again in crumbs. Fry in remaining ¼ cup shortening until brown, turning once. Serve with hot tomato sauce. Makes 6 servings.

Northwest Cheese and Corn Casserole

1 can (12 ounces) whole kernel corn
1 pimiento, chopped
½ pound process Cheddar
    cheese, grated
¾ cup cracker crumbs

½ cup milk
1½ tablespoons melted margarine
½ teaspoon salt
⅛ teaspoon pepper
8 crisp bacon slices

Heat oven to 375° F. Butter a 1½-quart baking dish. Arrange alternate layers of corn with pimiento, cheese, and cracker crumbs; repeat until all ingredients are used, ending with crumbs. Blend milk with margarine, salt, and pepper; pour over corn mixture. Bake 25 minutes. Serve hot with bacon slices.

Cheese Vegetable Rarebit

All it requires is thirty minutes of your time to put this nutritious dish together.

1 cup tomato juice	2 eggs, well beaten
1 tablespoon margarine, melted	3 cups grated Cheddar cheese
2 teaspoons Worcestershire sauce	12 slices fresh white bread, toasted
1½ teaspoons dry mustard	2 packages (10 ounces each)
½ teaspoon salt	frozen mixed vegetables
⅛ teaspoon pepper	½ teaspoon paprika

Blend tomato juice, margarine, Worcestershire sauce, mustard, salt, and pepper in top of double boiler; heat over boiling water. Add ¼ cup to eggs; return to sauce and cook, stirring, until mixture thickens, about 3 minutes. Add cheese; stir until melted. Place whole slices of bread on six individual serving plates; cut remaining 6 slices diagonally and place alongside of whole slices. Heat vegetables according to package directions; drain. Arrange hot vegetables on bread; pour cheese sauce over and sprinkle with paprika. Makes 6 servings.

Cheese Soufflés Marian

Even if you're penny-pinching, these soufflés will keep you within your budget while winning you a reputation as a superb cook.

2 tablespoons butter	2 teaspoons Worcestershire sauce
2 tablespoons flour	½ cup milk
⅓ teaspoon baking soda	1 cup grated cheese
1 teaspoon salt	4 eggs, separated
¼ teaspoon paprika	10 crisp bacon slices

Heat oven to 350° F. Butter well 10 custard cups. Melt butter in top of double boiler. Add flour, soda, salt, paprika, and Worcestershire sauce; stir until well blended. Gradually add milk, stirring constantly, and cook over boiling water until thickened. Remove from heat; stir in grated cheese and egg yolks which have been beaten until light and fluffy. Beat egg whites until stiff; fold into egg-yolk mixture. Turn into custard cups. Bake 12 minutes. Serve immediately with bacon. Makes 10 individual soufflés.

Cheese Soufflé

¼ cup butter	2 cups grated process
¼ cup flour	American cheese
1½ cups milk	6 eggs, separated
1 teaspoon salt	Tomato Vegetable Sauce
Dash pepper	(recipe below)

Heat oven to 300° F. Melt butter in top of double boiler; add flour and mix well. Add milk all at once. Cook, stirring constantly, until thickened. Add salt, pepper, and cheese. Stir constantly until cheese is melted and smooth. Remove from heat; cool slightly. Beat egg whites until stiff. Beat egg yolks until well blended. Add warm cheese mixture to egg yolks gradually, while stirring constantly. Pour cheese sauce over egg whites gradually, folding in quickly and lightly. Pour mixture into 2-quart soufflé or baking dish. Bake 45 minutes or until top is golden brown. Serve immediately with sauce.

Tomato Vegetable Sauce

2 tablespoons margarine	1 cup canned tomatoes
2 tablespoons minced onion	½ cup drained mixed vegetables
2 tablespoons finely chopped	⅛ teaspoon pepper
green pepper	½ teaspoon salt
2 tablespoons flour	

Melt margarine in small skillet; add onion and green pepper. Sauté until soft but not browned. Add flour and blend until smooth. Stir in tomatoes and mixed vegetables. Season with pepper and salt. Cook, stirring gently, until thickened. Makes 1½ cups.

Cheese Croute

When you serve this hearty dish with a tossed green salad, chunks of French bread, and buttered carrots, no one will miss not having meat.

5 slices bread
2 tablespoons margarine
½ teaspoon salt
⅛ teaspoon pepper
¼ cup sautéed sliced mushrooms
¼ cup sliced stuffed olives

1 cup shredded process
  Cheddar cheese
3 eggs
¼ teaspoon dry mustard
2⅓ cups milk

Heat oven to 300° F. Spread both sides of bread with margarine; cut into cubes. Place layer of bread cubes in 1½-quart deep casserole or soufflé dish. Sprinkle with salt and pepper. Cover with layer of ⅓ mushrooms, olives, and cheese. Repeat layering until all ingredients are used. Beat eggs with dry mustard and milk until thoroughly blended. Pour over bread mixture. Bake 40 to 45 minutes.

Puffy Cheese-Potato Casserole

Serve this hearty dish with stewed tomatoes, buttered asparagus, and a mixed green salad.

⅓ cup chopped onion
1 tablespoon margarine
1 package (12 ounces) frozen
  potato patties
¾ cup milk
¾ teaspoon salt

½ teaspoon paprika
⅛ teaspoon pepper
2 eggs, separated
¾ cup grated process
  Cheddar cheese

Heat oven to 350° F. Grease a round 1-quart casserole. Sauté onion in margarine in large skillet until soft. Add potato patties and milk. Cook over medium heat, stirring frequently and carefully breaking up patties with a fork. Add salt, paprika, and pepper; bring to boil. Remove from heat. Beat egg yolks until thick and fluffy. Gradually add a small amount of hot potato mixture to egg yolks, stirring constantly. Add to mixture in skillet. Add cheese; stir until cheese is melted. Beat egg whites until stiff; fold into potato mixture. Pour into casserole. Bake 35 minutes or until knife inserted in center comes out clean.

Soups du Jour: Meals in Themselves

The perpetual soup pot, once a fixture in many homes, is now a nostalgic memory for most Americans. Like the burnished coal-fed kitchen range it simmered on, the homemade soup disappeared from the scene for a while because the manufacturers took over stewing and brewing.

But now the big stew pot is once more making its appearance in many modern kitchens, for there is literally no fish, fowl, meat, or vegetable that cannot contribute to the soup pot. No recipe is so sacred, where soup is concerned, that the imaginative cook cannot give it the embellishment of her signature.

Soup can introduce a meal or accent it. Here, we are making it *the* meal. Light or hearty, hot or cold, its versatility in texture, taste, and service is unsurpassed.

For the homemaker with time to spare, soup made by a step-by-step process is well worth the time of preparation. For the busy woman we recommend the great soups found on supermarket shelves, but don't just follow the meager directions on the label—improvise all you can. Your personal touch will make all the difference and, when the budget's impossible, you can count on soup to save the day.

Country Corn Chowder

2 tablespoons margarine
2 tablespoons flour
1 quart milk
2 cups canned corn kernels
2 tablespoons chopped onion
1½ teaspoons salt

¼ teaspoon white pepper
⅛ teaspoon ground ginger
½ teaspoon whole celery seed
2 large eggs
3 slices crisp bacon, crumbled

Melt margarine in saucepan. Blend in flour; add milk all at once, stirring constantly. Heat to boil, stirring frequently. Add corn, onion, salt, pepper, ginger, and celery seed. Cook, covered, over low heat 20 minutes. Beat eggs; add 1 cup hot mixture to eggs. Return to soup; cook 3 minutes longer. Serve topped with crumbled bacon. Makes 6 servings.

Beef Barley Soup

1½ pounds beef shank
   bone and meat
2 marrow bones
2½ quarts water
¼ cup parsley flakes
¼ cup celery flakes
5 teaspoons salt

3 tablespoons chopped onion
¼ teaspoon pepper
½ teaspoon ground ginger
5 whole mushrooms
1 cup diced carrots
½ cup pearl barley

Place bones, meat, water, parsley and celery flakes, salt, onion, pepper, ground ginger, and mushrooms in large kettle. Simmer, covered, 2 hours. Remove bones. Add carrots and barley; simmer 2 hours longer or until barley is cooked. Makes 8 servings.

Frosty Tomato Soup

Cold and zesty—just the thing to beat the heat.

2½ cups tomato juice
1 teaspoon sugar
1 teaspoon horseradish
1 teaspoon lemon juice

Dash Tabasco
Dash onion salt
Dash celery salt

Combine all ingredients; mix well. Pour into refrigerator tray. Freeze firm; when ready to serve, break in chunks and beat with electric beater until smooth. Serve in chilled bowls.

Sausage Bean Chowder

The original recipe called for dry red beans and Mexican sausage.

½ pound bulk pork sausage
1 can (16 ounces) kidney beans
1½ cups canned tomatoes
2 cups water
1 small onion, chopped
1 bay leaf

¾ teaspoon salt
¼ teaspoon garlic salt
¼ teaspoon thyme
⅛ teaspoon pepper
½ cup diced potatoes
¼ chopped green pepper

Cook pork sausage in skillet until brown. Pour off fat. In large kettle combine kidney beans, tomatoes, water, onion, bay leaf, salt, garlic salt, thyme, and pepper. Add sausage. Simmer, covered, 1 hour. Add potatoes and green pepper. Cook, covered, 15 minutes or until potatoes are tender. Remove bay leaf and serve.

Creamy Cauliflower Soup

1 medium head cauliflower,
    cut in flowerets
¼ cup margarine
1 small onion, chopped
2 tablespoons flour
3 cups chicken broth

2 cups milk
1 teaspoon Worcestershire sauce
½ teaspoon salt
1 cup grated Cheddar cheese
1 tablespoon chopped green onion

Simmer cauliflower, covered, in small amount of salted water until just tender, about 15 minutes. Drain. Melt margarine in saucepan; sauté onions until soft. Add flour and blend. Gradually stir in chicken broth, then milk, Worcestershire sauce, and salt. Add cauliflower. Bring to boil. Stir in cheese. Serve hot, sprinkled with green onion. Makes 6 servings.

New York Potato Soup

A hearty luncheon soup served with Melba toast rounds, tossed green salad, and a fresh fruit cup.

3 cups thinly sliced potatoes
2 medium onions, thinly sliced
4 frankfurters
3 cups boiling water
4 beef bouillon cubes

2 cups milk
½ teaspoon salt
¼ teaspoon pepper
1 tablespoon chopped parsley

Place potatoes, onions, and frankfurters in deep kettle. Pour in water and cook, covered, 20 minutes or until potatoes are very tender. Remove frankfurters; cut into ½-inch slices. Drain potatoes and onions; reserve liquid. Press vegetables through fine sieve; return to liquid in kettle. Stir in bouillon cubes, milk, salt, pepper, parsley, and sliced frankfurters. Heat thoroughly.

Quick Borscht

1 can (1 pound) whole beets
¼ cup sugar
¾ teaspoon salt

5 tablespoons lemon juice
1 egg, well beaten
2 tablespoons sour cream

Drain contents of can of beets; reserve liquid. Finely chop beets and add to liquid in measuring cup, adding water to yield 1 quart. Heat beet mixture with sugar, salt, and lemon juice in saucepan to boiling point, stirring occasionally. Remove from heat; gradually add ¾ cup of hot mixture to beaten egg, stirring constantly; stir into beet mixture in saucepan. Return to heat; continue stirring and cook to boiling point, but do not boil. Serve hot or cold with dollops of sour cream.

Creamy Carrot Soup

6 tablespoons margarine
½ cup chopped onion
2 cups thinly sliced carrots
¾ teaspoon salt

3 chicken bouillon cubes
3 cups boiling water
¼ cup uncooked rice
2 cups milk

Heat margarine in saucepan; sauté onion until lightly browned. Add carrots and salt; toss to coat with margarine. Cook, covered, 20 minutes, stirring occasionally. Add bouillon cubes, water, and rice; stir. Simmer, covered, 1 hour, stirring occasionally, until carrots are very soft. Put mixture into an electric blender or pass through sieve; blend until smooth. Pour into saucepan; stir in milk and heat thoroughly.

Brown Flour Soup

This version of a Pennsylvania Dutch soup is similar in flavor to one popular in Switzerland.

¼ cup butter
½ cup flour
Dash pepper
5 beef bouillon cubes

5 cups water
¼ cup finely shredded
    Cheddar cheese

Heat butter in large saucepan; blend in flour and pepper. Cook until bubbly. Remove from heat. Combine bouillon cubes and water; add to flour mixture. Cook, stirring constantly, until slightly thickened. Reduce heat; simmer 20 minutes. Serve in individual soup bowls; sprinkle with cheese.

Old-Fashioned Bean Soup

2 cups navy beans
1 shank end of ham with bone
3 quarts water
⅓ cup mashed potatoes
2 large onions, finely diced
3 chopped carrots

4 stalks chopped celery
1 clove garlic, minced
1 tablespoon Worcestershire sauce
⅛ teaspoon rosemary
⅛ teaspoon red pepper
½ teaspoon salt

Soak beans overnight. Drain; add ham shank to beans in heavy kettle. Pour in water. Bring to boil; reduce heat and simmer 1½ hours or until beans are almost tender. Add mashed potatoes; mix thoroughly. Add remaining ingredients; cook 30 to 35 minutes longer or until vegetables are tender. Remove ham bone; cut off meat bits and add to soup; discard bone.

French Onion Soup

This adaptation of the Parisian classic is as delicious as if it were made the traditional way.

4 large onions, sliced very thin
2 tablespoons margarine
1 quart bouillon (canned,
    made with cubes or homemade)
1 teaspoon Worcestershire sauce

½ teaspoon salt
⅛ teaspoon pepper
6 slices French bread, toasted
½ cup grated Parmesan cheese

Cook onions in margarine until golden. Add bouillon, Worcestershire sauce, salt, and pepper. Bring to boil. Place bread slices in individual casseroles. Pour soup over bread. When bread comes to top, sprinkle with cheese. Place under broiler and brown lightly. Sprinkle with more cheese, if desired. Makes 6 servings.

Mulligatawny Soup

A flavorful variation of an old favorite subtly seasoned with spices.

1 medium onion, sliced
¼ cup margarine
1 medium carrot, sliced
1 stalk celery, sliced
1 medium apple, pared and diced
1 cup chopped cooked chicken
⅓ cup flour
1½ teaspoons curry powder

⅛ teaspoon mace
2 whole cloves
1 tablespoon minced parsley
2 cups chicken broth
1 cup canned tomatoes
1 teaspoon salt
⅛ teaspoon pepper

Sauté onion in margarine until tender. Add carrot, celery, apple, and chicken. Stir in flour, spices, and parsley. Stir in broth gradually, then tomatoes, salt, and pepper. Simmer, covered, 30 minutes or until vegetables are tender. Makes 8 servings.

Danish Cranberry Soup

A cool soup to keep you cool in the summer.

¼ cup quick-cooking tapioca
½ cup sugar
⅛ teaspoon salt

2 cups cranberry juice cocktail
½ cup dry white wine
¼ cup sour cream

Combine tapioca, sugar, salt, cranberry juice, and wine, in a saucepan. Cook over medium heat, stirring constantly, until mixture comes to boil. Remove from heat; cool, stirring once after 20 minutes. Chill well. Ladle into cups and top with sour cream.

California Orange Soup

The blend of citrus with peaches and bananas makes this summer soup an inviting dessert as well.

2 tablespoons quick-cooking tapioca
2½ cups orange juice
2 tablespoons sugar
Dash salt
2 cinnamon sticks

1½ cups orange sections
1 package (12 ounces) frozen
    sliced peaches, thawed
1 banana, sliced
¼ cup sour cream

Blend tapioca, orange juice, sugar, and salt in saucepan. Let stand 5 minutes. Add cinnamon sticks. Bring to boil over medium heat. Remove from heat; cool. Remove cinnamon sticks. Add orange sections, thawed peaches, and banana. Chill well. Ladle into chilled bowls. Garnish with sour cream. Makes 8 servings.

Pork and Vegetable Soup

Serve this hearty soup with cheese sandwiches for a nutritious and tasty meal.

½ pound lean pork, cut
    into strips
12 mushrooms, sliced
1½ cups fresh spinach,
    torn into small pieces
1 small carrot, cut into thin slices

3 tablespoons canned bamboo
    shoots, cubed
2 teaspoons soy sauce
1 teaspoon ground ginger
2 cans bouillon

Simmer pork in 1 cup water 10 minutes. Add mushrooms, spinach, carrot, bamboo shoots, soy sauce, ginger, and bouillon. Simmer until vegetables are crisp tender and flavors are blended. Makes 6 servings.

Cream of Green Vegetable Soup

Finely cut cabbage or green beans may be substituted for spinach.

2 tablespoons margarine	2 tablespoons flour
1 cup chopped spinach	1 quart milk
1 teaspoon salt	½ cup croutons

Heat margarine in large saucepan; add spinach and salt. Cook, covered, 10 minutes, stirring occasionally. Blend flour with ¼ cup milk; stir into spinach. Add remaining milk, stirring constantly, and cook until mixture is smooth and slightly thickened. Serve with croutons.

Savory Golden Soup

Beef bones make fine basic broth or stock—prepare them in advance and have them ready for a soup.

4 medium parsnips, pared, diced	⅛ teaspoon pepper
2 small sweet potatoes, pared, diced	1 cup cooked beef, cut up
3 cups Beef Stock (recipe below)	½ cup heavy cream
¾ teaspoon salt	½ cup chopped parsley

Add parsnips and sweet potatoes to Beef Stock in heavy deep skillet; season with salt and pepper. Cook 20 to 25 minutes or until vegetables are tender. Add meat and cream; heat thoroughly but do not boil. Serve garnished with parsley.

Beef Stock

Beef bones	1 bay leaf
1 onion, cut in pieces	1 teaspoon salt
2 stalks celery, sliced	3 cloves
5 cups water	5 peppercorns
2 sprigs parsley	

Buy 1½ pounds raw, or use leftover, roast beef bones. Put in heavy deep kettle. Add remaining ingredients. Simmer, covered, 1½ to 2 hours. Cool; skim off fat. Lift out bones and trim off every bit of meat. Discard bones. Strain broth; add meat. Makes 3 cups.

Spring Garden Soup

Sunday, Monday, and always, the family will cheer this vegetable soup.

½ head cauliflower	1 teaspoon salt
2 medium carrots, cubed	Dash pepper
3 cups Beef Stock (recipe page 220)	1 cup cooked beef, cut up
2½ cups canned tomatoes	¼ cup sour cream
½ teaspoon basil	

Break cauliflower into small sections and use tender green leaves that hug the head. Add to Beef Stock with carrots, tomatoes, basil, salt, pepper, and meat; cook over medium heat 15 to 20 minutes. Serve hot with scoop of sour cream on top.

Italian Minestrone

A hearty main dish soup. Serve chunks of buttered Italian bread and, for dessert, a luscious chocolate cake.

1 cup dried white beans	1 tablespoon flour
1 cup dried garbanzos	½ cup tomato purée
1 large potato, pared and diced	1 teaspoon sugar
1 cup finely chopped onion	1 cup uncooked noodles
1 clove garlic, minced	6 cups chicken broth
1 cup diced celery	1 teaspoon salt
3 leeks or green onions, diced	¼ teaspoon pepper
2 medium tomatoes, chopped	½ cup grated Parmesan cheese
3 tablespoons vegetable oil	

Soak white beans and garbanzos separately overnight in water to cover. Drain. Place beans in large heavy kettle and add fresh, lightly salted water. Cook until almost tender. Add potato; cook until potato and beans are soft. Drain; mash well. Sauté onion, garlic, celery, leeks or green onions, and tomatoes in hot oil until onion is tender. Sprinkle with flour. Add chicken broth, stirring constantly, until smooth and well blended. Add tomato purée, sugar, and soaked, drained garbanzos; stir well. Cook over low heat, 30 minutes or until garbanzos are almost tender. Add mashed bean and potato mixture, noodles, salt, and pepper. Cook 15 minutes or until noodles are tender. Serve in vegetable bowls; sprinkle cheese on top. Makes 8 servings.

Bouillabaisse Americana

The famous French soup is streamlined to suit American tastes and pocket-books.

1 small onion, thinly sliced
1 small clove garlic, minced
½ small bay leaf
¼ teaspoon thyme
2 tablespoons olive oil
1 can (10½ ounces)
    condensed tomato soup

1 soup can water
2 cups cooked seafood (leftover
    bits of fish, crab, shrimp, etc.)
1 teaspoon lemon juice
Dash Tabasco
4 thick slices French bread, toasted

Sauté onion, garlic, bay leaf, and thyme in oil until onion is tender. Add soup, water, seafood, lemon juice, and Tabasco. Bring to boil. Cover; simmer 5 to 6 minutes. To serve, ladle soup over toast in bowls.

Cream of Pea Soup

1 package (10 ounces) frozen peas
½ cup boiling water
1 teaspoon salt
¼ cup margarine
2 tablespoons finely minced onion

3 tablespoons flour
1 quart milk
⅛ teaspoon pepper
Leftover ham bits or
    frankfurter slices

Cook peas in boiling salted water until tender, retaining cooking water. Sieve peas with liquid. Melt margarine in saucepan; sauté onion until tender. Add flour; blend well. Add milk and cook, stirring constantly, until thickened and smooth. Add peas and pepper. Stir in ham bits or frankfurter slices. Serve in warm bowls.

Bay Clam Chowder

¼ pound salt pork, diced
1 medium onion, finely chopped
½ medium pepper, chopped
4 medium potatoes, pared and diced
1 pint clams, chopped, with liquid

1 small garlic clove, minced
1½ teaspoons salt
⅛ teaspoon white pepper
½ cup milk
½ cup light cream

Fry salt pork in skillet until well browned. Add onion and green pepper; sauté until lightly browned. Add 2 potatoes, clams, clam liquid, garlic, salt, and pepper; bring to boil. Reduce heat, simmer about 15 minutes or until potatoes are tender. Combine milk and cream; add remaining potatoes and cook over low heat until potatoes are very tender. Beat with electric beater until smooth and creamy. Add to clam mixture; simmer 5 minutes.

Turkey Soup Parmentiere

The soup of Provence is hearty and delicious.

1 large onion, minced	¼ teaspoon sage
3 cups sliced raw potato	¼ teaspoon thyme
3 cups turkey broth	1 teaspoon salt
1 cup peas and diced carrots	¼ teaspoon pepper
2 tablespoons margarine	2 cups finely diced cooked turkey
1½ cups light cream	¼ teaspoon paprika
1½ cups milk	2 tablespoons green onion, chopped

Cook onion and potato in broth for 20 minutes; add peas and carrots and cook 10 minutes longer. Add margarine, cream, milk, herbs and seasonings; stir. Add turkey. Heat thoroughly to boiling point. Serve with sprinkling of paprika and green onion.

Gazpacho Andalousian

Call it soup or salad, gazpacho is the most refreshing, light summer meal you can find. Toss the whole garden into this spicy vegetable mixture and serve it in icy cold mugs or chilled soup plates.

1 cup finely chopped drained, canned tomatoes	1 small clove garlic, minced
½ cup finely chopped green pepper	2 tablespoons tarragon wine vinegar
¼ cup finely chopped celery	2 tablespoons olive oil
¼ cup finely chopped red pepper	1 teaspoon salt
½ cup finely chopped cucumber	¼ teaspoon pepper
¼ cup finely chopped onion	½ teaspoon Worcestershire sauce
2 teaspoons chopped parsley	2 cups tomato juice
1 teaspoon chopped green onion	¾ cup croutons

Combine all ingredients, except croutons, in large bowl. Cover; refrigerate at least 4 hours. Serve in chilled cups or soup plates. Garnish with croutons. Makes 6 servings.

Sorrento Soup

1 quart water
1 cup rinsed large dry lima beans
2½ teaspoons salt
5 beef bouillon cubes
2½ cups canned
  tomatoes, with liquid
5 carrots, pared,
  quartered lengthwise
¼ pound green beans,
  sliced lengthwise

3 stalks celery, sliced
2 large onions, sliced
⅛ teaspoon pepper
½ teaspoon marjoram
1 teaspoon sage
¼ teaspoon onion salt
½ pound frankfurters,
  split lengthwise

Bring water to rolling boil in large kettle. Stir in lima beans; reduce heat, cover and simmer 30 minutes. Add 1 teaspoon salt; simmer 30 minutes longer. Add bouillon cubes, tomatoes, carrots, beans, celery, onions, pepper, and ½ teaspoon salt. Simmer, uncovered, for 30 minutes or until vegetables are just tender. Add herbs, onion salt, remaining salt, and frankfurters. Add more hot water, if necessary, for desired consistency. Heat thoroughly. Makes 6 servings.

Soup Bagdad

1 pound lentils
2½ quarts cold water
2 tablespoons salt
¼ teaspoon pepper
½ cup vegetable oil
2½ cups canned tomatoes
2 small onions, minced
2 tablespoons chopped fresh dill

2 cloves garlic, minced
1 tablespoon chopped celery leaves
1 bay leaf
1 pound ground lamb
1 egg, slightly beaten
¼ cup flour
¼ cup elbow macaroni

Wash lentils. Place in large kettle; add water, 1½ tablespoons salt, ⅛ teaspoon pepper, 6 tablespoons oil, tomatoes, onions, dill, garlic, celery leaves, and bay leaf. Cook, covered, over low heat for 1 hour and 35 minutes. Combine lamb with remaining salt and pepper, and egg; shape into 24 small balls. Roll balls in flour; brown in hot remaining oil. Add to soup along with macaroni; cook 20 minutes longer. Makes 6 servings.

Vegetables:
A Varicolored Variety

From artichokes to zucchini, you can buy vegetables fresh, frozen, and canned.

Vegetables bring never-ending variety to daily meals. Used wisely and skillfully, versatile and flavorful vegetables are among the most rewarding foods. And the way you plan to use them plays an important part in your selection, because vegetable preparation starts in the supermarket, not in the kitchen.

Almost no other food group in your daily bill of fare has so much to offer in meal enjoyment and health protection, and at the same time, can lose so much in taste, looks, and inner value so quickly. Losses occur through unwise planning for marketing, improper home storage, and careless cooking. Learn to select the vegetables for their tenderness, ripeness, freshness, and crispness. Store them properly as soon as they reach your kitchen and cook them in a minimum of water, with a minimum of heat and time. Learn to cook them only until crisp tender.

You can work magic with vegetable main dishes and if the unavoidable happens and you have leftovers, use them as soon as possible in salads, soups and, puréed, in sauces.

Vegetable Bake Marianna

Heated rye bread and fruit salad are the right partners for this flavorful dish.

4 medium onions
¼ pound sausage meat, crumbled
⅓ cup dry bread crumbs
¼ teaspoon salt

2 tablespoons chopped parsley
2 cups canned baked beans
½ cup canned tomatoes

Peel onions; cut a slice from top of each. Cook in boiling salted water to cover, about 25 minutes or until just tender. Cool. Scoop out centers; chop centers finely and combine with sausage, bread crumbs, salt, and parsley. Fill onion shells. Heat oven to 375° F. Pour beans in shallow 1½-quart baking dish; add tomatoes and mix slightly. Set stuffed onions in beans. Bake 30 minutes.

Creamed Mixed Vegetables

A nice way to serve leftover vegetables as a side dish, or in toast cups, or in a noodle ring as a luncheon entrée.

½ cup cooked carrots, diced
½ cup cooked green beans, sliced
½ cup cooked peas
½ cup cooked corn
1½ tablespoons margarine
3 tablespoons flour

½ cup milk
1 teaspoon salt
⅛ teaspoon pepper
1 teaspoon chopped onion
⅛ teaspoon savory
⅔ cup vegetable liquid or broth

Combine vegetables; set aside. Melt margarine in saucepan. Add flour and blend well. Add milk; cook, stirring constantly, until smooth and thickened. Add salt, pepper, onion, savory, and vegetable liquid or broth; stir until well blended. Add vegetables. Heat thoroughly but do not boil.

Upside-Down Vegetable Cake

2 cups flour
2 teaspoons baking powder
½ teaspoon salt
¼ cup shortening
1 egg, beaten

1 cup milk
4 cups mixed cooked vegetables
½ cup vegetable liquid
2 tablespoons margarine
1 cup hot canned tomato sauce

Heat oven to 425° F. Grease a shallow 2-quart baking dish. Combine flour, baking powder, and salt; cut in shortening with pastry blender. Combine egg and milk; add to dry ingredients, stirring until mixed. Arrange hot seasoned vegetables in baking dish. Pour vegetable liquid; dot with margarine. Cover with flour mixture. Bake 20 to 25 minutes. Turn out on hot serving platter with vegetables on top. Serve with hot tomato sauce. Makes 6 servings.

Breaded Vegetable Patties

1 cup mashed potatoes
½ cup cooked kernel
  corn, drained
¾ cup cooked peas, drained
¼ cup diced cooked
  carrots, drained

1 teaspoon salt
¼ teaspoon marjoram
1 egg
1 tablespoon water
1 cup dry bread crumbs
Vegetable oil

Combine potatoes, corn, peas, carrots, salt, and marjoram; mix well. Shape into patties. Beat egg slightly with water. Dip patties into egg, then into bread crumbs. Deep-fry in hot vegetable oil until golden brown.

Vegetable Casserole

Serve with leftover meat or cold cuts and you have a complete meal in record time.

¼ cup chopped green pepper
1 small onion, choppped
¼ cup margarine
2 tablespoons ketchup
½ teaspoon salt
⅛ teaspoon pepper

1 cup drained canned tomatoes
1 can (8 ounces) small
  whole onions, drained
1 can (1 pound) cream style corn
1 cup cooked rice

Heat oven to 350° F. Cook green pepper and onion in margarine until tender. Add ketchup, salt, pepper, tomatoes, onions, corn, and rice; mix gently. Turn into 1-quart casserole. Bake 40 minutes.

Stuffed Acorn Squash

2 acorn squash, cut in half
1½ teaspoons chopped onion
1½ teaspoons chopped green pepper
¼ cup melted butter
1 cup grated Cheddar cheese

2 cups soft bread crumbs
½ teaspoon salt
⅛ teaspoon pepper
½ cup dry bread crumbs
3 tablespoons margarine

Heat oven to 375° F. Bake acorn squash until soft. Cool; remove squash from shells and mash. Sauté onion and green pepper in 2 tablespoons butter. Add squash; cook 5 minutes, stirring occasionally. Remove from heat. Add cheese, soft bread crumbs, salt, pepper, and remaining 2 tablespoons melted butter; mix well. Place mixture in squash shells in baking dish. Sprinkle with bread crumbs; dot with margarine. Bake 20 minutes or until browned.

Asparagus Glory Casserole

Cinnamon pears, a mixed green salad, and butterscotch brownies make this casserole dish a dandy for an informal meal.

3 eggs
¼ cup milk
1 can (10½ ounces) cream
   of mushroom soup
1½ cups cooked rice

2 cups grated process
   American cheese
8 cooked asparagus spears
8 crisp bacon slices

Heat oven to 325° F. Grease a 1½-quart baking dish. Beat eggs slightly; add milk, soup, rice, and cheese and mix well. Turn into baking dish. Lay asparagus spears across top. Bake 1 hour and 30 minutes. Serve at once with bacon slices.

Asparagus Jubal

2 pounds fresh asparagus
Boiling salted water
½ cup slivered almonds
½ cup butter

½ teaspoon salt
1 tablespoon lemon juice
Dash paprika

Cook asparagus in boiling salted water until crisp tender; drain. Arrange on heated serving platter; keep hot. Sauté almonds in butter over low heat, stirring occasionally, until golden. Remove from heat; stir in salt and lemon juice. Pour over hot asparagus. Sprinkle with paprika. Makes 8 servings.

Asparagus Timbale

You can work magic with asparagus and this dish can be the focal point of any meal.

2 tablespoons margarine	⅛ teaspoon pepper
2 tablespoons flour	1⅓ cups cooked asparagus,
⅔ cup milk	finely chopped
½ teaspoon salt	2 eggs, beaten

Heat oven to 350° F. Lightly grease 4 custard cups. Melt margarine in saucepan; blend in flour until smooth. Slowly add milk; cook, stirring constantly, until sauce is smooth and thickened. Season with salt and pepper. Mix asparagus into the sauce. Add 2 tablespoons of sauce to eggs; then gradually stir mixture into sauce. Spoon into custard cups. Set in pan of hot water; bake 20 minutes or until set.

Baked Bean Loaf

A Western pioneer recipe which was served on lean days when meat was not available.

1½ cups beans	1 cup soft bread crumbs
3 cups cold water	1 teaspoon Worcestershire sauce
¼ cup chopped onion	¾ teaspoon salt
½ cup chopped celery	⅛ teaspoon pepper
½ cup liquid from beans	1 cup hot canned tomato sauce
1 egg, beaten	

Soak beans in water overnight. Cook beans until they are tender in water in which they were soaked. Boil liquid to ½ cup, and chop beans very fine. Add remaining ingredients, except tomato sauce. Heat oven to 400° F. Grease a 9 × 5 × 3-inch loaf pan. Pack bean mixture into loaf pan. Bake 30 minutes. Serve with hot tomato sauce. Makes 8 servings.

Scalloped Snap Beans

Serve as a vegetable to accompany an entrée, or with crisp bacon slices as a main dish.

2 tablespoons margarine
3 tablespoons flour
1 cup milk
½ cup liquid drained from beans
¼ cup finely cut process
   American cheese

½ teaspoon salt
⅛ teaspoon pepper
1 tablespoon prepared mustard
2 cups canned snap beans, drained
¼ cup buttered bread crumbs

Heat oven to 350° F. Grease a 1-quart baking dish. Melt margarine in skillet; add flour and blend well. Slowly add milk; cook, stirring constantly, until smooth and thickened. Stir in beans liquid, mustard, and cheese; simmer, stirring, until cheese is melted. Add salt and pepper. Put alternate layers of beans and sauce into baking dish. Top with buttered bread crumbs; bake 30 minutes.

Harvard Beets

½ cup sugar
2 tablespoons flour
¼ cup water
½ cup vinegar

½ teaspoon salt
2 tablespoons margarine
3 cups cooked beets, diced

Combine sugar and flour in saucepan. Add water and vinegar. Cook over medium heat, stirring constantly, until smooth and thickened, about 10 minutes. Add salt, margarine, and beets; stir. Cover; continue cooking 10 minutes longer.

Beets in Orange Sauce

2 tablespoons margarine
2 tablespoons flour
¾ cup water
1½ teaspoons grated orange rind
¾ cup orange juice

¼ teaspoon salt
⅛ teaspoon pepper
2 teaspoons sugar
3½ cups cooked beets, sliced

Melt margarine in saucepan; stir in flour and blend well. Add water slowly; blend. Add orange rind, juice, salt, pepper, and sugar. Cook, stirring constantly, until thickened. Add beets and heat thoroughly. Makes 8 servings.

Broccoli Amandine

1 package (10 ounces) frozen
  broccoli spears
¼ cup margarine

1½ tablespoons lemon juice
¼ teaspoon salt
¼ cup slivered blanched almonds

Cook broccoli according to package directions. Melt margarine in saucepan. Add remaining ingredients; simmer 5 minutes, stirring occasionally. Drain broccoli; arrange in serving dish. Top with sauce.

Broccoli-Celery Mélange

A combination of vegetables always perks up a meal and gives extra nutrition, too.

4 large stalks celery
1 package (7 ounces) frozen
  chopped broccoli
¼ cup water

2 tablespoons margarine
½ teaspoon salt
⅛ teaspoon pepper

Slice celery and place in medium skillet; add frozen broccoli, water, margarine, and seasonings. Cover; bring to boil. Reduce heat; cook 5 minutes. Break up broccoli with fork. Cook, covered, 5 to 8 minutes longer, or until vegetables are crisp tender.

Casserole of Brussels Sprouts

Vegetables bring never-ending variety to daily meals—try this conversation-piece casserole.

1½ tablespoons margarine
½ cup chopped celery
¼ cup chopped onion
1½ tablespoons flour
½ teaspoon salt

⅛ teaspoon pepper
1 cup canned tomatoes
1½ cups cooked brussels sprouts
½ cup fine bread crumbs
1½ tablespoons melted margarine

Heat margarine in skillet; sauté celery and onion until soft. Blend in flour, salt, and pepper. Add tomatoes; stir and cook until mixture is thick. Heat oven to 350° F. Grease a 1-quart baking dish. Put brussels sprouts in baking dish. Add tomato mixture. Sprinkle bread crumbs over top which have been mixed with melted margarine. Bake 30 minutes.

Polish Sour Cream Cabbage

The original recipe came over with the Polish immigrants to Cleveland, Ohio, where it is still considered the only proper way to serve cabbage.

1 small (about 1½ pounds)
  head cabbage
2 tablespoons margarine
1 clove garlic, minced
¼ cup water

½ cup sour cream
1 tablespoon vinegar
1 tablespoon sugar
1 teaspoon salt
1 egg, beaten lightly

Shred cabbage medium fine; set aside. Heat margarine in skillet; sauté garlic. Add cabbage and water. Cover tightly; bring to boil. Reduce heat; simmer 10 minutes. Combine sour cream with vinegar, sugar, salt, and egg; blend thoroughly. Pour over cabbage; bring to quick boil and serve immediately.

Hungarian Cabbage

An old-country recipe adapted to new-world methods, it will bring compliments whenever it is served.

1 medium head (about 1½ pounds)
  red cabbage
1 tablespoon vinegar
1 teaspoon salt
¼ pound mushrooms, sliced
1 small onion, chopped
3 tablespoons shortening
½ cup uncooked oatmeal

¼ cup tomato juice
1 egg yolk
2 tablespoons sour cream
¼ teaspoon chopped caraway
  seeds
⅛ teaspoon marjoram
2 tablespoons grated
  Parmesan cheese

Wash and drain cabbage head; cut out stem end and hollow out center. Chop up pulp; set aside. Parboil cabbage shells 5 minutes in boiling water to which vinegar and salt have been added; remove and drain. Heat oven to 350° F. Grease a 1-quart baking dish. Sauté mushrooms and onion in shortening in skillet; add chopped cabbage, oatmeal, and tomato juice. Cook over medium heat, 10 minutes, stirring constantly; cool mixture slightly. Blend egg yolk, sour cream, and seasonings; add to oatmeal mixture. Stuff into cabbage shell in baking dish. Bake 30 minutes. Remove to heated serving platter; sprinkle with cheese.

Tennessee Carrot Loaf

A versatile meatless dinner dish served plain or with a creamy cheese sauce.

1½ cups cooked carrots, diced
1½ cups cooked turnips, diced
2 tablespoons chopped parsley
¼ cup finely chopped onion
1½ tablespoons melted shortening
3 eggs, well beaten
1½ cups soft break crumbs

1 cup evaporated milk
½ cup water or liquid from
   vegetables
1 teaspoon salt
⅛ teaspoon pepper
Cheese Sauce (recipe below)

Heat oven to 350° F. Combine carrots, turnips, parsley, and onion in bowl. Add cooled shortening to eggs; stir in bread crumbs. Pour evaporated milk and water into egg mixture. Add to vegetable mixture with salt and pepper; mix well. Turn into well greased 1-quart baking pan. Set in pan of hot water. Bake 50 to 60 minutes or until knife inserted in center comes out clean. To serve, cut in squares and serve with Cheese Sauce. This may also be made in a 9 × 5 × 3-inch loaf pan or a 4-cup ring mold. Makes 6 servings.

Cheese Sauce

2 tablespoons margarine
3 tablespoons flour
1½ cups milk

¾ teaspoon salt
⅛ teaspoon pepper
½ cup grated Cheddar cheese

Melt margarine in saucepan; add flour and blend well. Add milk, salt and pepper. Cook, stirring constantly, until thickened. Remove from heat. Add cheese; stir until melted.

Corn À La King

4 slices bacon
1 cup chopped green pepper
2 tablespoons chopped onion
3 tablespoons chopped pimiento
1 can (1 pound, 1 ounce) whole
   kernel corn

1 can (10½ ounces) condensed
   cream of celery soup
1 tablespoon margarine
¼ teaspoon salt
⅛ teaspoon paprika
4 slices toasted white bread

Fry bacon in skillet until crisp; drain on absorbent paper. Measure 1 tablespoon bacon drippings and discard balance. Sauté pepper and onion until soft. Add remaining ingredients, except white bread and bacon. Heat thoroughly but do not boil. Serve over toasted bread. Crumble bacon, sprinkle on top.

Corn and Pepper Fritters

A Midwestern specialty, especially good with ham.

2 cups cut cooked corn
2 tablespoons sugar
½ teaspoon salt
½ cup evaporated milk
2 eggs, beaten

¼ cup chopped green pepper
1½ cups flour
1½ teaspoons baking powder
Vegetable oil
Hot canned tomato sauce

Combine corn, sugar, and salt; add evaporated milk, eggs, and green pepper. Combine flour with baking powder; add to corn mixture and beat well. Drop by tablespoonfuls into greased skillet. Cook slowly until puffed and browned. Serve hot with tomato sauce.

Vinaigrette Dandelion Greens

Spring dandelion greens are highly prized when they are young and tender as they are an excellent source of vitamin A, iron, calcium, and the B vitamins.

1 teaspoon minced onion
6 tablespoons margarine, melted
½ teaspoon prepared mustard
2 tablespoons lemon juice
¾ teaspoon salt

⅛ teaspoon pepper
2 hard-cooked eggs, chopped
2½ pounds chopped, unseasoned,
    cooked dandelion greens

Sauté onion in 1 tablespoon margarine until tender. Add mustard, lemon juice, salt, pepper, and eggs. Heat thoroughly. Pour over dandelions; toss and serve.

Nordic Eggplant Scallop

A new way to serve eggplant that's company-good and economical.

2 tablespoons finely chopped onion
1 small eggplant, pared and cubed
¼ cup margarine
1½ cups canned tomatoes
1 tablespoon sugar

2 tablespoons flour
½ cup sour cream
½ teaspoon salt
⅛ teaspoon pepper

Sauté onion and eggplant in margarine in large skillet until lightly brown. Add tomatoes and sugar; cook until about half the liquid has evaporated.

Cover; simmer until eggplant is tender, about 20 minutes. Blend flour and sour cream. Add to eggplant mixture. Cook, stirring gently, until just thickened. Season with salt and pepper. Serve at once.

Planked Eggplant

An Italian speciality worth the effort of preparing it.

1 large eggplant	1 tablespoon finely chopped onion
2 tablespoons butter	1 tablespoon ketchup
2 tablespoons flour	2 eggs, separated
1 cup milk	½ teaspoon salt
1½ cups grated American cheese	⅛ teaspoon pepper
1½ cups soft bread crumbs	

Heat oven to 350° F. Wash eggplant, cut lengthwise into halves; scrape out centers leaving ½-inch shells. Cook pulp in small amount of water until tender; drain and mash. Melt butter in saucepan; blend in flour until smooth. Gradually add milk; cook, stirring constantly, until thickened. Add mashed eggplant pulp, cheese, bread crumbs, onion, ketchup, and egg yolks; mix well. Beat egg whites until stiff; fold eggplant mixture into egg whites. Fill shells. Bake 1¼ hours.

Peas Du Provence

A summer-fresh flavor you'll enjoy. Bake this Continental vegetable dish in the oven along with your meat entrée.

1 package (10 ounces) frozen green peas	1 tablespoon margarine
½ teaspoon salt	1 lettuce leaf
½ teaspoon sugar	½ cup thinly sliced radishes

Heat oven to 350° F. Place peas in small baking dish; sprinkle with salt and sugar. Dot with margarine. Place lettuce leaf on top. Bake, covered, 20 to 25 minutes or until peas are just tender. Remove lettuce; stir in radish slices and serve.

Peppers Tricolino

4 medium peppers	1 tablespoon margarine
Boiling water	½ teaspoon salt
1 cup cooked lima beans, drained	⅛ teaspoon dry mustard
¾ cup cooked kernel corn, drained	⅛ teaspoon paprika

Wash peppers and remove seeds; cover with boiling water and boil 5 minutes. Drain. Combine remaining ingredients; stuff mixture into pepper shells. Heat oven to 350° F. Grease a 1½-quart baking dish. Place pepper shells in dish. Bake 10 to 12 minutes or until thoroughly heated. Serve at once.

Southern Potatoes and Turnips

2 large potatoes, pared, quartered	¼ cup margarine
2 large turnips, pared, quartered	2 tablespoons flour
1½ cups water	¼ teaspoon pepper
1½ teaspoons salt	

Place potatoes and turnips in saucepan; pour in water and add 1 teaspoon salt. Cook over moderate heat until tender, about 15 minutes. Drain and mash. Heat margarine in skillet; blend in flour, remaining ½ teaspoon salt and pepper. Slowly add ¼ cup cold vegetable liquid. Cook, stirring constantly, until smooth and thickened. Add turnip and potato mash. Beat until light and fluffy. Serve immediately Makes 6 servings.

Baked Squash

Give meals an extra sparkle by serving a specially prepared vegetable.

2 acorn squashes, cut in half	1 tablespoon brown sugar
1 tablespoon melted butter	2 tablespoons heavy cream
¾ teaspoon salt	Dash nutmeg

Heat oven to 350° F. Remove squash seeds and stringy portions of vegetables. Score inside surface by making several gashes with sharp knife. Brush with butter; sprinkle with salt and brown sugar. Place in shallow baking dish, cut side up. Bake 1 hour or until tender. Pour a little cream into each half; sprinkle lightly with few grains of nutmeg and bake 10 minutes longer.

Tomato Pies Ana

½ cup canned tomatoes
½ can (6 ounces) tomato paste,
　about ⅓ cup
¼ teaspoon garlic salt
¼ teaspoon salt
⅛ teaspoon pepper
¾ teaspoon oregano

¼ teaspoon thyme
¼ cup milk
1 tablespoon melted margarine
1 cup packaged biscuit mix
¾ cup cottage cheese
3 tablespoons grated Parmesan
　cheese

Heat oven to 425° F. Combine first 7 ingredients; set aside. Add milk and margarine to biscuit mix; stir quickly with fork until mix is just moistened. Knead gently 8 times. Divide dough into 4 pieces. Pat each into a 4½-inch circle on lightly greased cooky sheet. Pinch up edges to make slight rims. Spread cottage cheese on circles; cover with tomato mixture. Sprinkle with Parmesan cheese. Bake 10 minutes. Reduce heat to 350° F. Bake 10 minutes longer. Serve hot.

Green-and-Red Tomato Surprise

A richly flavored vegetable dish—or use the Red Sauce as a condiment with meats.

2 medium green tomatoes
1½ teaspoons celery salt
⅛ teaspoon pepper
⅛ teaspoon onion salt

¾ cup cracker crumbs
2 tablespoons bacon drippings
Red Sauce (recipe below)

Slice tomatoes about ½ inch thick. Combine celery salt, onion salt, and pepper; sprinkle both sides of slices. Roll in cracker crumbs. Sauté slowly in bacon drippings until tender and golden on both sides, but not mushy. Spoon sauce over slices.

Red Sauce

4 firm, medium, red tomatoes,
　chopped fine, peeled
1 can (4 ounces) green chili
　peppers, drained, chopped

1 medium onion, finely chopped
¼ teaspoon salt
⅛ teaspoon pepper
2 tablespoons cider vinegar

Combine all ingredients; mix well. Let stand 2 to 3 hours before serving.

Tomato-Cheese Custard

1 can (1 pound) tomatoes
1 tablespoon minced onion
1 tablespoon butter
1 teaspoon salt

¼ teaspoon pepper
3 slices day-old bread, crumbled
2 eggs, slightly beaten
½ cup shredded Cheddar cheese

Heat oven to 375° F. Butter a 1-quart baking pan. Combine tomatoes, onion, butter, salt, pepper, and bread in saucepan; heat thoroughly but do not boil. Remove from heat; let stand until cool. Add eggs; mix well. Pour into baking dish. Top with cheese. Set in pan of hot water; bake about 40 minutes.

Tomatoes in Savory Sauce

A delicious luncheon dish when tomatoes are placed on toast rounds and garnished with crisp bacon.

¼ cup butter
6 medium tomatoes, peeled, halved
6 tablespoons flour
2 teaspoons sugar
½ teaspoon dry mustard

1½ cups milk
⅛ teaspoon Worcestershire sauce
½ teaspoon salt
⅛ teaspoon pepper

Melt butter in skillet; fry tomatoes until lightly browned and just tender. Remove all but two halves and keep warm. Mash remaining two halves. Blend flour with sugar and mustard; add to mashed tomato, stirring well. Add milk all at once. Cook, stirring constantly, until thickened. Season with Worcestershire sauce, salt, and pepper. Pour over tomatoes and serve.

Louisiana Tomato Aspic

1 envelope unflavored gelatin
2 cups tomato juice
½ teaspoon salt
Few drops bottled hot pepper sauce
1 tablespoon grated onion

1 tablespoon lemon juice
1 tablespoon sugar
Dash Worcestershire sauce
Lettuce greens

Soften gelatin in ½ cup cold tomato juice. Combine remaining tomato juice with salt, pepper sauce, and onion; bring to a boil. Stir in lemon juice, sugar, and Worcestershire sauce. Add to gelatin; stir until dissolved. Pour into individual molds. Chill 4 hours or overnight. Unmold on lettuce greens.

Stuffed Tomatoes Gabriel

4 firm, medium tomatoes
2 teaspoons minced onion
1 teaspoon shortening
½ teaspoon salt
⅛ teaspoon pepper
1 cup soft bread crumbs

1 egg, slightly beaten
2 tablespoons chopped
  green pepper
2 tablespoons chopped celery
3 tablespoons chopped cabbage

Heat oven to 375° F. Grease a 1-quart baking dish. Cut off tops of tomatoes, but do not discard; scoop out centers. Chop pulp. Sauté onion in shortening until tender. Combine with tomato pulp and remaining ingredients; mix well. Fill tomato shells with mixture; replace tops. Place in baking dish. Bake 30 minutes.

Golden Turnip Scallop

Piquant turnip, mellowed with apple, bakes buttery-sweet in this easy vegetable dish.

1½ pounds shredded
  yellow turnips
1 medium apple, pared,
  quartered, chopped

2 tablespoons brown sugar
1 teaspoon salt
⅛ teaspoon pepper
¼ cup margarine

Heat oven to 350° F. Combine turnip with ¾ chopped apple; mix well with brown sugar, salt, and pepper. Turn into 1-quart baking dish. Sprinkle remaining chopped apple on top. Dot with margarine. Cover. Bake 1½ hours or until turnip is tender.

Baked Turnip Puff

A delicious way to serve potatoes and turnips—whether fresh or leftovers.

1½ cups hot, mashed potatoes
1½ cups hot, mashed, yellow turnips
1½ teaspoons salt
⅛ teaspoon pepper

2 tablespoons margarine
2 tablespoons minced onion
1 egg, well beaten

Heat oven to 400° F. Combine all ingredients. Bake in greased 1-quart casserole 30 minutes.

Salad Showmanship

Is there anything brighter, easier to serve, or more inviting than a crisp salad? Salads are so versatile—they can be made with crisp greens or vegetables, tangy fruit, snappy cheese, nourishing eggs, and peppery herbs, then tossed with a glistening dressing.

Salads bring year round springtime to your table and with their tantalizing taste and gay garnishes give a fresh and lively lift to your meals.

There is a great parade of salads from which to choose—from appetizers to desserts—colorful gelatins, garden-fresh greens, mellowed coleslaw, gaily fruited or heartily whole-meal.

Select your salad according to its function: fresh fruit salad as an appetizer, chef's salad as a whole meal, molded gelatin to accompany a hearty dinner, coleslaw with sandwiches, and rich frozen-fruit salad that can double as dessert.

Salads contribute to your very good health and should be included in every meal. They're economical and quick to prepare, and remember that the darker salad vegetables offer larger amounts of vitamins A and C and are richer in iron than the pale ones.

With salads you can be as adventuresome as you wish.

Caesar's Salad

A French specialty of a famous restaurant in Paris.

½ clove garlic
2 tablespoons vegetable oil
Dash cumin
4 cups crisp salad greens
⅓ cup safflower oil
⅓ cup grated Parmesan cheese

⅓ cup crumbled blue cheese
¾ teaspoon salt
⅛ teaspoon pepper
1 raw egg
¼ cup fresh lemon juice
1½ cups dry croutons

Combine garlic and vegetable oil in small glass; let stand 1 hour. Place salad greens in large bowl. Add safflower oil, cheeses, salt, and pepper. Break raw egg over all. Sprinkle lemon juice. Toss salad well. Remove garlic from oil; pour oil over croutons and sprinkle on top of salad. Makes 8 servings.

Sacramento Salad

Here's a versatile salad in which you can use any leftover meat—ham, chicken, tongue, turkey—in place of the salami, the cheese doesn't have to be Swiss, and you can even add leftover green beans or peas.

1 small iceberg lettuce,
    torn in bite-size pieces
1 medium tomato, cut into eighths
1 medium cucumber, sliced

1 medium onion, sliced
½ cup hard salami strips
½ cup Swiss cheese strips
Sacramento Dressing (recipe below)

Place lettuce in salad bowl. Arrange tomato, cucumber, and onion on top of lettuce. Sprinkle salami and cheese strips. Pour Sacramento Dressing over all and toss lightly.

Sacramento Dressing

½ cup mayonnaise
2 tablespoons ketchup
1 tablespoon vinegar
½ teaspoon paprika

¼ teaspoon salt
¼ teaspoon curry powder
⅛ teaspoon pepper
¼ cup milk

Combine all ingredients; chill. Makes ¾ cup.

Pepper Cabbage Salad

Cabbage is almost as versatile as lettuce in making salads. We all know about coleslaw, but cabbage can be basic to many other salad dishes.

1 small (about 1¼ pounds) cabbage	½ cup sugar
1 medium green pepper	¼ cup vinegar
1 medium sweet red pepper or carrot	¼ cup water
1 stalk celery	2 teaspoons salt

Grate cabbage fine. Chop peppers and celery; mix with cabbage. Combine sugar, vinegar, water, and salt. Pour over vegetables; toss lightly and chill 30 minutes before serving.

Mediterranean Salad

1 can (1 pound 4 ounces) garbanzos	½ medium green pepper,
¼ cup bottled Italian dressing	cut into strips
½ teaspoon salt	2 tablespoons chopped celery
⅛ teaspoon pepper	1 tablespoon chopped parsley

Heat garbanzos and liquid in saucepan; drain. Toss with Italian dressing. Cover; refrigerate several hours or overnight. Sprinkle with salt and pepper. Add green pepper and celery; toss lightly. Sprinkle with parsley.

Crisp Greens with Avocado Dressing

Use avocados when they are plentiful and cheap to make this delightful dressing.

1 tablespoon lemon juice	6 drops Tabasco
2 tablespoons evaporated milk	¾ cup sieved avocado
½ teaspoon salt	Crisp salad greens
1 teaspoon prepared mustard	

Add lemon juice to milk; beat well. Add salt, mustard and Tabasco; blend thoroughly. Add avocado and beat. Refrigerate 1 hour. Place salad greens in bowl; pour on dressing.

Note: If dressing is too thick blend in a little light cream.

Aspic Avocado

1 tablespoon unflavored gelatin
2 tablespoons cold water
1 cup boiling water
1 cup sieved avocados
4 teaspoons lemon juice

½ teaspoon Worcestershire sauce
⅛ teaspoon salt
Dash Tabasco
½ teaspoon celery salt
1 pimiento, minced

Soften gelatin in cold water; dissolve in boiling water and cool. Add avocados, lemon juice, Worcestershire sauce, salt, Tabasco, celery salt, and pimiento; blend well. Turn into 4 individual molds. Refrigerate until firm. Unmold on bed of shredded lettuce, chopped celery tops, or watercress.

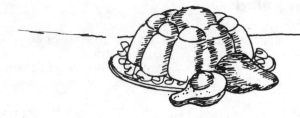

Garden Fresh Salad

½ pound washed, dried spinach
1 small Bermuda onion, sliced
¼ cup diced celery

4 hard-cooked eggs, sliced
Heirloom French Dressing
   (recipe below)

Tear spinach into bite-size pieces. Combine all ingredients, except dressing, in salad bowl. Toss lightly with French Dressing.

Heirloom French Dressing

2 tablespoons olive oil
2 tablespoons vegetable oil
2 tablespoons tarragon vinegar

1 teaspoon salt
1 small clove garlic, minced
⅛ teaspoon pepper

Combine oils and toss salad greens. Combine remaining ingredients. Toss again.

Deluxe Coleslaw

Here's a chance to use your herbs and spices on the pantry shelf.

1 teaspoon prepared mustard	1 teaspoon sesame seed
1 teaspoon water	1 tablespoon sugar
3 cups shredded cabbage	6 tablespoons salad oil
½ teaspoon onion salt	2 tablespoons white vinegar
½ teaspoon celery salt	1 tablespoon chopped green pepper
1 teaspoon mustard seed	1 tablespoon chopped pimiento
1 teaspoon celery seed	

Moisten mustard with water; let stand. Place cabbage in bowl. Combine remaining ingredients with mustard. Pour over cabbage and toss lightly. Chill in refrigerator.

Cabbage-and-Apple Salad

1 package lemon-flavored gelatin	½ teaspoon salt
2 cups hot water	1 cup diced red apples
½ cup shredded cabbage	¼ cup chopped walnut meats
4 teaspoons vinegar	Lettuce greens

Dissolve gelatin in hot water. Chill until slightly thickened. Combine cabbage, vinegar, and salt; let stand 20 minutes. Fold seasoned cabbage, apples, and nuts into gelatin. Turn into individual molds; chill until firm. Unmold on crisp lettuce.

Salad Suprême

A meal-in-one salad, perfect for lunch or supper.

1 quart mixed salad greens	½ cup julienne strips
2 small tomatoes, peeled,	luncheon meat
cut in wedges	½ cup julienne strips
1 hard-cooked egg, quartered	Swiss cheese
2 tablespoons finely	¼ cup diced cooked chicken
sliced green onion	Bottled French dressing

Pull apart chilled greens into bite-size pieces and place in large bowl. Add tomato wedges, egg, onion, luncheon meat, cheese, and chicken. Pour on enough dressing to coat ingredients. Toss lightly.

Tomato Cottage Cheese Salad

Use two molds and serve one as a salad for dinner and the other as an entrée for lunch.

2 cups canned tomatoes
1 teaspoon salt
Dash pepper
1 small bay leaf
3 whole cloves
3 tablespoons minced onion
1 package (3 ounces)
　lemon-flavored gelatin

1 tablespoon vinegar
2 tablespoons cold water
1¼ cups cottage cheese
2 tablespoons minced green pepper
½ cup diced celery
2 cups finely shredded cabbage
⅓ cup mayonnaise

Combine tomatoes, salt, pepper, bay leaf, cloves, and onion in saucepan. Simmer 20 minutes. Force through sieve; measure and add enough hot water to make 1½ cups. Dissolve gelatin in hot tomato mixture. Add vinegar. Measure ½ cup of mixture; add 2 tablespoons cold water and turn into 2 molds. Chill until firm. Chill remaining gelatin mixture until slightly thickened. Combine cottage cheese with remaining ingredients and fold into thickened gelatin mixture. Turn into molds over firm gelatin layer; chill until firm. Unmold on crisp lettuce or watercress. Makes 8 servings.

Earth Goddess Salad

1 cup coarsely shredded spinach
1 cup bite-size pieces
　raw cauliflower
⅓ cup grated carrot

¼ cup sour cream
½ teaspoon salt
⅛ teaspoon pepper

Combine spinach, cauliflower, and carrot in salad bowl. Fold in sour cream lightly, just enough to mix. Season with salt and pepper.

Wilted Lettuce Salad

3 slices bacon, diced
1 small head iceberg lettuce
1 tomato, diced
¼ cup green onion, sliced

½ teaspoon salt
½ teaspoon oregano
¼ teaspoon pepper
2 tablespoons vinegar

Fry bacon in skillet until crisp; remove to absorbent paper. Discard all but 1 tablespoon fat. Tear lettuce into bowl; add tomatoes, onion, and seasonings. Combine vinegar and bacon drippings; bring to a boil. Toss with salad. Crumble bacon over salad.

Hot Potato Salad

A German-style potato salad bouncing with flavor.

2 strips bacon
½ small onion, minced
½ small green pepper, minced
½ cup mayonnaise
1½ teaspoons cider vinegar
1 tablespoon water

1½ teaspoons Worcestershire sauce
¼ teaspoon dry mustard
1½ cups cooked sliced potatoes
2 hard-cooked eggs, chopped
¼ cup chopped celery
2 tablespoons chopped dill pickle

Fry bacon in skillet until crisp; remove to absorbent paper and crumble. Add onion and green pepper to skillet drippings; sauté until tender. Add mayonnaise, vinegar, water, Worcestershire sauce, and dry mustard. Cook over very low heat 3 minutes. Add remaining ingredients. Toss well to coat all pieces with dressing. Sprinkle with crumbled bacon.

Peppy Tomato Scallop

1 large green pepper,
  cut into chunks
1 medium onion, sliced
2½ cups canned tomatoes
¼ teaspoon salt
⅛ teaspoon pepper

1 tablespoon brown sugar
1 bay leaf
1 tablespoon margarine, melted
2 tablespoons flour
¼ cup dry bread crumbs

Heat oven to 350° F. Grease a 1-quart baking dish. Combine green pepper, onion, and drained tomatoes. Add salt, pepper, brown sugar, and bay leaf; mix well. Turn into baking dish. Combine margarine and flour and blend to smooth paste. Add ½ cup liquid from drained tomatoes. Pour over tomato mixture. Sprinkle with bread crumbs. Bake 45 minutes.

Bohemian Salad

½ teaspoon dry mustard
½ teaspoon onion juice
¾ cup French dressing
1 cup cooked diced potatoes
1 cup cooked diced green beans
1 cup cooked diced beets

⅓ cup mayonnaise
Crisp lettuce greens
1 hard-cooked egg
2 tablespoons chopped green onion
1 teaspoon chopped pickle

Add mustard and onion juice to French dressing. Marinate vegetables separately in ¼ cup of dressing for each; chill in refrigerator 1 hour. To serve, combine potatoes and beans with mayonnaise; place them in a bowl lined with lettuce greens. Arrange beets over beans and potatoes. Chop egg over these. Sprinkle with green onion and pickle.

Caliph's Salad

When avocados and apples are in abundance in local markets, it's an ideal time to treat the family to this exotic salad.

⅓ cup vegetable oil
1½ teaspoons grated lemon rind
¼ cup lemon juice
1 teaspoon curry powder
¾ teaspoon dry mustard
1 tablespoon sugar
½ teaspoon salt

1 avocado
1 cup diced red-skinned apple
1 banana, diced
1 green onion, sliced
3 cups cooked rice, chilled
¼ cup peanuts
Lettuce greens

Combine oil, lemon rind, lemon juice, curry powder, mustard, sugar, and salt in a jar with tight-fitting cover; shake well and set aside. Cut avocado into slices; brush with lemon dressing. In large bowl combine apple, banana, green onion, rice, and peanuts; toss lightly with dressing. Mound onto lettuce greens; top with avocado slices. Makes 8 servings.

Lettuce and Broccoli Salad

Make your vegetable part of the salad and serve it cold as it was done in colonial times when it was called "sallet."

1 small head iceberg lettuce
1 pound fresh or 1 package
   (10 ounces) frozen broccoli, cooked,
   drained, chilled
1 medium tomato, quartered

8 cucumber slices
⅓ cup French dressing
1 teaspoon prepared horseradish
1 tablespoon water
1 teaspoon Worcestershire sauce

Core lettuce; wash in cold water and drain well. Separate outer lettuce leaves to line 4 salad plates. Arrange broccoli spears, tomato wedges and cucumber on lettuce. Combine French dressing with horseradish, water and Worcestershire sauce; pour over salad.

Green Bean Salad Italiano

1 package (9 ounces) quick-frozen
   Italian green beans
⅓ cup thinly sliced onion
2 tablespoons vegetable oil
2 tablespoons lemon juice
½ teaspoon salt

1 teaspoon sugar
⅛ teaspoon pepper
¼ teaspoon paprika
1 tablespoon finely diced pimiento
2 tablespoons chopped dill pickle

Cook beans according to package directions; drain. Add onions. Combine remaining ingredients; mix well. Add to bean mixture and toss. Chill before serving.

Mediterranean Salad Bowl

Cumin, the dried fruit of an Egyptian plant, gives an exotic touch to this salad.

4 medium tomatoes, peeled
2 small cucumbers, pared,
   thinly sliced
⅓ cup finely chopped onion

1 small green pepper, chopped
16 pitted ripe olives
Cleopatra's Dressing (recipe below)

Slice tomatoes and cut in ¾-inch chunks. Mix with cucumbers, onion, pepper, and olives in large bowl. Pour dressing and marinate 1 hour before serving.

Cleopatra's Dressing

½ cup olive oil
¼ cup lemon juice
¾ teaspoon salt
1½ teaspoons sugar

¼ teaspoon seasoned pepper
½ teaspoon cumin
1 small clove garlic, halved

Blend first six ingredients in small jar; add garlic. Let stand 3 or 4 hours in regrigerator. Remove garlic and discard before using dressing. Makes ¾ cup.

Vegetable Delight Salad

Serve this plain as a salad or transform it into a main dish by filling the center with chicken salad.

1 package (10 ounces) frozen
  mixed vegetables
1 envelope unflavored gelatin
1¼ cups water
1 bouillon cube
2 tablespoons sugar

1 can (8 ounces) tomato sauce
1 tablespoon lemon juice
1 tablespoon grated lemon rind
1 clove garlic, minced
½ teaspoon Worcestershire sauce

Cook vegetables according to package directions; chill. Soften gelatin in ¼ cup cold water; add bouillon cube and sugar. Add 1 cup boiling water to softened gelatin mixture; stir until dissolved. Add remaining ingredients; mix well. Cool until syrupy; add chilled vegetables. Turn into 9-inch ring mold. Refrigerate until firm.

Chef's Salad Del Mar

1 small head romaine lettuce
½ pound spinach
1 small head Boston lettuce
1 can sardines in oil
¼ pound cheese, cut in strips

2 hard-cooked eggs, sliced
6 tablespoons mayonnaise
1 tablespoon lemon juice
1 teaspoon heavy cream

Wash greens thoroughly; drain and chill. Tear into bite-size pieces. Place in salad bowl. Add drained sardines, cheese, and eggs. Combine mayonnaise with lemon juice and cream; toss salad lightly.

May Basket Salad

½ cup pitted dates
4 oranges
¼ cup chopped green onion

1 cup finely chopped
  romaine lettuce
Creamy Mustard Dressing
  (recipe below)

Cut dates into slivers. Cut 1 inch cap off stem end of oranges. Carefully remove fruit pulp with sharp knife; cut into pieces. Combine fruits, onion, and lettuce; toss. Pile mixture into orange shells. Spoon dressing into shells.

Creamy Mustard Dressing

½ teaspoon dry mustard
½ teaspoon sugar
¼ teaspoon salt
1½ teaspoons flour
1 egg

¼ cup milk
1½ teaspoons margarine
2 tablespoons vinegar
½ cup sour cream

Combine mustard, sugar, salt, and flour. Beat egg and milk together; stir into flour mixture. Cook over low heat, stirring constantly until thickened. Stir in margarine and vinegar; cool. Blend sour cream.

Peanut-y Fruit Salad

The perennial favorite, peanut butter, moves into the salad kingdom for an unusual dressing.

2 fresh pears
1 banana, sliced
2 tablespoons lemon juice
¼ cup peanut butter

2 tablespoons mayonnaise
2 tablespoons chopped onion
Lettuce greens

Halve, core, and cut each pear lengthwise into 8 slices. Brush pear and banana slices with lemon juice. Combine peanut butter, mayonnaise and onion; mix until well blended. Cover 4 individual salad plates with lettuce greens. Arrange 4 pear slices and 4 banana slices on each. Spoon peanut butter dressing over fruits.

Peach-Cheese Salad

Anyone who has enjoyed cottage cheese served in cling peach halves has a new treat in store with this new-styled salad.

1 can (1 pound) cling peach
    slices, drained
1 cup cottage cheese
1 envelope unflavored gelatin

1 cup milk
½ teaspoon grated lemon rind
2 tablespoons lemon juice
Crisp lettuce greens

Chop peach slices coarsely. Sieve cheese. Soften gelatin in ½ cup milk in saucepan; stir over low heat until dissolved. Remove from heat; stir in cheese, lemon rind and juice, and remaining milk. Chill until mixture begins to thicken; fold in peaches. Turn into 3-cup mold; chill until firm. Unmold onto salad greens. Makes 6 servings.

Sunny Orange Salad

Flower-fresh and blooming with color, this salad just looks like summer.

1½ cups shredded fresh spinach
½ medium head iceberg
   lettuce, shredded
1 tablespoon diced red onion
1 tablespoon diced green pepper

1 large orange, sliced
¼ medium unpared cucumber,
   scored, sliced
Sunshine Dressing (recipe below)

Toss together in large bowl spinach, lettuce, onion, and green pepper. Arrange in layers, spinach mixture, orange slices, and cucumber. Pour dressing over all.

Sunshine Dressing

½ cup mayonnaise
2 tablespoons honey

1 tablespoon lemon juice
¾ tablespoon caraway seed

In small bowl combine mayonnaise with honey and lemon juice; beat with rotary beater until smooth. Stir in caraway seed. Makes ¾ cup.

Red Applesauce Salad

1 package lemon-flavored gelatin
¼ cup red cinnamon candies
1¼ cups boiling water
1 cup unsweetened applesauce
1½ teaspoons lemon juice
½ teaspoon grated lemon rind
⅛ teaspoon cloves

¼ cup chopped walnuts
1 package (3 ounces) cream cheese
2 tablespoons light cream
1 tablespoon bottled Italian
   salad dressing
Crisp lettuce greens

Dissolve gelatin and candies in boiling water, stirring frequently. Stir in applesauce, lemon juice and rind, cloves, and walnuts. Pour into 6-inch square pan. Blend cream cheese, milk, and salad dressing. Spoon mixture on top of gelatin; with a spoon swirl cheese mixture through gelatin mixture. Chill until firm. Cut into 4 individual portions and serve on lettuce greens.

Date-Pineapple Slaw

½ cup dates, pitted, sliced
½ cup diced canned pinapple
2½ cups finely shredded cabbage
⅓ cup mayonnaise

1 tablespoon fresh lemon juice
¼ teaspoon salt
¼ teaspoon dry mustard

Combine dates with pineapple and cabbage. Combine mayonnaise and lemon juice; stir in remaining ingredients and toss lightly with cabbage mixture.

Temptation Salad

If fresh pears are not available, use canned pear halves and omit sugar.

2 large fresh pears, sliced
1 tablespoon sugar
1 tablespoon lemon juice
1 medium cucumber, thinly sliced

⅛ teaspoon salt
Lettuce greens
Bottled creamy French dressing

Toss pears with sugar and lemon juice. Combine cucumber and salt. Chill both mixtures. Arrange pears and cucumbers on lettuce leaves. Serve with French dressing.

Confetti Salad

Watermelon balls join fruit cocktail for an inviting and colorful salad to lure warm-weather appetites.

1 package (3 ounces)
   lemon-flavored gelatin
1 cup boiling water
½ cup cold water
3 tablespoons lemon juice

½ cup sour cream
1 can (1 pound 1 ounce)
   fruit cocktail
½ cup watermelon balls
Lettuce greens

Dissolve gelatin in boiling water; add cold water and lemon juice. Blend in sour cream; chill until slightly thickened. Drain fruit cocktail thoroughly; fold into gelatin mixture with watermelon balls. Turn into 1-quart mold. Chill until firm. Unmold on bed of lettuce greens.

Dessert Delights

Many homemakers in the rush and flurry of busy everydays will labor over a main-dish course and then just toss store-bought cookies on the table for dessert.

Dessert leaves a lasting impression, whether it's the fancy finale of a glamorous dinner party or the plain end to a simple supper in the backyard.

Desserts are important because they supply sugar for quick energy and should be included in the meal. Everyone hankers for a sweet now and then, even those who are watching their calories, and today's homemaker should set her standards high because dessert is one of the most important courses of a meal. It can tone up a less-than-stupendous dinner and it adds the final touch of glory to a really superb meal. Good friends, good cheer, and a dessert, are the makings of many a memorable evening. When the coffee's brewed and the dessert makes its appearance, all attention is focused on it.

So go all out with an extra-special treat now and then, for, frankly, who doesn't look forward to dessert as the high point of a meal, or the ending of a visit. Treat everyone to sweet splurges that are exciting to eat. The desserts following are economical to make and easy to fix.

Plum Betty

A quickie dessert which may be served hot or cold.

4 cups day-old bread, torn
  into coarse crumbs
½ cup vegetable oil
2 pounds tart red plums, pitted

⅔ cup sugar
¼ teaspoon salt
Hard Sauce (recipe below)

Heat oven to 350° F. Grease an 8-inch square baking dish. Place bread in bowl; drizzle with 6 tablespoons oil. Combine plums with sugar and salt. Arrange alternate layers of bread mixture and plums in baking dish, beginning and ending with bread. Drizzle remaining 2 tablespoons vegetable oil over the top. Cover; bake 20 minutes. Uncover; bake 30 minutes longer. Serve with Hard Sauce.

Hard Sauce

¼ cup shortening
⅛ teaspoon salt
¼ teaspoon cinnamon

⅛ teaspoon nutmeg
1 cup confectioners' sugar
1½ teaspoons heavy cream

Combine all ingredients; mix well. Spread into a 4-inch square pan; chill. Cut in squares and serve.

Hi-Hat Fudge Pudding

A pluperfect dessert fit for little princes and princesses.

1 cup flour
2 teaspoons baking powder
½ teaspoon salt
¾ cup sugar
6 tablespoons cocoa
¼ teaspoon cloves
1 teaspoon vanilla

½ cup milk
2 tablespoons margarine, melted
½ cup coarsely chopped walnuts
1¼ cups light brown sugar
2 cups hot water
1 cup whipped cream
¼ teaspoon nutmeg

Heat oven to 350° F. Combine flour, baking powder, salt, sugar and 2 tablespoons cocoa in mixing bowl. Sprinkle cloves on top. Combine vanilla, milk, margarine, and walnuts; add to dry ingredients; stir until well blended. Turn into an 8-inch square pan. Mix brown sugar with remaining cocoa. Sprinkle over batter. Pour hot water over entire surface. Bake 40 to 45 minutes. Serve warm; garnish with whipped cream and nutmeg.

Cherry Cake Pudding

1½ cups cake flour	2 eggs, well beaten
2 teaspoons baking powder	½ cup milk
¼ teaspoon salt	¼ cup cherry juice
4 tablespoons margarine	½ teaspoon vanilla
½ cup sugar	2 cups canned red cherries, pitted

Heat oven to 400° F. Lightly grease a 1½-quart baking dish. Combine cake flour with baking powder and salt. Cream margarine; add sugar and cream until light and fluffy. Add eggs; beat until blended. Add dry ingredients alternately with combined milk and cherry juice, beating smooth after each addition. Stir in vanilla. Place drained cherries in baking dish. Pour batter over cherries. Bake 30 to 35 minutes or until done. Serve warm, plain or with whipped cream.

Butterscotch Bread Pudding

An unusual flavor for bread pudding which should appeal to all.

3 cups milk, scalded	2 eggs, slightly beaten
1½ cups bread cubes	¼ teaspoon salt
¾ cup brown sugar	1 teaspoon vanilla
3 tablespoons melted butter	½ teaspoon almond flavoring

Heat oven to 325° F. Butter a 1-quart baking dish. Pour scalded milk in bowl; soak bread in milk. Cool. Cook brown sugar with butter, stirring until melted; add to milk mixture. Add remaining ingredients; blend. Turn into baking dish. Bake 45 to 50 minutes or until set.

Fruit Crisp

Delicious when served hot with milk or cream.

4 cups sliced tart apples	3 tablespoons flour
⅓ cup water	¼ cup rolled oats
1 tablespoon lemon juice	½ cup brown sugar
½ teaspoon nutmeg	⅓ cup peanut butter
¼ teaspoon allspice	2 tablespoons melted margarine

Heat oven to 350° F. Arrange sliced apples in 1-quart baking dish. Add water and lemon juice; sprinkle with spices. Combine flour, rolled oats, brown sugar, peanut butter, margarine. Spread over apples. Bake 40 minutes.

Oatmeal Rhubarb Crumble

3 cups diced rhubarb
¼ cup sugar
¼ teaspoon cinnamon

1 tablespoon margarine
¼ cup water
Oatmeal Topping (recipe below)

Heat oven to 350° F. Grease a shallow baking dish. Arrange rhubarb in bottom of dish. Sprinkle with sugar and cinnamon. Dot with margarine. Pour water over all. Spread topping evenly over rhubarb. Bake 40 minutes. Serve warm with light cream or whipped cream.

Oatmeal Topping

⅔ cup flour
⅛ teaspoon salt
¼ teaspoon baking soda

⅔ cup rolled oats
⅓ cup sugar
¼ cup melted shortening

Combine flour, salt and baking soda. Mix oatmeal and sugar together; add to flour mixture. Blend shortening into dry ingredients until a crumbly mixture is formed.

Sweet Crumb Souffle

A delicious way to use leftover cake.

2 cups milk
½ cup soft bread, cake,
   or cookie crumbs
2 tablespoons sugar
3 tablespoons margarine

½ teaspoon vanilla
½ teaspoon lemon flavoring
2 eggs, separated
⅛ teaspoon salt

Heat oven to 350° F. Butter a 1-quart baking dish. Pour milk on crumbs, add sugar and margarine; heat to boiling. Remove from heat; add flavorings and beaten egg yolks. Add salt to egg whites and beat until stiff. Fold cooked mixture into egg whites and mix lightly but thoroughly. Pour into pan. Set in pan of hot water. Bake 1 hour. Makes 6 servings.

Pear and Apple Scallop

An exciting dessert will climax any meal with a flourish.

¼ cup sugar	4 cups thinly sliced, pared apples
1 teaspoon cinnamon	2 cups thinly sliced, pared pears
¼ teaspoon allspice	Brown Sugar Topping (recipe below)
¼ teaspoon ground cloves	Sweetened whipped cream

Heat oven to 350° F. Combine sugar, cinnamon, allspice, and cloves. Arrange alternate layers of apple and pear in 1½-quart shallow baking dish. Sprinkle each layer with spice mixture. Cover with Brown Sugar Topping. Bake 45 minutes or until fruit is tender. Serve warm with whipped cream.

Brown Sugar Topping

¼ cup flour	¼ cup margarine
½ cup brown sugar	½ cup oatmeal

Combine flour with sugar. Cut in margarine with pastry blender. Mix in oatmeal thoroughly. Divide dough into two parts; roll each on lightly floured board to about ⅛-inch thickness. Fit on top of fruit mixture.

Pears Limoges

A Parisian dessert streamlined to a thrifty spectacular.

½ cup sugar	½ cup confectioners' sugar
1½ cups water	2 tablespoons sherry wine
2 fresh pears, pared, halved, cored	½ cup heavy cream
2 egg yolks	Chocolate shavings

Combine sugar and water in saucepan; heat until sugar dissolves. Add pears; cover and simmer 30 to 35 minutes or until tender. Remove from heat. Place pears in bowl; pour over ½ cup syrup and refrigerate 6 hours. In top of double boiler beat egg yolks, confectioners' sugar, and wine until light. Place over hot water. Cook, stirring constantly, for 8 to 10 minutes. Refrigerate for 6 hours. Beat heavy cream until soft peaks form. Fold in chilled sauce. Drain pears; serve, topped with sauce. Garnish with chocolate shavings.

Cracker Torte

Cut in 9 squares and use as dessert or in 16 small squares and use as tea dainties.

3 egg whites
1 cup sugar
¼ teaspoon baking powder

10 soda crackers, rolled fine
¾ cup chopped walnuts
1 teaspoon vanilla

Heat oven to 350° F. Beat egg whites until stiff; slowly add sugar and baking powder and beat 1 minute. Add cracker crumbs, walnuts, and vanilla. Turn into 9-inch square pan. Bake 25 minutes. Cool; cut into squares and serve plain or with whipped cream.

Peanut-y Bars

1 package (4 ounces) chocolate
  pudding and pie filling
1⅓ cups packaged biscuit mix
⅓ cup sugar

¾ cup milk
3 tablespoons vegetable oil
½ cup salted peanuts

Heat oven to 350° F. Grease a 9-inch square pan. Combine pudding with biscuit mix and sugar. Add milk and oil; mix with spoon until blended. Turn into pan. Sprinkle peanuts on top. Bake 25 to 30 minutes. Cut into squares. Makes 16 squares.

Apple Crisp

Stretch the leftover portion by serving it with ice cream.

4 cups sliced, pared apples
¼ cup water
¾ cup flour
1 teaspoon cinnamon

1 teaspoon salt
1 cup sugar
⅓ cup margarine

Heat oven to 350° F. Butter an 8-inch square baking pan. Spread apples in pan; sprinkle with water. Combine flour with cinnamon and salt. Blend in sugar and margarine. Sprinkle this mixture over apples. Bake 35 to 40 minutes. Makes 6 servings.

Caramel Ice Cream

1½ cups milk
½ cup sugar
2 eggs, separated
⅛ teaspoon salt

⅓ cup dark corn syrup
1 teaspoon vanilla
¼ cup chopped nuts

Scald milk. Place sugar in skillet over low heat and cook, stirring occasionally until a light brown syrup is formed. Pour into scalded milk; stir until syrup is dissolved. Beat egg yolks; pour into hot milk and cook over low heat until mixture coats spoon. Add salt. Cool. Turn into refrigerator tray; freeze until almost firm, about 1½ to 2 hours. Put egg whites and corn syrup in bowl; beat until mixture is creamy and thick. Remove frozen custard to a bowl; beat until smooth but not melted. Fold in egg white mixture, vanilla and nuts. Return to refrigerator tray; freeze until firm. Makes 6 servings.

Scotch Shortbread

A jiffy-to-make recipe of an old-time favorite.

1 cup shortening
¾ cup confectioners' sugar
1½ cups flour

½ teaspoon salt
1 tablespoon lemon juice

Heat oven to 375° F. Cream shortening and sugar. Combine flour and salt; stir into shortening mixture along with lemon juice. Roll to ¼-inch thickness on floured board. Cut in desired shapes with floured cutter and place on cookie sheet. Bake 20 to 25 minutes. Makes 4 dozen 2-inch cookies.

Butterscotch Apple Dumplings

You'll love them baked this way in their own luscious "scotch" sauce.

1½ cups flour
2 teaspoons double-acting
   baking powder
½ teaspoon salt
1½ tablespoons sugar
¼ cup shortening
½ cup milk
2 medium apples, pared,
   cored and halved

¼ cup sugar
½ teaspoon cinnamon
⅛ teaspoon nutmeg
⅓ cup brown sugar
5 tablespoons margarine
Dash salt
1 cup boiling water

Combine flour with baking powder, salt and 1½ tablespoons sugar. Cut in shortening with pastry blender until mixture resembles coarse meal. Add milk, mixing until soft dough is formed. Knead dough on lightly floured board 1 minute. Heat oven to 375° F. Grease a 9-inch square pan. Divide dough in half. Roll each half to ⅛-inch thickness and cut into two squares 5 × 5 inches. Place apple half on each square. Sprinkle each with 1 tablespoon of combined sugar, cinnamon, and nutmeg. Moisten edges of dough and bring corners up over apples, pressing edges together. Place in pan with joined edges on top. Mix together brown sugar, margarine, and salt; add water, stir and bring to a boil. Pour over dumplings in pan. Bake 45 to 50 minutes or until apples are tender. Serve warm.

Lemon Cream Tarts

The filling may be used for cup cakes or cake shells—it's delicious.

1 cup milk
¼ cup cornstarch
½ cup sugar
Dash salt
1 egg, separated

3 tablespoons lemon juice
½ teaspoon grated rind
1 tablespoon butter
4 baked tart shells

Scald milk. Blend cornstarch, sugar, and salt. Gradually add milk to dry ingredients. Cook over low heat, stirring constantly until thickened. Beat egg yolk, add a little of hot mixture. Return to the hot mixture and cook 2 minutes longer. Remove from heat; add lemon juice, lemon rind, and butter. Cool. Fold in stiffly beaten egg white. Fill tart shells.

Fruit Filled Éclairs

An elegant dessert for a special occasion—blackberries, loganberries, raspberries, or strawberries may be used instead of blueberries.

½ cup boiling water	2 eggs
¼ cup butter	Fruit Filling (recipe below)
¼ teaspoon salt	¾ cup sweetened whipped cream
½ cup flour	

Heat oven to 400° F. Combine water, butter, and salt; bring to a boil. Add flour all at once to boiling liquid. Cook until transparent, about 5 minutes, stirring constantly. Remove from heat; cool to lukewarm. Add eggs one at a time, beating thoroughly after each addition. Shape on cookie sheet to make six éclairs. Bake 40 minutes or until well browned. Cool. Cut tops from éclairs, fill with Fruit Filling mixture; replace top. Top with whipped cream. Makes 6 servings.

Fruit Filling

½ cup sugar	1 tablespoon margarine
2 tablespoons cornstarch	1 tablespoon lemon juice
¼ teaspoon salt	½ teaspoon grated lemon rind
2½ cups canned blueberries, or sweetened fresh	

Combine sugar, cornstarch, and salt in top of double boiler. Add syrup drained from blueberries. Cook, stirring, until thickened. (If fresh fruit is used, add ½ cup corn syrup.) Continue cooking 10 minutes. Remove from heat. Stir in margarine, lemon juice, and rind. Stir in blueberries. Cool.

Holiday Bread

For tea time or any time, this bread is a treat; serve buttered or plain.

1 cake compressed yeast
¼ cup lukewarm water
1 can (6 ounces) evaporated milk
¼ cup butter
¼ cup sugar
1 teaspoon salt

1 can (1 pound) fruit cocktail
5½ cups flour
½ cup diced citron
½ cup raisins
8 cardamom seeds, crushed
½ cup chopped nuts

Soften yeast in lukewarm water. Scald milk, add butter, sugar, salt, and syrup drained from fruit. Add about half the flour; beat well. Add yeast, citron, raisins, cardamom seeds, nuts, and fruit. Mix; add enough flour to make soft dough. Knead in bowl 3 minutes. Turn out onto floured board; knead 2 minutes. Place in greased bowl; cover. Let rise until double in bulk, about 2½ hours. Shape into two loaves and place into 2 greased 9 × 5 × 3-inch loaf pans. Let rise until double in bulk, about 1 hour. Bake 1 hour, or until browned. Let stand 2 minutes; turn onto cooling racks.

Cherry Apricot Betty

A king-size dessert, for a crowd, which will win you compliments.

6 tablespoons melted butter
2 cups soft bread crumbs
1 can (1 pound 10 ounces)
    water-pack pitted red cherries
1 can (1 pound) apricot halves
½ cup brown sugar

2 tablespoons lemon juice
1 teaspoon grated lemon rind
½ teaspoon cinnamon
½ teaspoon nutmeg
¼ teaspoon salt
Fruit Sauce (recipe below)

Heat oven to 375° F. Pour butter over crumbs; mix until all are buttered. Drain syrup from cherries and apricots; reserve for sauce. Place a layer of crumbs in 1½-quart baking dish. Add a layer of fruit over crumbs; sprinkle with ⅓ sugar, lemon juice and rind, spices, and salt; repeat until all ingredients have been used, reserving a few crumbs for top. Bake 30 minutes. Serve warm with Fruit Sauce. Makes 10 to 12 servings.

Fruit Sauce

1 cup cherry and apricot syrup
1 tablespoon cornstarch
⅛ teaspoon salt
¼ teaspoon nutmeg

¼ cup sugar
½ cup heavy cream
½ teaspoon vanilla
Few drops lemon flavoring

Blend ¼ cup of fruit syrup with cornstarch until smooth. Heat remaining syrup to boiling; stir in cornstarch mixture. Cook until thickened and clear, stirring constantly. Add salt, nutmeg, and sugar; stir until well blended. Remove from heat; cool. Whip cream; fold into sauce with lemon flavoring.

Cocoa Cup Cakes

Thrifty, energy-giving, after-school pickups.

1½ cups flour
1¼ cups sugar
½ cup cocoa
1 teaspoon salt
1 teaspoon baking soda
⅔ cup shortening

1 cup milk
¾ teaspoon baking powder
2 eggs
1 teaspoon vanilla
Bittersweet Icing (recipe below)
¼ cup grated chocolate

Heat oven to 375° F. Combine flour, sugar, cocoa, salt, soda, shortening, and ⅔ cup milk; beat at medium speed 2 minutes. Stir in baking powder. Add 1 whole egg and 1 egg yolk, saving white for icing, remaining ⅓ cup milk, and vanilla. Beat 2 minutes. Fill, one-half full, cup-cake cups which have been set onto cookie sheets. Bake 15 to 20 minutes. Cool. Ice with Bittersweet Icing; sprinkle with grated chocolate.

Bittersweet Icing

¾ cup sugar
¼ teaspoon cream of tartar
1 egg white

2 tablespoons water
½ teaspoon vanilla

Place all ingredients in top of double boiler. Beat constantly over hot water with rotary beater until icing will hold in peaks.

Banbury Turnovers

This New England specialty is a favorite of young and old alike.

Pastry for 2-crust 9-inch pie
½ cup sugar
1 tablespoon flour
1 egg, slightly beaten

1 cup seedless raisins
¼ cup chopped nuts
1 tablespoon lemon juice
2 teaspoons grated lemon rind

Heat oven to 425° F. Roll pastry ⅛ inch thick; cut into 4-inch squares. Combine sugar and flour; stir into egg. Combine remaining ingredients and blend into egg mixture. Place 1 tablespoonful of filling on half of each square; fold pastry to form triangle. Seal edges and flute with fork. Cut or prick small steam vents. Place on cookie sheet. Bake 15 minutes. Makes 12 turnovers.

Frugal Coconut Squares

⅓ cup shortening
1 cup flour
¼ teaspoon salt

½ cup brown sugar
1 egg
Coconut Topping (recipe below)

Heat oven to 425° F. Cut shortening into combined flour, salt, and sugar with pastry blender. Add egg; blend well. Turn into 8-inch square pan. Bake 8 to 10 minutes or until lightly browned. Cover with Coconut Topping. Reduce temperature to 375° F. Bake 30 minutes longer. Makes 16 2-inch squares.

Coconut Topping

1 cup brown sugar
2 tablespoons flour
¼ teaspoon salt
¼ teaspoon baking powder

1 egg
1 teaspoon vanilla
½ cup coconut

Combine sugar, flour, salt and baking powder. Blend with egg, vanilla, and coconut.

Cinnamon Pinwheels

Serve warm from the oven with a glass of milk for an energy snack and save balance for a breakfast treat the following morning.

2 cups flour
3 teaspoons baking powder
1 teaspoon salt
⅓ cup shortening

¾ cup milk
2 teaspoons cinnamon
½ cup sugar
2 tablespoons margarine

Heat oven to 425° F. Butter, lightly, cookie sheets. Combine flour, baking powder, and salt. Cut in shortening with pastry blender until mixture looks like coarse cornmeal. Remove 1 cup of mixture to another bowl; blend with milk to form a paste. Add paste to shortening mixture and mix just enough to hold dough together. Turn onto floured board; knead lightly 10 times. Roll dough to oblong shape, about 10 × 18 inches. Sprinkle with cinnamon and sugar; dot with margarine. Roll lengthwise like a jelly roll; seal edges tightly. Cut slices about 1 inch thick; place on cookie sheet. Bake 12 to 15 minutes. Makes 16 pinwheels.

Applesauce Crunch Cookies

Simply delicious, and just perfect for dessert, picnics, snacks, and parties.

1¾ cups flour
½ teaspoon double-acting
  baking powder
1 teaspoon baking soda
½ teaspoon salt
1 teaspoon cinnamon
½ teaspoon cloves

½ teaspoon nutmeg
¾ cup shortening
1 cup sugar
1 egg
1 cup sweetened applesauce
½ cup raisins
½ cup ready-to-eat cereal

Heat oven to 375° F. Grease cookie sheets. Combine flour, baking powder, soda, salt, and spices. Cream shortening; add sugar and cream blending well. Add egg; beat well. Add flour mixture alternately with applesauce to shortening, mixing thoroughly. Add raisins and cereal; blend. Drop by teaspoonful on cookie sheets, 2 inches apart. Bake 15 minutes or until done. Makes about 3½-dozen cookies.

Skillet Fruit Cake

⅓ cup shortening	2 cups cake flour
⅔ cup brown sugar	1 teaspoon salt
1 cup drained crushed pineapple	3 teaspoons double-acting
1 cup drained apricot halves	baking powder
½ cup margarine	¾ cup milk
1 cup sugar	1 teaspoon vanilla
2 eggs	¾ cup sweetened whipped cream

Heat oven to 375° F. Melt shortening and brown sugar in 10-inch skillet. Place pineapple and apricots in skillet. Cream margarine and sugar until light and fluffy. Add eggs; blend thoroughly. Combine flour, salt, and baking powder. Add dry ingredients alternately with milk and vanilla to egg mixture; beat until smooth. Pour batter of fruit in skillet. Bake 40 to 45 minutes. Serve warm inverted onto serving plate. Top with whipped cream.

Viennese Chocolate Cake

Really a gem! Adapted from an old Continental prize-winning recipe.

½ cup butter	½ teaspoon salt
1 cup sugar	¾ cup milk
½ cup egg yolks, well beaten	½ teaspoon vanilla
1⅔ cups cake flour	1 cup apricot jam
3 teaspoons baking powder	Caramel Frosting (recipe below)

Heat oven to 375° F. Grease a jelly-roll pan, 10 × 15 inches. Cream butter and sugar until light and fluffy. Add egg yolks; beat well. Combine dry ingredients. Add alternately with combined milk and vanilla, in thirds, beating until smooth after each addition. Spread in jelly-roll pan. Bake 25 minutes. Turn out onto cake rack; cool. Cut into 4 pieces crosswise. Split each piece in two making 8 layers. Spread apricot jam between layers. Top with Caramel Frosting.

Caramel Frosting

½ cup confectioners' sugar	½ cup and 2 tablespoons corn syrup
½ cup cocoa	2 tablespoons margarine
⅛ teaspoon salt	½ teaspoon vanilla

Combine sugar, cocoa, and salt. Combine corn syrup and margarine in saucepan. Cook over medium heat until mixture comes to a full boil. Remove from heat. Add dry ingredients all at once. Beat with wooden spoon until smooth. Add vanilla; blend well. Pour and spread on cake.

Hot Milk Cake

2 eggs
1 cup sugar
1 cup cake flour
⅛ teaspoon salt

1 teaspoon baking powder
½ cup hot milk
1 tablespoon shortening

Heat oven to 350° F. Grease and dust with flour an 8 × 8-inch pan. Beat eggs until light and thick. Slowly add sugar and beat until foamy. Combine flour, salt, and baking powder. Fold into egg and sugar mixture all at one time. Combine milk and shortening; stir until melted. Add to flour mixture all at once. Turn into prepared pan. Bake 30 minutes. Serve plain, dusted with confectioners' sugar, or frosted with your favorite icing.

Dynasty Cake

No frosting is needed when the delicious praline topping is baked on this cake.

2 cups cake flour
2 teaspoons double-acting
  baking powder
¾ teaspoon salt
1 cup sugar

⅓ cup shortening
¾ cup milk
1 teaspoon vanilla
1 egg
Praline Topping (recipe below)

Heat oven to 350° F. Grease a 9-inch square pan; line bottom with waxed paper and grease again. Combine flour, baking powder, salt and sugar. Measure shortening into a mixing bowl. Add dry ingredients with ½ cup milk, vanilla, and egg; mix until flour is dampened. Beat 1 minute. Add remaining milk; blend and beat 2 minutes longer. Turn batter into pan. Bake 35 minutes. Spread Praline Topping; bake 5 minutes longer. Cool and cut cake in pan.

Praline Topping

¼ cup brown sugar
2 teaspoons flour
⅓ cup chopped nuts

2 tablespoons melted margarine
1 tablespoon water

Combine all ingredients.

Raisin Pie Romanoff

½ cup sugar
3 tablespoons flour
¼ teaspoon cloves
½ teaspoon cinnamon
¼ teaspoon salt
2 cups raisins, rinsed, drained

2 cups water
2 tablespoons cider vinegar
2 tablespoons butter
Pastry for 9-inch pie shell
and lattice top
¼ cup sour cream

Combine sugar, flour, cloves, cinnamon, and salt; mix well. Stir in raisins. Combine water, vinegar, and butter in saucepan. Stir in raisin mixture. Bring to boil; cook, stirring constantly, until thickened, about 4 to 5 minutes. Cool slightly. Heat oven to 450° F. Pour raisin mixture into pastry shell. Cover top with strips of pastry. Bake 25 to 30 minutes or until pastry is lightly browned. Remove from oven; cool. Serve with daubs of sour cream.

Angel Ice-Cream Pie

A no-crust pie you can prepare in advance and keep in the freezer until ready to serve.

1½ pints strawberry ice cream
1½ cups leftover angel
food cake, cubed

½ ounce (½ square) bitter
chocolate, shaved

Have ice cream slightly softened. Place ½ of angel food cake cubes in bottom of 9-inch pie pan. Spoon ½ of ice cream over them. Add remaining cake cubes and ice cream. Smooth ice cream to edges of pie pan. Sprinkle chocolate on top. Cover with freezer wrapping and freeze until needed.

Pink Cloud Pie

23 vanilla wafers
1 package (4 ounces)
lemon-flavored pie filling
1 envelope unflavored gelatin
1 teaspoon grated lemon rind

2½ cups water
⅓ cup sugar
2 eggs, separated
1 package (10 ounces) frozen
sliced strawberries, thawed

Arrange vanilla wafers in bottom and around the sides of a 9-inch pie plate. Mix lemon-flavored pie filling, gelatin, and grated lemon rind; gradually add water. Add sugar and slightly beaten egg yolks; mix well. Cook over medium heat, stirring constantly, until mixture thickens. Remove from heat;

cool. Chill until thick and syrupy. Beat egg whites until stiff. Fold into lemon mixture; chill until thick. Spoon into pie plate; chill until firm. Spoon some of sliced strawberries over lemon filling; pass the remainder around in a bowl.

Tropical Pie

Warm-weather way with tangy citrus flavor.

¾ cup sugar
⅓ cup flour
¼ teaspoon salt
1¼ cups milk
3 egg yolks
½ cup orange juice

2 tablespoons lemon juice
1 tablespoon grated orange rind
1 tablespoon grated lemon rind
1 9-inch baked pastry shell
Tropical Meringue (recipe below)

Combine sugar, flour, salt, and milk. Cook over hot water until thick. Beat egg yolks, add a little of the hot milk mixture and return to first mixture, stirring constantly. When thick, remove from heat. Add orange and lemon juice and rind. Turn into baked pastry shell. Let stand until cool. Top with Tropical Meringue.

Tropical Meringue

3 egg whites
¼ cup sugar

4 maraschino cherries, quartered
2 tablespoons shredded coconut

Beat egg whites with sugar until stiff enough to hold peaks. Place meringue on pie; carefully decorate with maraschino cherries and coconut.

Easy Pumpkin Pie

A national favorite which is also delicious made the Western way, with winter squash, or the Southern way, with sweet potatoes.

1 9-inch pastry shell, unbaked
2 cups cooked mashed pumpkin
¾ cup light brown sugar
1 teaspoon cinnamon
¾ teaspoon ginger

½ teaspoon nutmeg
¾ teaspoon salt
2 eggs, slightly beaten
1½ cups milk

Heat oven to 425° F. Prepare pastry shell. Combine remaining ingredients; mix well. Pour into shell. Bake 1 hour or until done. Serve warm or cold, plain or with whipped cream.

Honey Pecan Pie

A Kentucky specialty so easy to make and so good to eat!

⅓ cup honey	3 eggs, beaten
¾ cup brown sugar	1 teaspoon vanilla
3 tablespoons shortening	1½ cups chopped pecans
3 tablespoons margarine	1 8-inch pastry shell, unbaked

Heat oven to 425° F. Heat honey and sugar together to form a smooth syrup. Stir in shortening and margarine. Add eggs, vanilla, and pecans. Pour into pastry shell. Bake 10 minutes; reduce temperature to 350° F. and bake 25 to 30 minutes longer.

Rhubarb Chiffon Pie

2 teaspoons unflavored gelatin	2 eggs, separated
2 tablespoons cold water	Red food coloring
1 pound rhubarb, thinly sliced	¼ teaspoon salt
1¾ cups sugar	1 9-inch baked pastry shell
1 tablespoon warm water	

Soften gelatin in cold water. Cook rhubarb with 1 cup sugar and warm water for 10 minutes or until rhubarb is tender. Combine egg yolks with ½ cup sugar in top of double boiler and cook over very low heat until thickened. Stir in gelatin. Combine egg yolk mixture with rhubarb sauce; cool until thickened but not stiff. Stir in few drops red food coloring. Beat egg whites and salt until soft peaks form. Add remaining ¼ cup sugar gradually while beating until stiff peaks form. Fold into rhubarb mixture. Turn into baked pie shell. Chill until set, about 2 hours.

Jam Pie French-Style

Unbaked pastry shell	3 eggs, separated
¾ cup plum preserves	½ cup milk
¾ cup butter	1¼ cups flour
1 cup sugar	1 teaspoon vanilla

Heat oven to 350° F. Make a rich pie crust and line a deep pie plate. Cover bottom with preserves. Cream butter and ¾ cup sugar. Add beaten egg yolks, milk, flour, and ½ teaspoon vanilla. Pour into pie shell. Bake 35 minutes or until center is firm. Beat egg whites until stiff, add remaining sugar and vanilla. Spread on pie; return to oven and brown 10 to 12 minutes.

Caramel Custard Pie

Something special for custard-pie lovers!

½ cup sugar, caramelized
3 cups milk, scalded
3 eggs, slightly beaten
¼ teaspoon salt

6 tablespoons sugar
1 teaspoon vanilla
1 9-inch unbaked pastry shell

Heat oven to 425° F. Caramelize sugar by heating it slowly in heavy skillet, stirring constantly, until melted and golden brown, about 5 minutes; remove from heat. Add slowly to scalded milk, stirring constantly. Combine eggs, salt, and 6 tablespoons sugar. Add milk mixture, stirring constantly. Add vanilla. Pour into pastry shell. Bake 25 to 30 minutes or until knife inserted comes out clean. Cool before serving.

Mississippi Nut Pie

If pecans are too expensive for your pocketbook, use any other nuts to make this tasty pie.

1 cup dark corn syrup
¾ cup sugar
3 eggs, slightly beaten
3 tablespoons margarine

1 teaspoon vanilla
1 cup pecans, coarsely broken
1 9-inch unbaked pastry shell

Heat oven to 375° F. Combine corn syrup and sugar in saucepan; boil 2 minutes. Pour slowly over eggs, stirring constantly. Add margarine, vanilla, and nuts; blend well. Turn into pastry shell. Bake 50 minutes or until done. Pie will be done when completely puffed across top. Cool before serving.

Dutch Apple Crunch Pie

The crunch topping over the pastry makes this a special company dessert.

Pastry for 2-crust 9-inch pie
5 cups pared sliced apples
¾ cup sugar
¼ teaspoon cinnamon
¼ teaspoon salt

1 tablespoon flour
1 tablespoon lemon juice
1 tablespoon shortening
Crunch Topping (recipe below)

Heat oven to 425° F. Roll pastry ⅛-inch thick. Line 9-inch pie plate with ½ crust and trim edge. Combine apples with remaining ingredients, except Crunch Topping. Turn into pie plate. Top with pastry; fold edge under, seal, and flute edge. Cut small steam vents on top. Sprinkle with Crunch Topping. Bake 10 minutes; reduce temperature to 350° F. and continue baking 25 to 30 minutes longer.

Crunch Topping

1 tablespoon shortening
1 tablespoon sugar

3 tablespoons flour
¼ teaspoon salt

Blend all ingredients together until crumbly.

Winter Fruit Pie

A great way to use winter nuts when they are plentiful and economical.

Pastry for 2-crust, 9-inch pie
1 cup dried apricots
1 cup raisins
1 cup water
2 tablespoons lemon juice

1 tablespoon grated lemon rind
2 tablespoons flour
½ cup sugar
1 cup chopped nuts
2 tablespoons margarine

Heat oven to 425° F. Roll pastry ⅛ inch thick. Line a 9-inch pie plate with pastry; trim edge. Simmer dried fruit and raisins in water until tender, about 15 minutes. Drain; measure fruit liquid and add enough water to make ¾ cup. Combine with lemon juice and rind; pour over drained fruit. Add remaining ingredients, except margarine, stirring lightly, until well blended. Turn into pastry lined pie plate. Top with pastry; prick top. Trim off edges, fold, and flute. Bake 10 minutes. Reduce temperature to 350° F; continue baking 35 minutes longer.

Old-Fashioned Buttermilk Pie

A thrifty Pennsylvania Dutch favorite with a flavorful, creamy filling.

⅔ cup and 2 tablespoons sugar
1 tablespoon flour
1 tablespoon margarine
2 eggs, separated
1 tablespoon lemon juice

Grated rind of 1 lemon
⅛ teaspoon salt
1 cup buttermilk
1 8-inch unbaked pastry shell

Heat oven to 425° F. Combine ⅔ cup sugar with flour and margarine; cream until light and fluffy. Beat egg yolks until fluffy; add to flour mixture. Add lemon juice and rind, salt, and buttermilk; blend well. Turn into pastry shell. Bake 30 minutes. Beat egg whites until they form soft peaks; add remaining 2 tablespoons sugar and beat until stiff. Reduce temperature to 325° F. Spread meringue on top of pie. Bake about 15 minutes or until meringue is delicately browned.

Index